The Smoky Mountains

photographer's guide

by Bill Campbell
and Nye Simmons

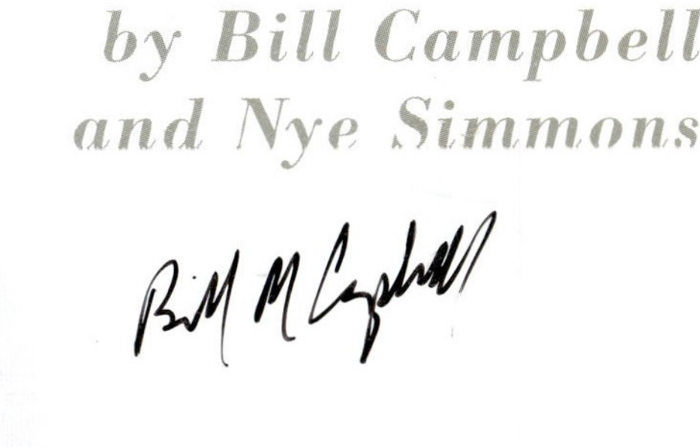

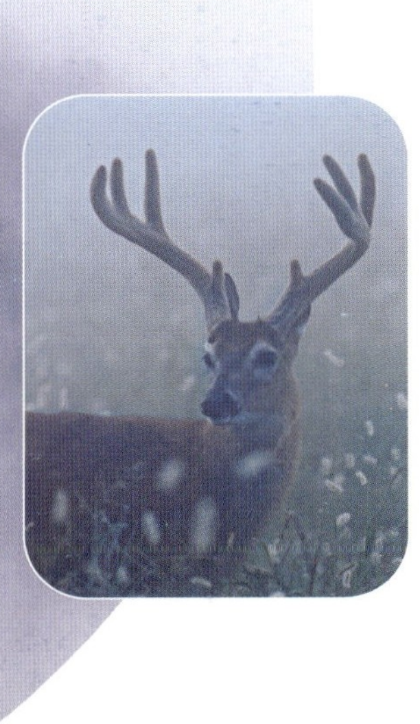

Contents

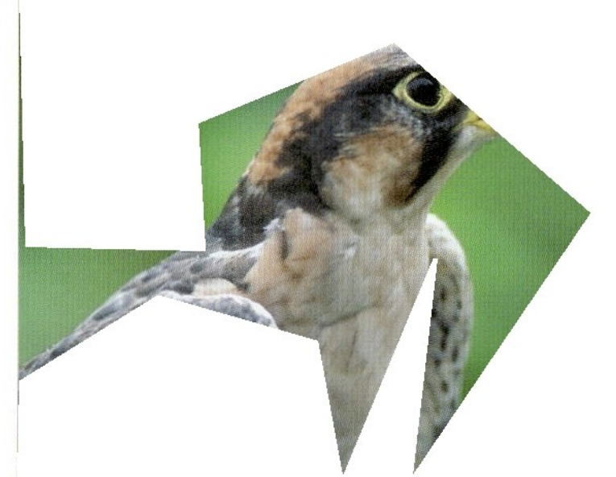

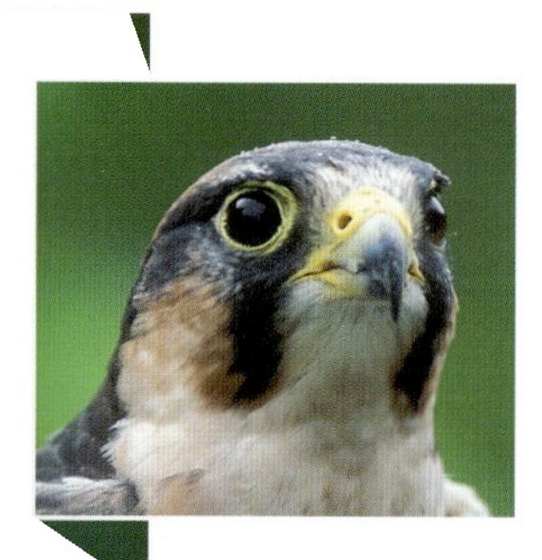

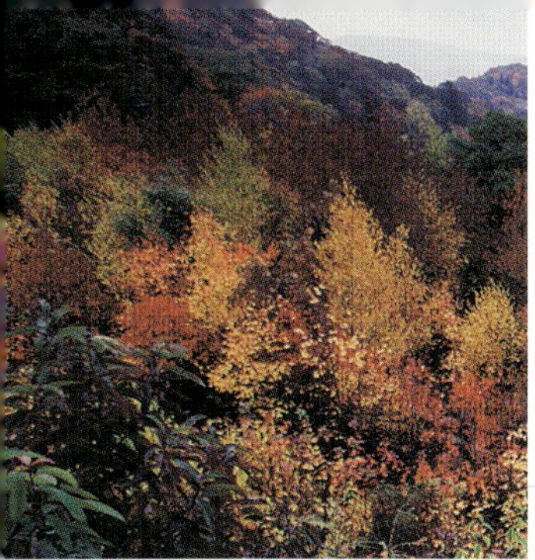
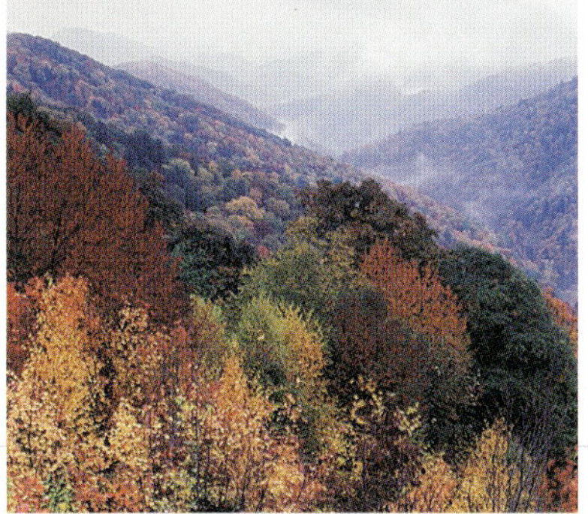
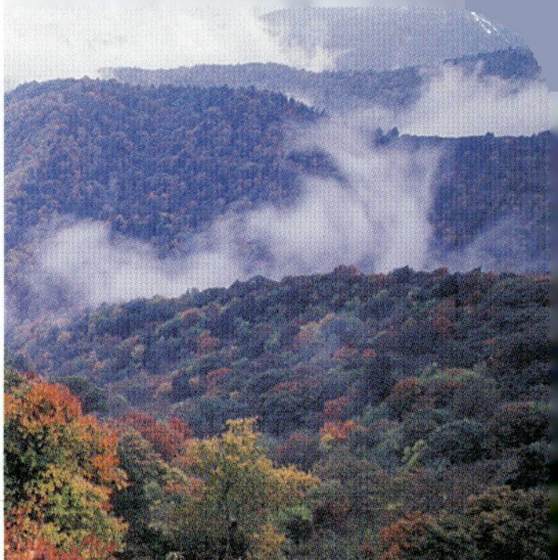

Page 2 images by Bill Campbell; page 3 image by Nye Simmons.

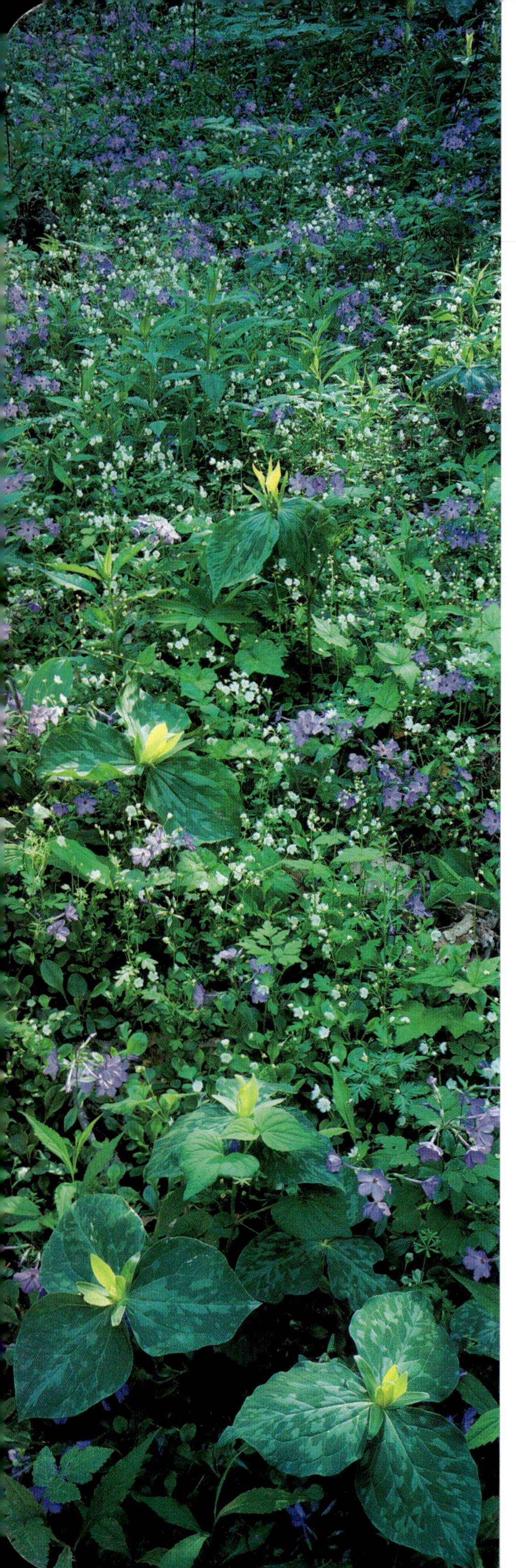

Images and text by Bill Campbell and Nye Simmons
Edited by Steve Kemp
Book and cover design by Lisa Horstman
Production by Jim Wells
Printed in Hong Kong

1 2 3 4 5 6 7 8 9

ISBN 9745526-0-7

Acknowledgments

Many more people deserve thanks and recognition than space allows for the help they gave seeing this project through to completion. My wife and sons, Deborah, Nye, and Lee, could have said "are you done yet?" far more often than they did, nor did they complain (too much) about the many days and nights I spent away from home in pursuit of images. Thanks for so many things go to my parents Charles and Lorraine, not the least of which was their love for the English language. Special thanks go to Dr. Bob Singh for years of friendship and encouragement. Thanks also to our production team, Lisa, Jim, and our editor Steve, who made this such a grand fun adventure.—*NS*

Thanks is such a trivial word that does not even come close to the feeling I have for all my friends who have been supportive in this endeavor and my career. But the most important thanks goes to my family, both immediate and extended. My wife Mary is the essence of support and love and my hope is that we survive many more books like this together. My boys, Matt, Luke and Joe, have been wonderful companions on many trips and are learning to love and respect nature with the same zeal that I feel.

My mom and dad, Joe and Gail Campbell, are two of my biggest fans and I appreciate everything they have taught me over the years. My Palmer parents, Dan and Henrietta, have been equally supportive as I was incorporated into the Palmer clan. My brother and sister, Andy and Robin and my brothers and sisters-in-law; Sandra, Lynn, Jim, Dan, Amy, James, Gwen, Nancy, Teresa, Reza, Mark, Steve and Cindy have been a circle of love and hope and support and I thank them.

I would like to dedicate this book to Teresa Zare, Mary's sister, who has shown all of us what courage and strength really mean when faced with overwhelming odds. We love you.—*BC*

Page 4 image by Nye Simmons; page 5 image by Bill Campbell.

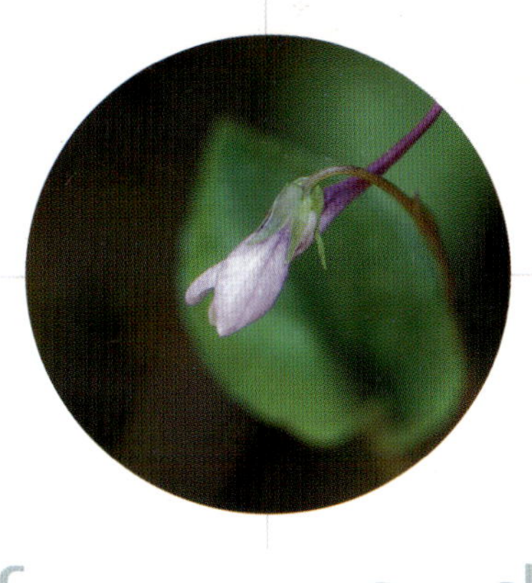

foreword

The Great Smoky Mountains National Park is definitely on the short list of places for all nature photographers to visit. The diversity of flora and fauna within the park gives anyone with a camera more than ample opportunities to photograph. Four complete seasons, each full of subtle changes, allows great photography during any month of the year. I have had many wonderful experiences photographing in the park.

With today's hectic schedules and the daunting size of the park, many visitors will appreciate this guide to the most popular photographic locations, plus an introduction to places off the beaten path. The hints on photographic technique, suggestions on planning each day to maximize photo opportunities, and short lessons in the area's natural history offer the photographer control over the where and when of photographing in the Smokies. This book deserves a spot on the shelf or in the pack of anyone considering a trip to the Great Smoky Mountains.

—John Shaw

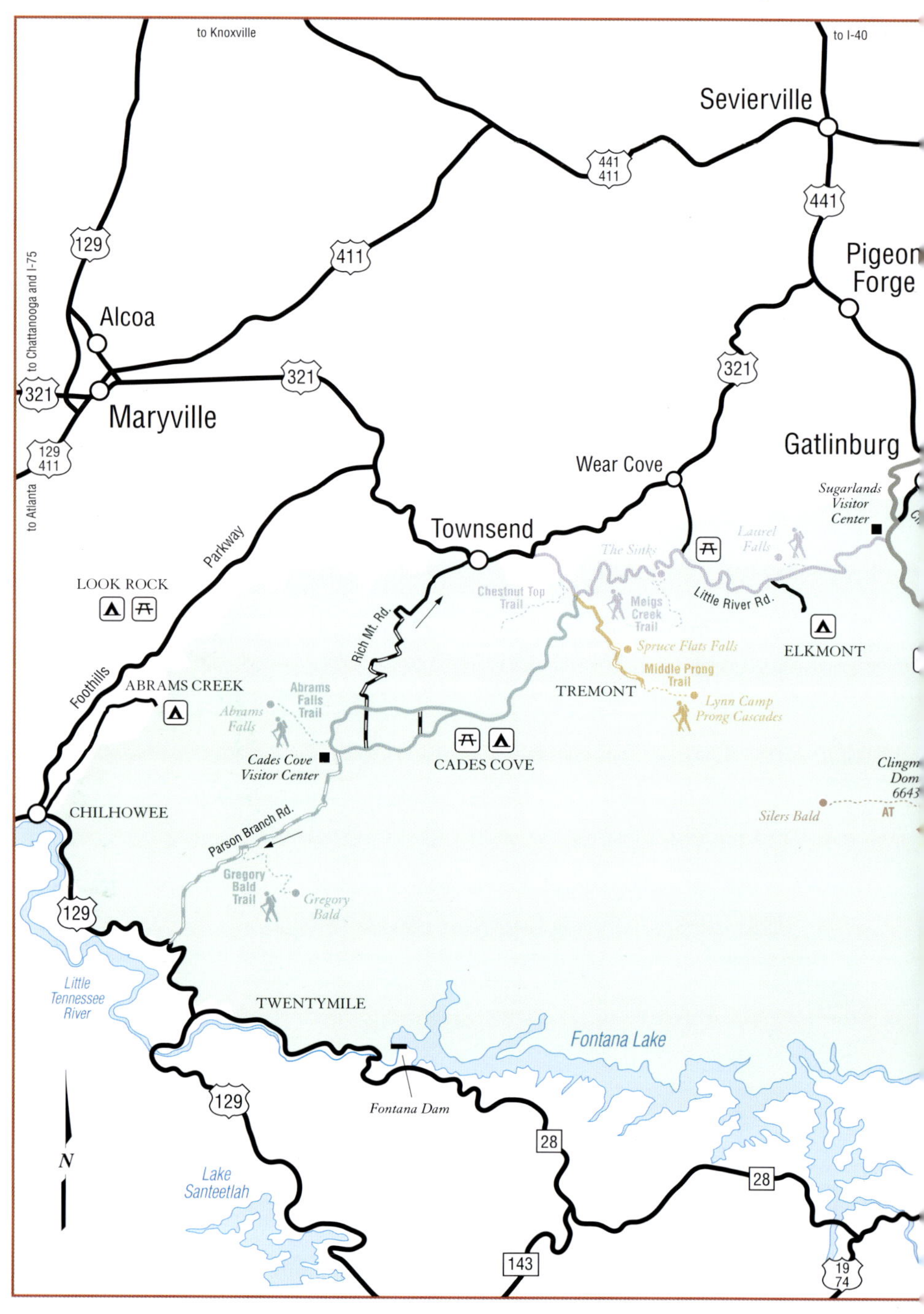
to Knoxville
to I-40
Sevierville
441
411
441
Pigeon
Forge
129
411
Alcoa
to Chattanooga and I-75
321
321
321
Maryville
129
411
to Atlanta
Gatlinburg
Wear Cove
Sugarlands
Visitor
Center
Townsend
Parkway
The Sinks
Laurel
Falls
LOOK ROCK
Chestnut Top
Trail
Meigs
Creek
Trail
Little River Rd.
Rich Mt. Rd.
Spruce Flats Falls
ELKMONT
Foothills
ABRAMS CREEK
Abrams
Falls
Trail
Abrams
Falls
TREMONT
Middle Prong
Trail
Lynn Camp
Prong Cascades
Cades Cove
Visitor Center
CADES COVE
CHILHOWEE
Silers Bald
AT
Parson Branch Rd.
Gregory
Bald
Trail
Gregory
Bald
129
Little
Tennessee
River
TWENTYMILE
Fontana Lake
Fontana Dam
129
N
28
28
Lake
Santeetlah
143
19
74

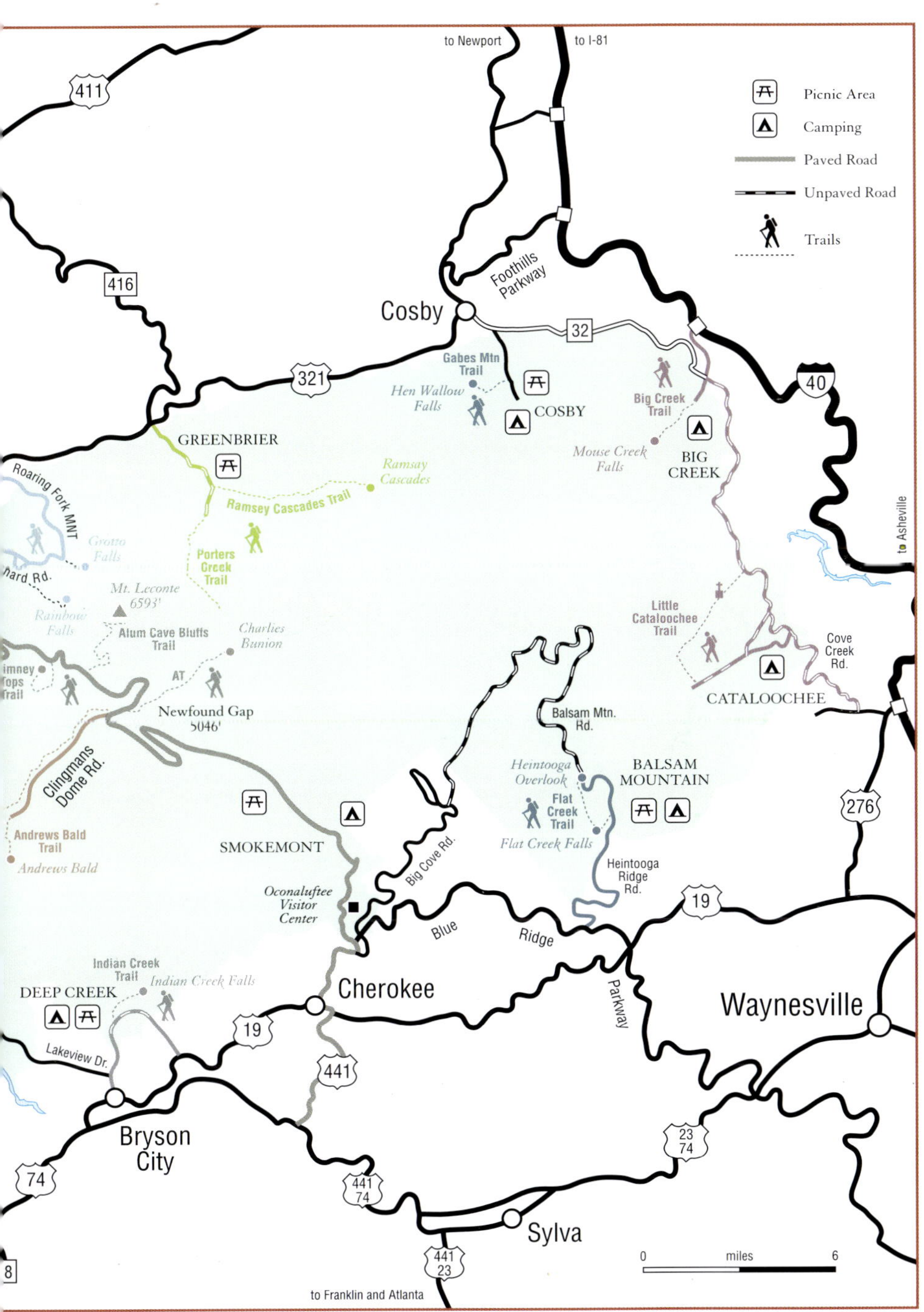
to Newport
to I-81
Picnic Area
Camping
Paved Road
Unpaved Road
Trails
411
416
Foothills Parkway
Cosby
32
321
Gabes Mtn Trail
Hen Wallow Falls
COSBY
40
Big Creek Trail
Mouse Creek Falls
BIG CREEK
GREENBRIER
Ramsay Cascades
Ramsey Cascades Trail
Roaring Fork MNT
Grotto Falls
Porters Creek Trail
to Asheville
Mt. Leconte 6593'
Rainbow Falls
Alum Cave Bluffs Trail
Charlies Bunion
Little Cataloochee Trail
Cove Creek Rd.
CATALOOCHEE
AT
Newfound Gap 5046'
Balsam Mtn. Rd.
Clingmans Dome Rd.
Heintooga Overlook
BALSAM MOUNTAIN
Flat Creek Trail
Flat Creek Falls
276
Andrews Bald Trail
Andrews Bald
SMOKEMONT
Big Cove Rd.
Heintooga Ridge Rd.
Oconaluftee Visitor Center
19
Blue Ridge Parkway
Cherokee
Indian Creek Trail
Indian Creek Falls
DEEP CREEK
Waynesville
19
Lakeview Dr.
441
Bryson City
74
23 74
441 74
Sylva
441 23
0 miles 6
to Franklin and Atlanta

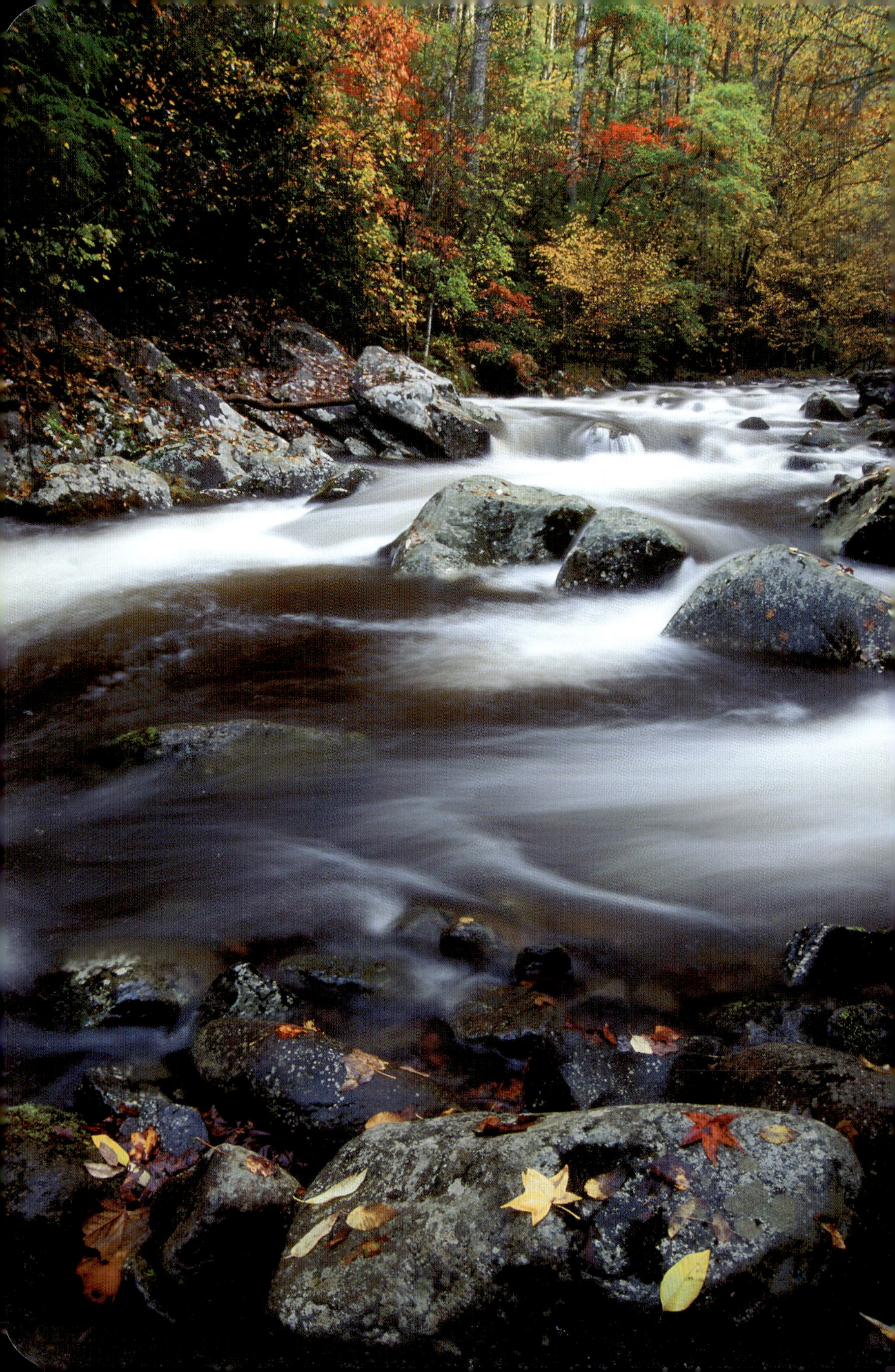

Fall along the Middle Prong of the Little River in Tremont is an excellent time to use soft light to explore various views of water and fall color. Overcast days allow longer exposure for that silky look.—*BC*

Introduction

THE SOFT GURGLE of a mountain stream. The stillness of the open forest. The haunting call of a Pileated Woodpecker. The gentle movement of a young buck in the morning mist. The kaleidoscope of autumn color that drapes the shoulders of majestic peaks. The rebirth of the forest as spring paints her delicate pastels on the easel of budding flowers. These are but a few of the countless scenes that you will encounter as you wander the vast expanses of Great Smoky Mountains National Park in eastern Tennessee and western North Carolina.

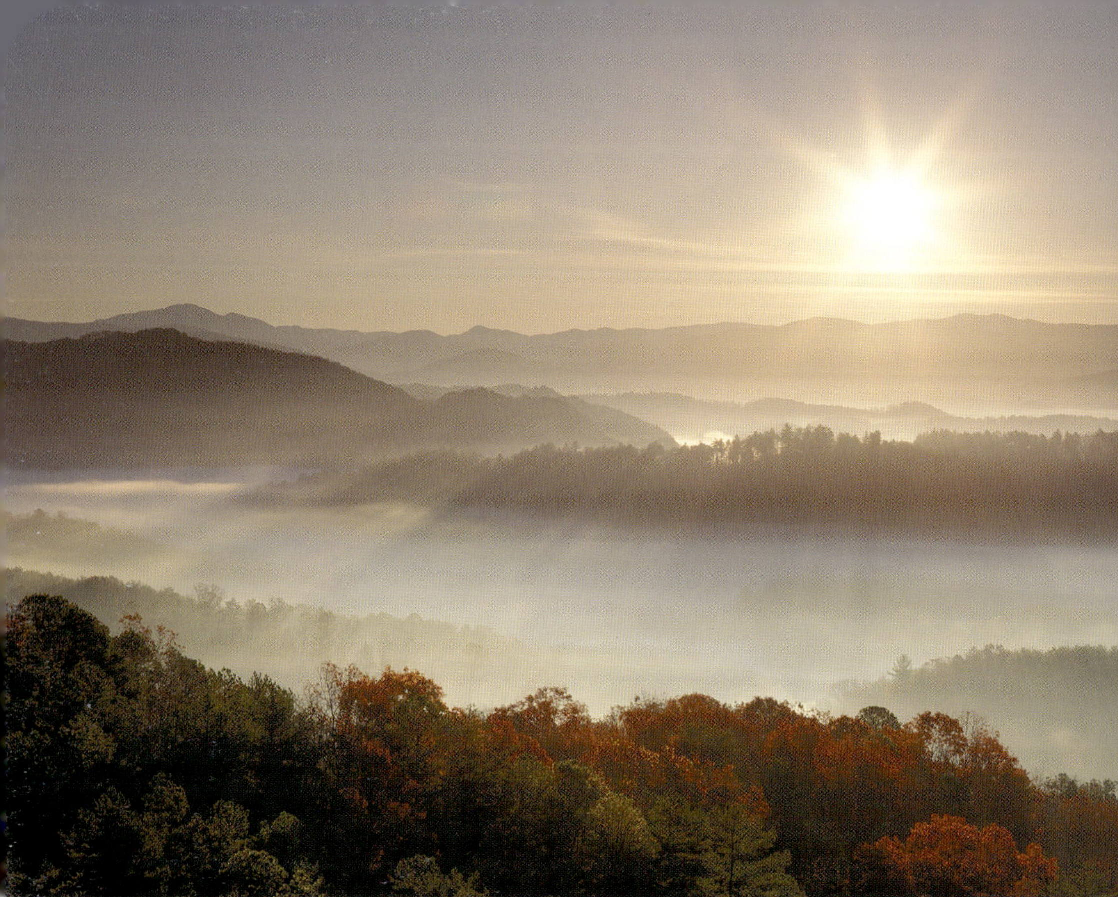

The Smokies is considered by many to be the most biologically diverse national park in America. Containing as many species of native trees as all of Northern Europe and called the "salamander capital of the world," it is not surprising that more species are added to the list on a regular basis. The All Taxa Biodiversity Inventory (ATBI) sponsored by Discover Life in America, has already added over 3000 new species to the park's list and over 300 new species to science. Talk about walking through uncharted and undiscovered territory, you could be photographing a salamander, fungus, or fern previously unknown to science.

Rising over 5000 feet to a peak of 6643 feet at Clingmans Dome, the Smokies encompass over 500,000 acres and 800 miles of hiking trails. The Great Smoky Mountain range runs about 70 miles east-west on the North Carolina-Tennessee border and is surrounded in part by the Cherokee, Nantahala and Pisgah national forests. Rainfall may average over 85 inches a year, and temperatures range from highs in the 80s in summer to lows well below freezing in the winter at the lower elevations. Higher elevations experience even lower temperatures, a grateful relief in summertime.

With such diversity of climate and ecology, it is no wonder that the Smokies are the most visited national park. The number of visitors has now surpassed 10 million a year, each one eager to take home a remembrance of this grand park. With the adage "take only photographs, leave only footprints," the most logical way to carry back a piece of the park is through our photographs. To this

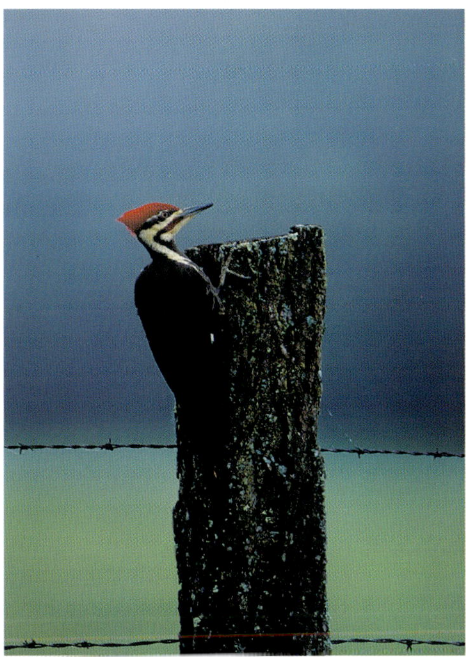

Opposite page: Foothills Parkway West is one of the best sunrise locations in the area and has many moods. A 3 stop Singh-Ray grad balanced the contrast range.—*NS*

Pileated woodpeckers are shy of people; use the vehicle as a blind and brace your lens on the window for a closer approach than you can make on foot.—*NS*

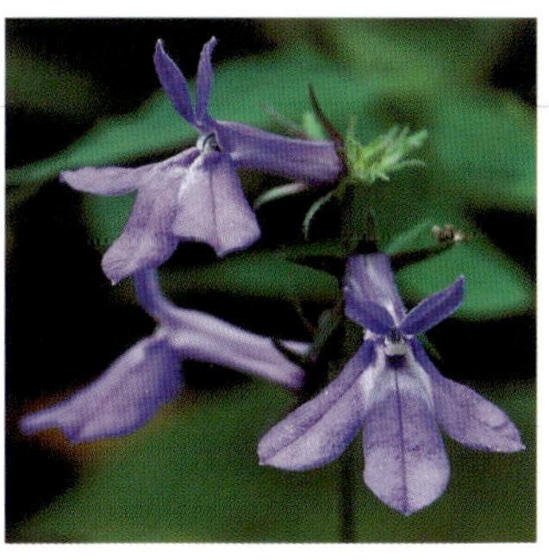

Downy Lobelia blooms in early fall along Rich Mountain Road out of Cades Cove.—*BC*

end we have put together this book to help direct those people who would like to take home the best images they can, but don't have an abundance of time to explore for photo opportunities.

Better nature photography begins with better understanding of nature. To increase your chances of great images, the best advice is to become a better naturalist. Reading books about the areas and environments you visit, collecting flora and fauna guides to the same areas, and spending time observing the ebb and flow of nature are great ways to improve your chances of being able to design images which express how you feel about your subject.

Along with a better understanding of the natural world comes a deepening connection to nature

Using this book

You will find this book organized into regions based on the road that leads through that area. We have mentioned just a few of the countless backcountry opportunities that abound within the park, as the majority of visitors rarely venture very far from their vehicle. Almost all the locations we will discuss are less than a mile's venture from your car, most within 100 yards. Each location's description will tell you about the area and give some guidelines as to time of day, season and lighting situations for each area. These are just general guidelines to maximize your time photographing in the Smokies and are not absolutes about each area.

For information about photographic techniques, look at chapters ten and twelve, and also the captions of images within each section. We have tried to give teaching hints all throughout the book on how to improve your photography. For specific help on the best wildflower locations, go straight to page 72, Wildflowers.

around us. Awareness brings a feeling of responsibility to protect our environment. Stewardship of nature compels us to be vigilant in all aspects of conduct while photographing our natural environment. The North American Nature Photography Association has drawn up their ***Principles of Ethical Field Practices*** which we have reprinted on the inside cover. Please look over these suggestions and consider how any of your actions will be perceived by others around you. The last statement, "Be a good role model, both as a photographer and a citizen," goes far in helping us remember all the other suggestions.

There are as many different ways of seeing as there are photographers, each a personal expression in its own right. BC has been teaching photography for years and sees a broad variety of possibilities in any location. He has published numerous articles about digital photography and also teaches digital imaging for photographers. For the past several years, NS has concentrated on landscape photography with a 4x5 inch view camera; the longest focal length equivalent is 135mm for a 35mm system. His vision leans toward a wider view that the view camera captures so well, but he still finds time to use his 35mm and 6 x 7 cm cameras for those closer and longer viewpoints. We tend to look (and therefore see) within the confines of the equipment we are using; adding a new focal length to our system tends to develop new vision.

We hope this book will make your visit to Great Smoky Mountains National Park more enjoyable and that you can experience some of the wonder of discovery that we felt when we made our favorite images.

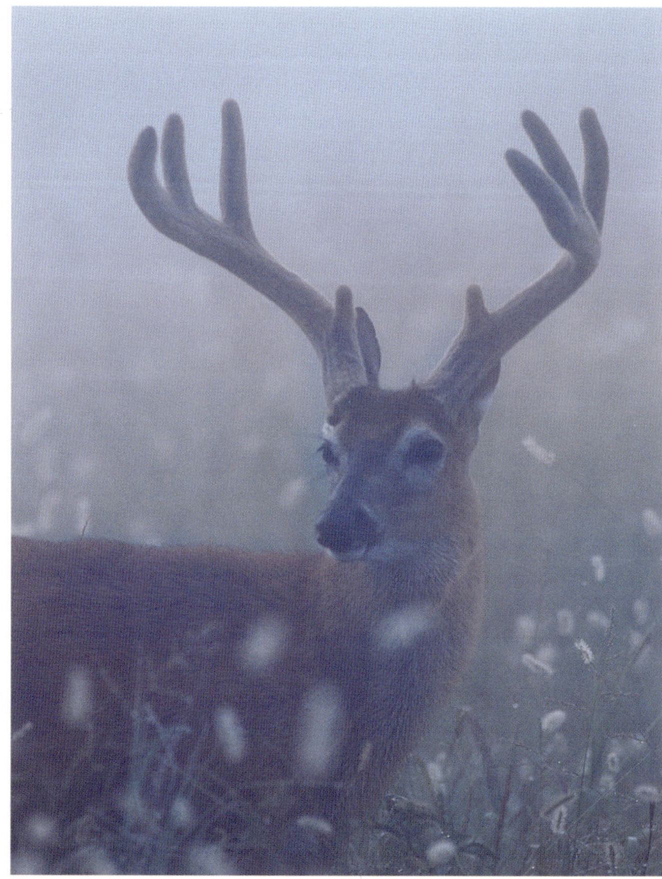

ABOVE: The soft light of morning fog lends an ethereal quality to wildlife images as well as landscapes. Expose for your primary subject, here the buck's face.—*NS*

OPPOSITE PAGE, LEFT: A Snail on a carpet of moss. Look for these small invertebrates after it rains.—*BC*

OPPOSITE PAGE, RIGHT: Long spurred violet is one of the many species of violets found in the Smokies.—*BC*

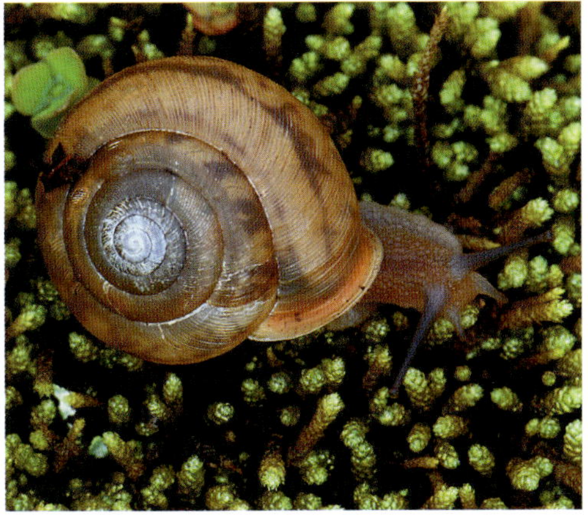

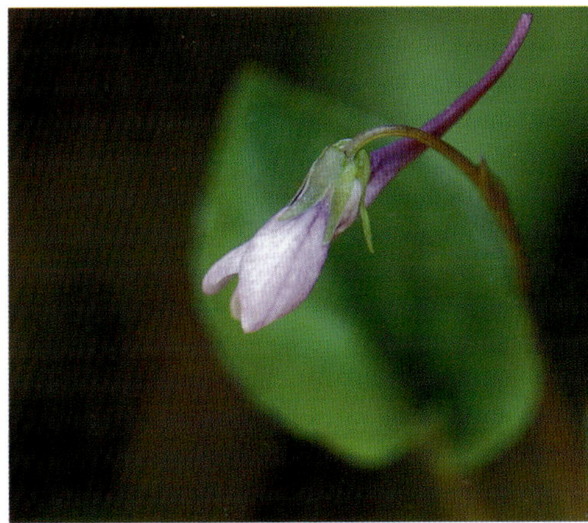

Safety Issues

Safety in a park that experiences 10 million plus visits a year is a paramount concern, especially for park officials. A few suggestions will help you have a trouble free visit to our park:

1) Obey posted speed limit signs and traffic control lines.

2) Respect those behind you and pull off at a convenient spot if you are slower or desire to stop and look at the scenery.

3) Be extremely careful around the many streams and waterfalls. Rocks are very slick and injuries and deaths have occurred within the park related to stream and waterfall activities.

4) Don't leave food out and unattended at a campsite or picnic area. Food smells attract bears. Feeding bears is against park rules and endangers both bear and human. Remember that a fed bear is a dead bear.

5) If hiking alone (not necessarily recommended), leave information about your planned itinerary.

6) Give all animals a respectful distance and leave the area if it appears that the animal is in any way disturbed by your presence.

7) Know that weather conditions can change quickly and be prepared for the worst type of weather during the season you are visiting. Streams can rise quickly in the summer during a heavy thunderstorm and lightening is a common occurrence during these storms. Snow can fall in blizzard proportions from November to April.

8) Watch where you walk, as trails can be close to vertical drop offs and venomous snakes do inhabit the park. Both Timber Rattlesnakes and Northern Copperheads are venomous, but usually not aggressive, and bites seem to occur from stepping on an unseen reptile.

9) Take plenty of fluids to drink during the summer to avoid dehydration. Any water taken from local sources within the park needs to be treated before drinking.

10) If an emergency occurs, contact the nearest ranger or call 865-436-9171, the National Park information number. 911 is also available in many areas, but please use only in true emergencies.

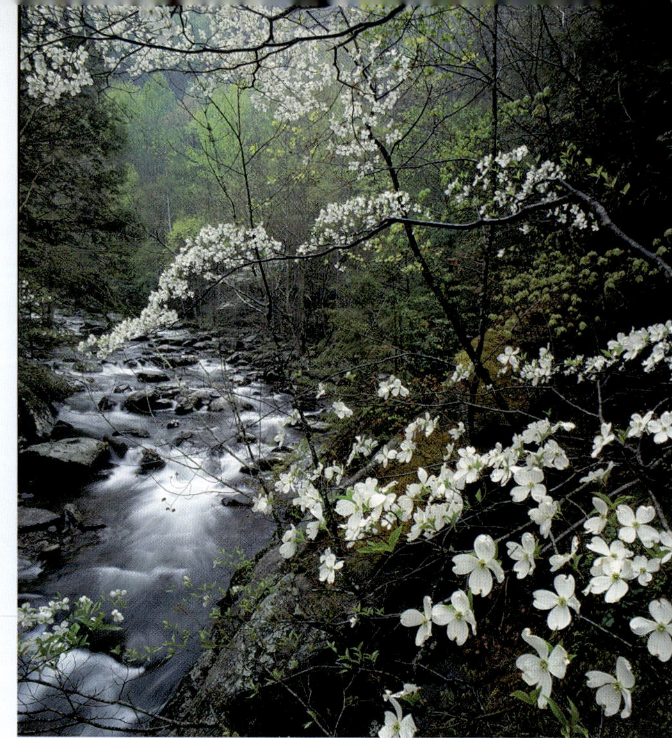

TOP: Scenes like this are vanishing at an alarming rate; although controversial, resistant hybrids may be the only long term solution—*NS*

BOTTOM: Well-watered trees in moist locations have been especially susceptible to the dogwood anthracnose disease—*NS*

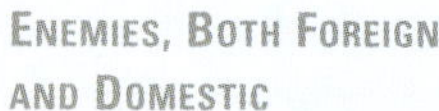

Enemies, Both Foreign and Domestic

Our Park is under siege. The enemy, an insect or disease, is often invisible with names difficult to pronounce, and sometimes all too familiar. Adelgids, tiny little aphid like insects, nearly unseen, have decimated the Fraser fir, leaving behind ghostly skeletons in the high country. They seem ever so comfortable here, and have asked their cousin that likes hemlocks to move on down. More skeletons are eminent. Chestnut blight, Dutch elm disease, Beech Bark disease, Dogwood Anthracnose, the list continues, and doesn't even touch the other non-native species like the exotic European Boar, Japanese grass, and wisteria. All are foreign invaders that find little host resistance. The native Southern pine beetle kills in cycles, emerging when winters aren't cold enough to kill them off. This insect is a natural part of the ecosystem; its beneficial effects are obscure to the casual observer while the dead trees are evident to everyone. The full cycle of re growth won't be completed for many years.

The flowering dogwoods we love so dearly are sick; many have died (up to 100% in some Park locations). Many of the survivors look healthy today, but be forewarned, one of our favorite trees looked great the spring before it died. As visitors and photographers, we miss the blossoms in spring that make the forest and streams so special and the intense reds in

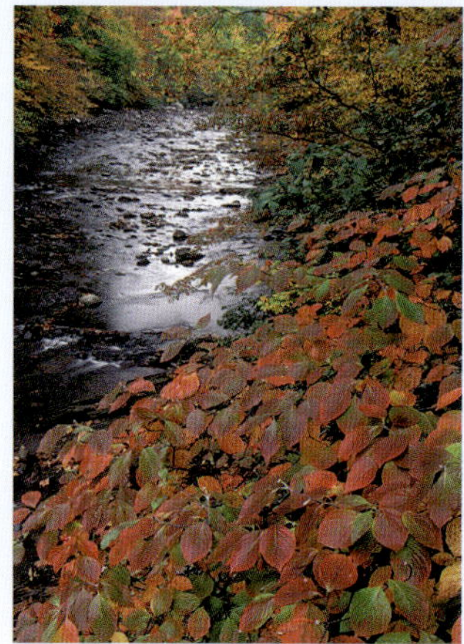

fall. Their loss has a ripple effect on the forest community that used the dogwood for food and shelter as well. No one can fully predict the consequences to an out of balance ecosystem.

In 1999, poachers entered Cades Cove and killed two of the most magnificent white tailed bucks in the park. The delicate lady

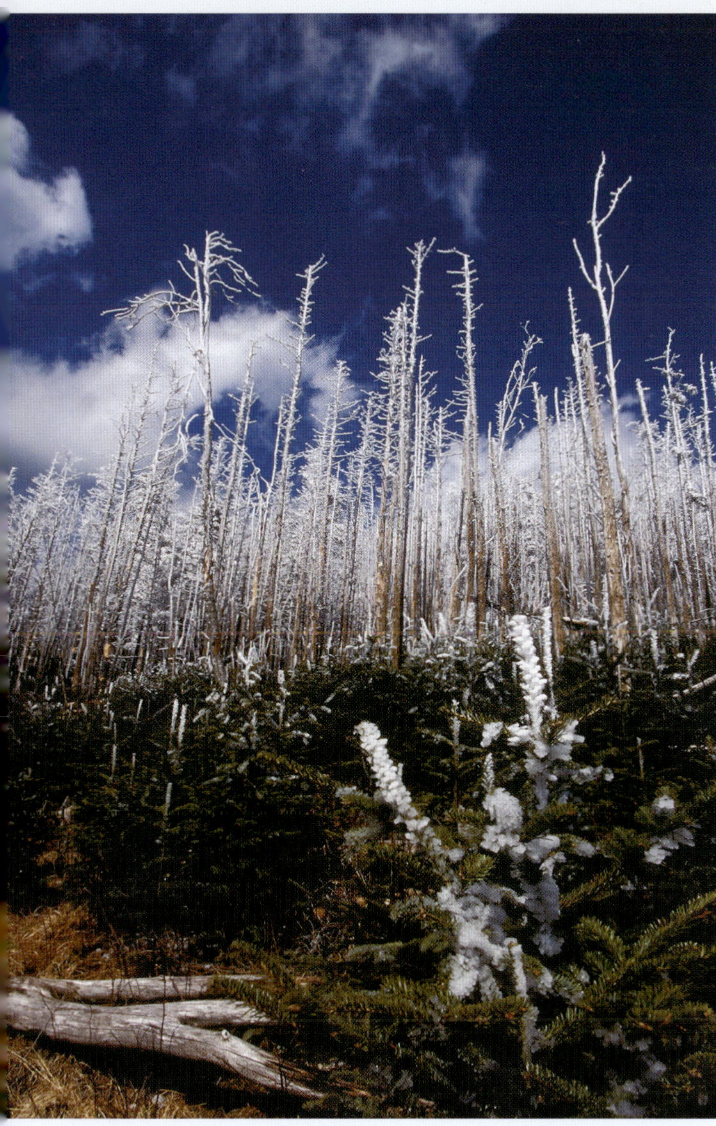

Fraser firs at Clingmans Dome stand as skeletal reminders of the ravaging Balsam Wooly Adelgid. More than 70% of the mature firs are now affected within the park.—*BC*

slipper is a victim of poaching also and has been hard hit, dug up to be transplanted to gardens far away. Black bears have a hard enough time finding something to eat and dodging cars without having to worry about someone wanting their gall bladder for an aphrodisiac.

Air pollution threatens the Park's resources as well as impacting human health. Visibility impairment, ozone, and acid rain are serious problems created by pollution emitted from power plants, industry, and automobiles. Views from scenic overlooks have been degraded over the years. On a good day you can see about 25 miles, down from 93 miles when the park was created. During some episodes visibility is reduced to less than 1 mile at Newfound Gap. High levels of ozone pollution damage resources and cause us respiratory problems. Acid rain has widespread effects.

But there is hope. Not all bugs are invincible, not all trees die. Many are joined in the effort to protect the Park. Friends of the Smokies and Great Smoky Mountains Association funded an effort to assist the Park in controlling the hemlock adelgid. There is much that still needs to be done. You can help.

***Your** attitude and **your** voice are ultimately the only defense that refuges like this will ever have. Make your opinion known to political leaders, and back it up with a vote. Urge Congress to make adequate funds available to support our parks. Friends of Great Smoky Mountains National Park and the Great Smoky Mountains Association are two non profit organizations that support the Park and deserve your support through membership and financial contributions. They can both be found on line at* **http://www.smokiesstore.org** *and* **www.friendsofthe smokies.org**.

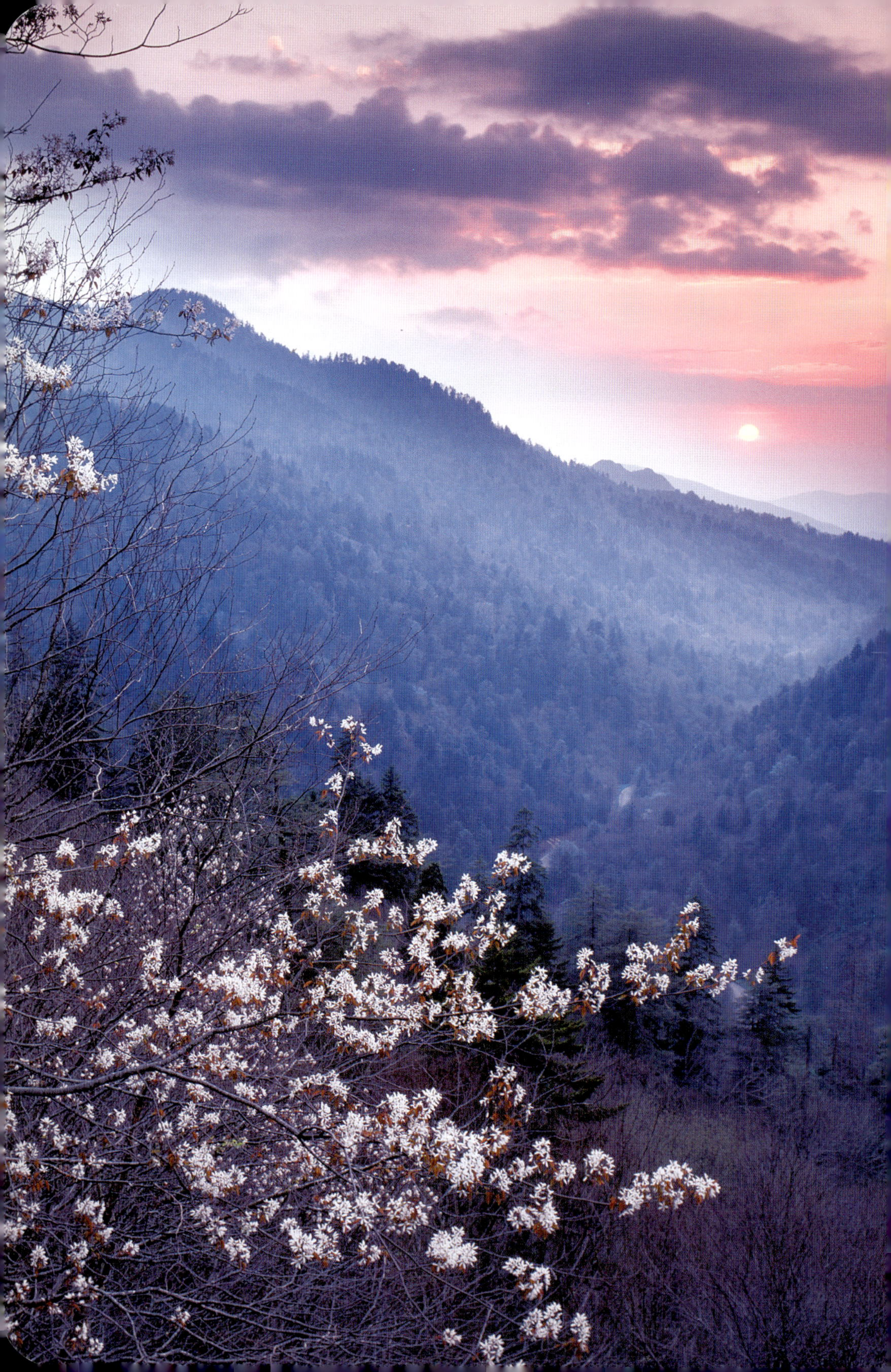

Classic Smokies grand scenics

Sunrises & sunsets

Stream scenes

Wildflowers

Winter ice formations

Photo hikes

Chapter One

Newfound Gap Road

Blooming sarvis at Morton Overlook lasts only a few days in late April. Several photographers ignored this lovely tree to make telephoto images of the setting sun; 3 stop Singh Ray grad.—*NS*

MOST PEOPLE COME TO THE PARK through Gatlinburg, TN or Cherokee, North Carolina, making the road that connects them a logical place to start your photographic journey. Each side of the park has its own unique personality, and it is quite possible to become ensnared by the beauty of one feature and lose track of time, only to run short later in the day or week. Hwy 441 (Newfound Gap Road) is your access to many of the classic Smokies scenes, including views of Mount Le Conte, the Chimneys, and Morton Overlook. 441 brings you to the Newfound Gap and Oconaluftee Overlooks,

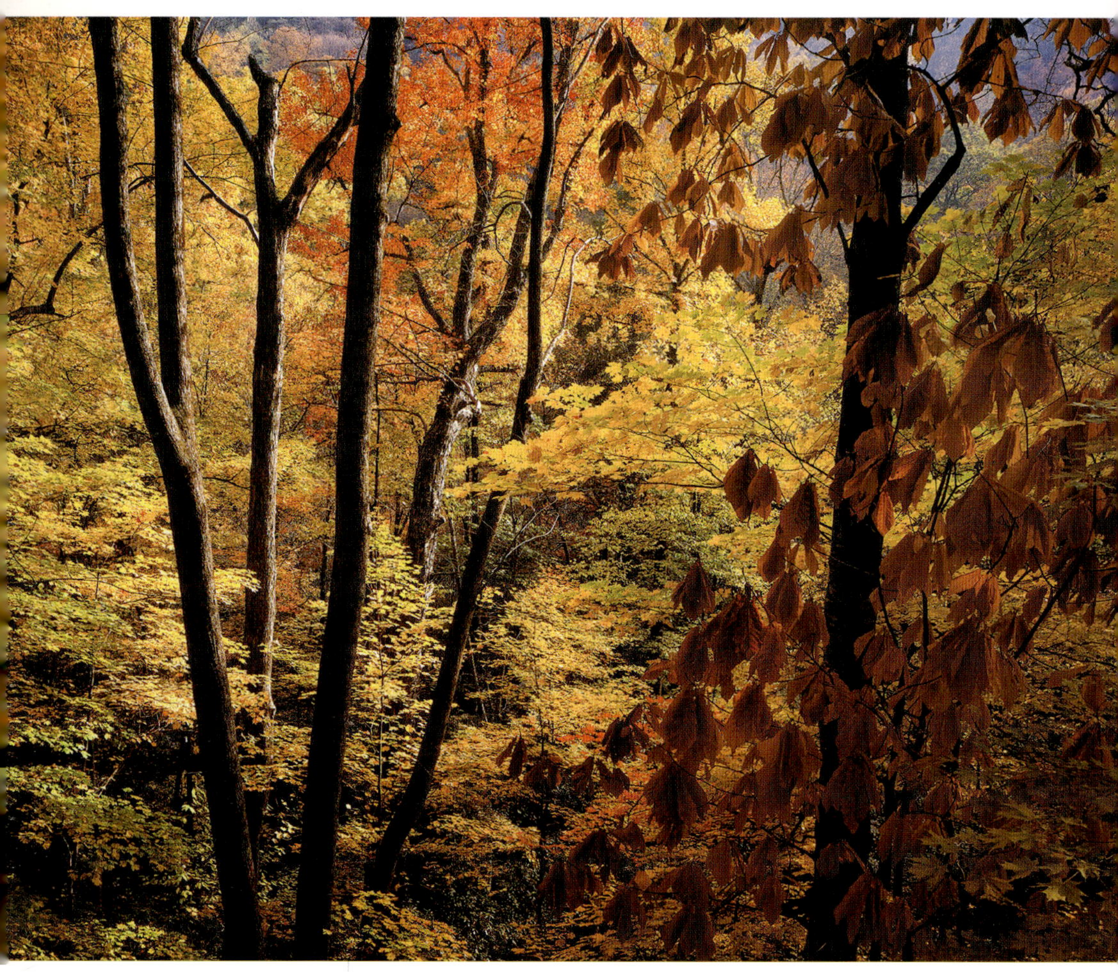

Fall forest—Shapely tree trunks add graphic interest to this softly backlighted scene; no filtration was needed; the edge of "peek a boo" light added a magic glow.—*NS*

the high ridges on the North Carolina side, and down to the Mountain Farm Museum with its visitors center on the North Carolina side. You'll find many hiking options along this road; 441 is also your access to the Appalachian Trail at Newfound Gap and Clingmans Dome.

Starting at the Sugarlands Visitor Center on the Tennessee side, at the junction of Little River road and US 441, follow the road towards Cherokee. Set your odometer to 0.0 at this intersection and head south towards Newfound Gap. Reverse mileage if you are starting at Oconaluftee where you zero your odometer.

Just up the road you will find two quiet walkways giving you access to the West Prong of the Little Pigeon River below. A short walk takes you to intimate forest and river scenes; spring wildflowers can be excellent here.

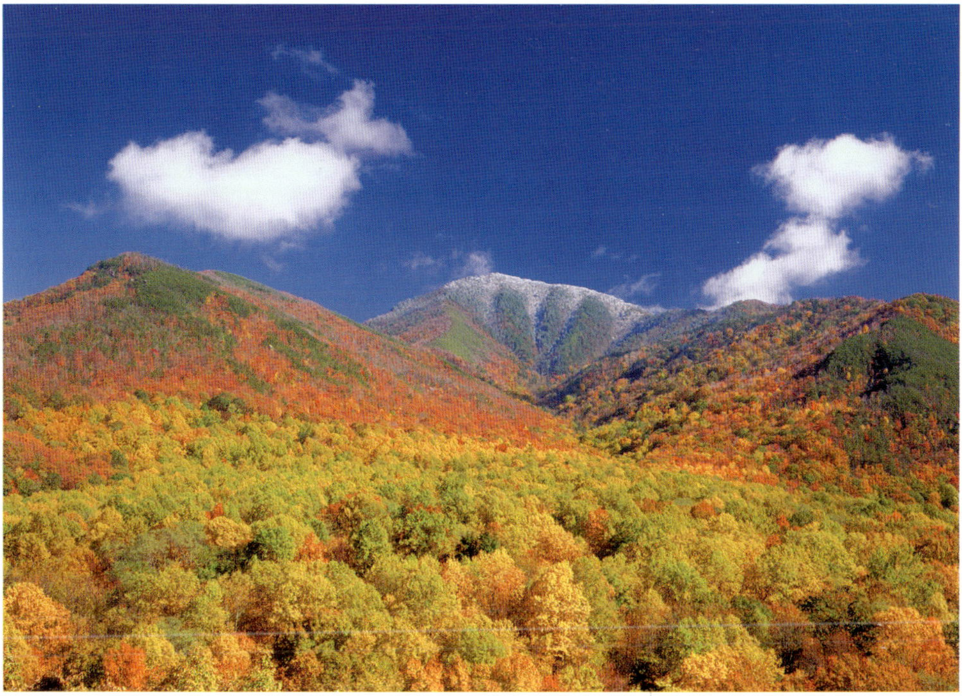

Campbell Overlook
2.2 (27) miles

Not far into the park you will find on your left two large turnouts with classic views of Mount Le Conte, elev. 6593 feet. Campbell Overlook proper is the second of the two; each offers slightly different compositions. Le Conte is stunning when helped by pretty fall leaves, snow, frost, or a rainbow, though some of these props are rare events. You will have an elevated view of the hardwood forest on the lower flanks of the mountain as well.

Early to mid-afternoon light is flattering; the sun comes up behind the mountain leaving the face in deep shadow. An early crescent moon will linger in the morning sky here at the right time of the month. Polarizers help here. If the sky is dead, try a telephoto to compose sections of hillside. Up the road a very short distance on the left (Campbell Overlook proper) there is another similar parking area and view with slightly different perspective and foreground.

Above: Mount LeConte was losing snow fast in this early afternoon composition. A Singh-Ray polarizing color intensifier filter popped the clouds and the colors with minimal color cast.—*NS*

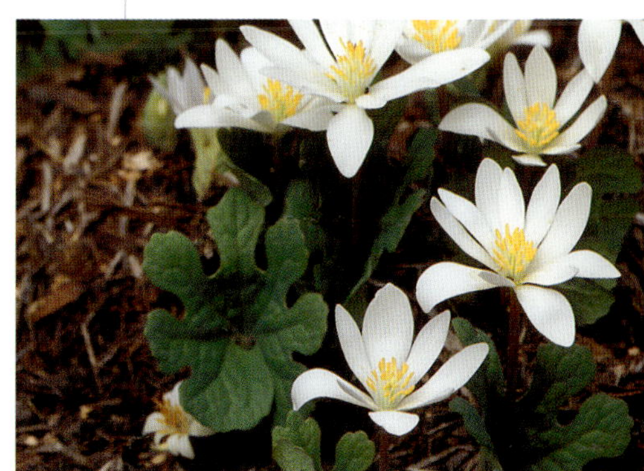

Bloodroot blooms early and low to the ground. Optimal appearance only lasts several days, and fragile leaves are easily knocked off by heavy rain.—*BC*

HIKE IT

Chimney Tops Picnic Area

4.6 (24.6) miles

You'll find restrooms (closed in winter), a picnic area, and sometimes a bear (looking for garbage and handouts—please don't feed them). During mid to late April, the fringed phacelia and many other species bloom here and literally carpet the ground, sometimes resembling snow. A self-guiding nature trail winds up hill from the parking area near the gate offering a chance to stretch your legs and look for compositions (more on that in the wildflower section.) Just up the road are two more pullouts where you can park and find abundant wildflowers on the uphill side. Recent deadfalls have cluttered the larger scenes but many intimate flower scapes remain.

***The West Prong of the Little Pigeon River** runs through the picnic area and is attractive from the bridge. Bridges of any kind give a perspective from midstream that can only otherwise be achieved by wading out into the river, and you should investigate these opportunities whenever possible. Watch out for traffic.*

Chimney Tops Viewing Areas

5.4 (23.8) miles

Up a steep hill with an abrupt hairpin turn from the picnic area you will find a series of turnouts on the right (west) side of the road with a clear view of the Chimney Tops and the hillside on the opposite side of the river. The first is very small and comes at you quickly; the next ones are close enough to the first and easier to enter and exit. There are several more in the next half-mile, each with its own character.

Spring forest colors are subtle here, with beautiful pastels and greens. Fall colors are unusually intense here near peak season, and often linger until early November. An early rising moon can be seen above the Chimneys late on a fall afternoon, 3-4 days before full moon. Morning light hits the ridge later in the day, and is usually good until you lose it behind the ridge in the afternoon. Further up the road, you can frame the chimneys with back lighted leaves in late morning to early afternoon in the fall. The far hillsides hold snow well, but it melts off quickly on foreground branches. Be here early if that accent is important to your image.

OPPOSITE PAGE, TOP: The West Prong Little Pigeon River suffered from very flat light. A Singh-Ray Color Polarizer (Gold N Blue) adds a splash of color to the water in an otherwise bland scene.—*NS*

OPPOSITE PAGE, BOTTOM LEFT: The Chimneys in fall color. Different light, different snow, different mood. Even a dusting works to your advantage; an added plus is the road may stay open after a light snow.—*NS*

OPPOSITE PAGE, BOTTOM RIGHT: Great Horned Owls are usually nocturnal creatures. The feather configuration on their wings makes them silent but deadly predators.—*BC*

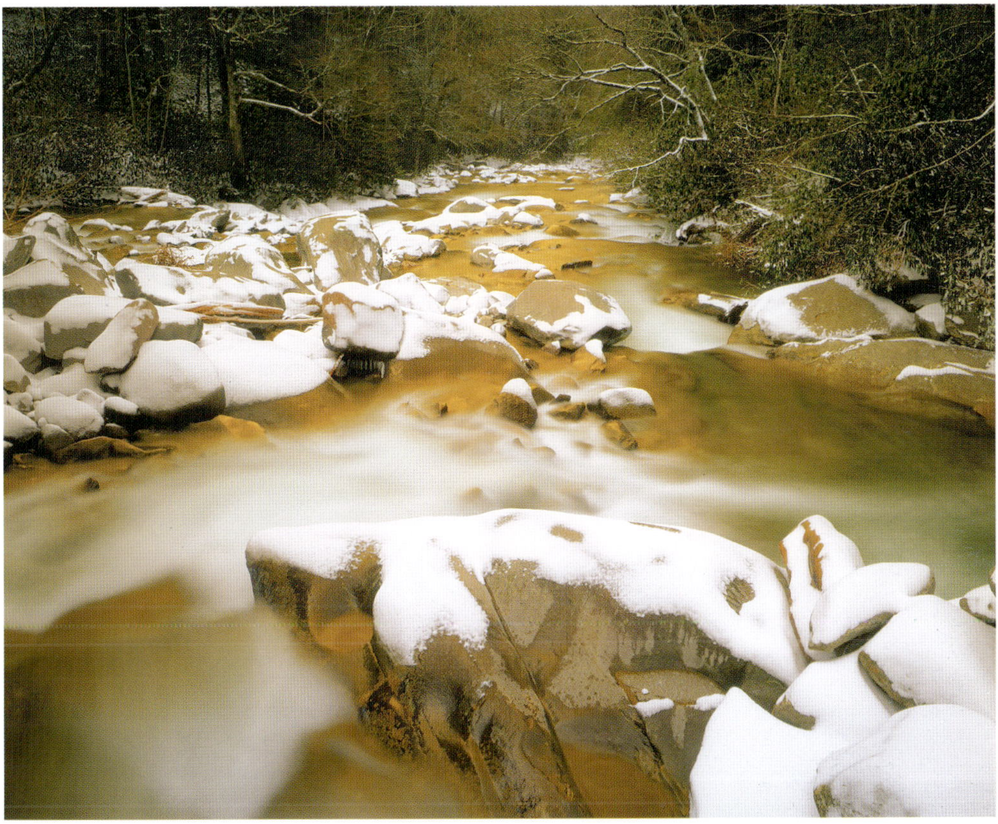

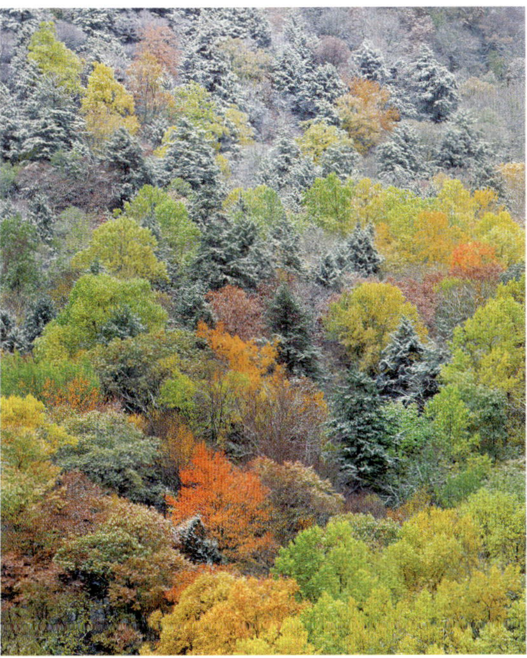

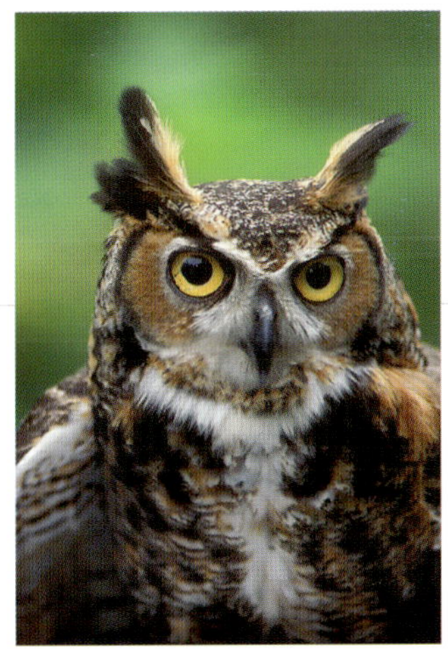

Chimney Tops Trailhead
7.1 (22.1)miles

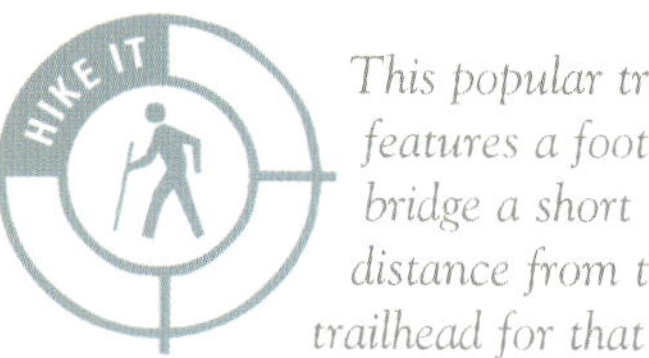

This popular trail features a footbridge a short distance from the trailhead for that aerial perspective of the West Prong from mid-stream. Multiple options can be found at all seasons for stream bed shots with rhododendron, mountain laurel, fall colors, snow and ice, or whatever else Mother Nature is serving up on your visit. Soft light is the usual recommendation for stream scenes, but late afternoon light bounces off the east slopes putting a color wash on the water for a while. Follow the trail across the footbridge, and then across another bridge spanning a side stream to the signpost sending you uphill to the left for the hike to the top. When photographing from the footbridge, make sure no one will step on the bridge during the exposure, as the vibrations will ruin your image.

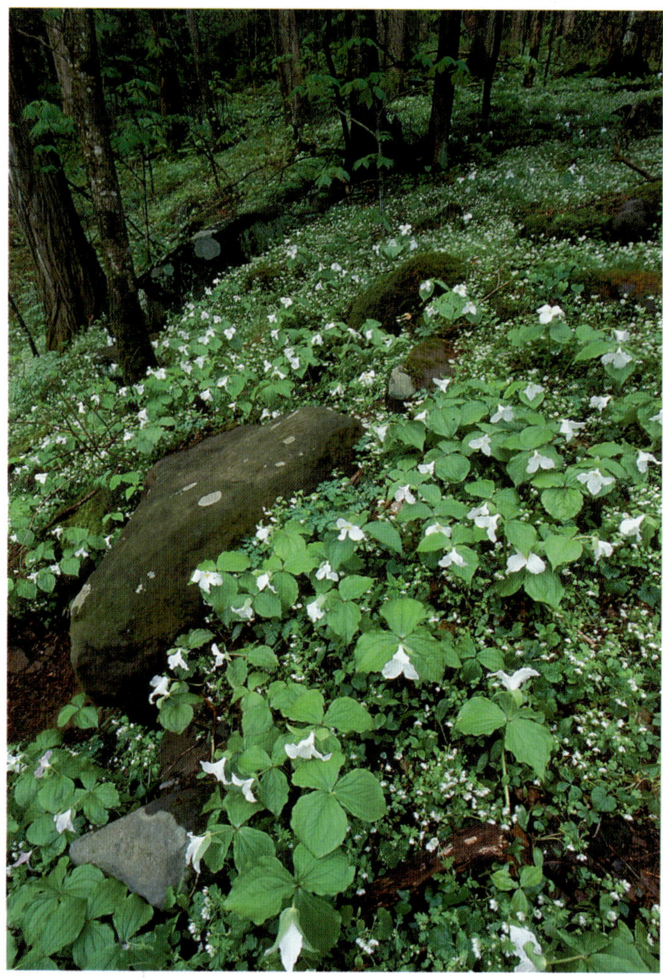

Large-flowered Trillium can be found blooming in mass at Chimney Tops Picnic Area around the middle of April. Explore the Cove Hardwood trail here for a variety of wildflowers.—*BC*

For those wanting a workout, the hike to **the Chimneys** *offers outstanding views at the end of a steep climb. This is not a "granny trail" and not for the heavily laden, climbing almost 1500 feet in 2 miles.*

In Between *Multiple scenes can be photographed in the next five miles on the way to Morton Overlook. Several turnouts offer views of the West Prong, now dwindling to a trickle at higher elevations. Serviceberry trees (sarvis) bloom here in spring and rosebay rhododendron in June and July.*

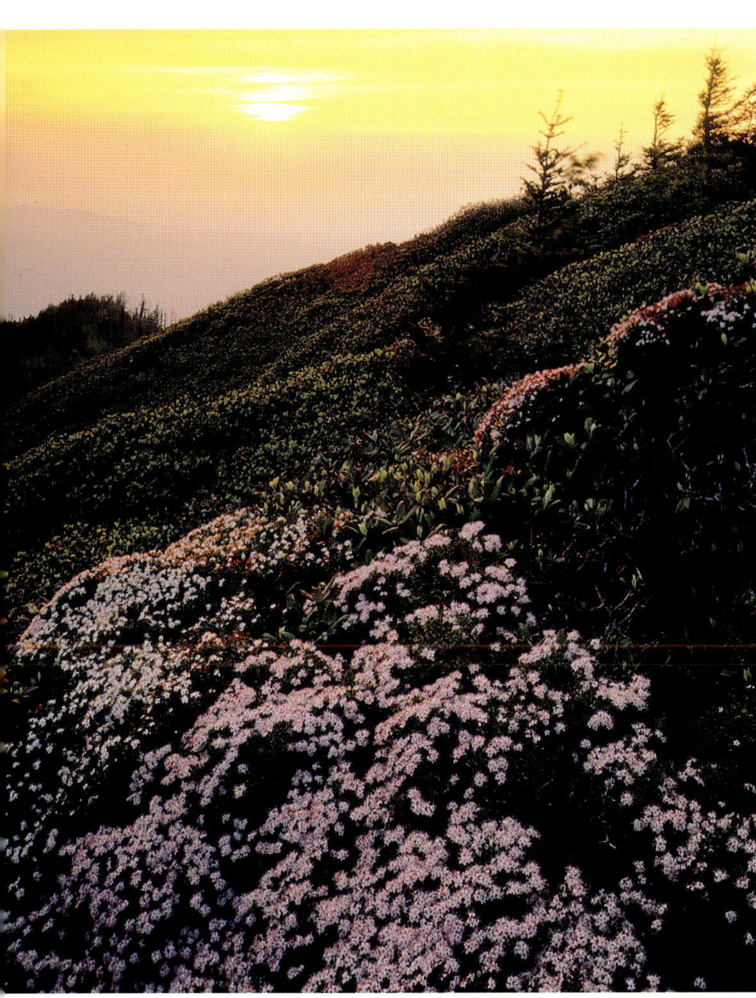

Sand Myrtle on Mount Le Conte bloom in late May and early June. A 3 stop Singh Ray grad balanced exposure for the setting sun and foreground blossoms.

HIKE IT

Alum Cave Bluffs Trailhead

mile 8.8 (20.4)

This is the shortest and easiest route to Mount Le Conte. It's about 5 miles each way, with 2,500 feet elevation gain, so pare down your camera gear to the bare essentials, and allow extra hiking time for the extra burden. Storm gear is a must, as the weather is fickle; it also gets 10-20 degrees colder at night than down in the valley. Even summers can be very chilly. The footbridge near the parking area offers another mid-stream view for those not inclined to hike. For photographers wanting the best light, plan to spend the night at Le Conte Lodge (advanced reservations required, often a year in advance—865-429-5704) or at the shelter (reservations up to 30 days out—865-436-1231). The Lodge is privately owned and operated as a concession; the shelter is a backcountry style structure like the ones on the AT, maintained by the Park Service. Evening light is typically best at Cliff Tops and morning at Myrtle Point, both of which involve short additional hikes. The lovely heather-like sand myrtle blooms in late May to early June; October is popular for fall color and generally good weather.

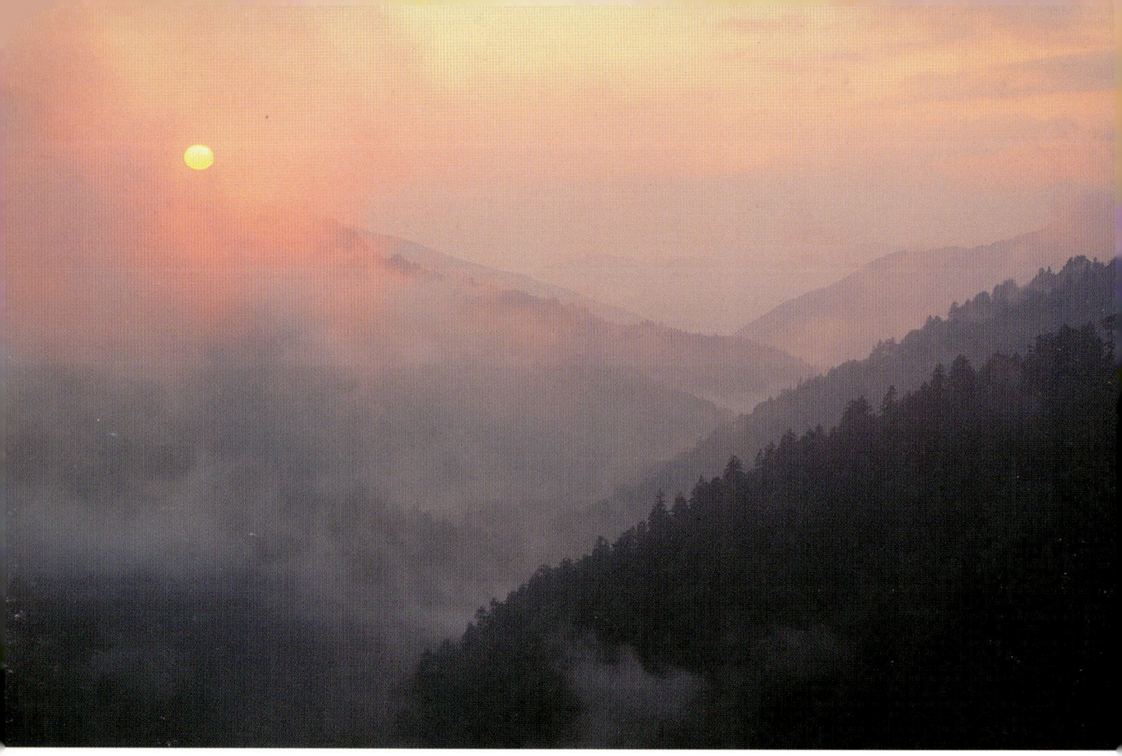

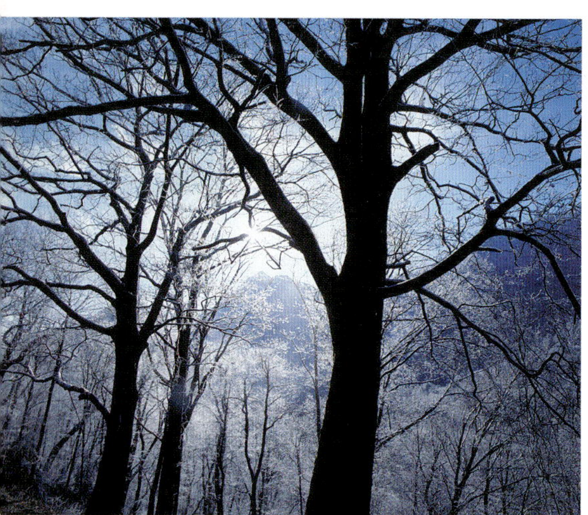

Above: Winter silhouette—Almost a duotone; like a black and white image, it relies on shapes and balance rather than just color to make a statement. The main verticals approximate the rule of thirds.—*NS*

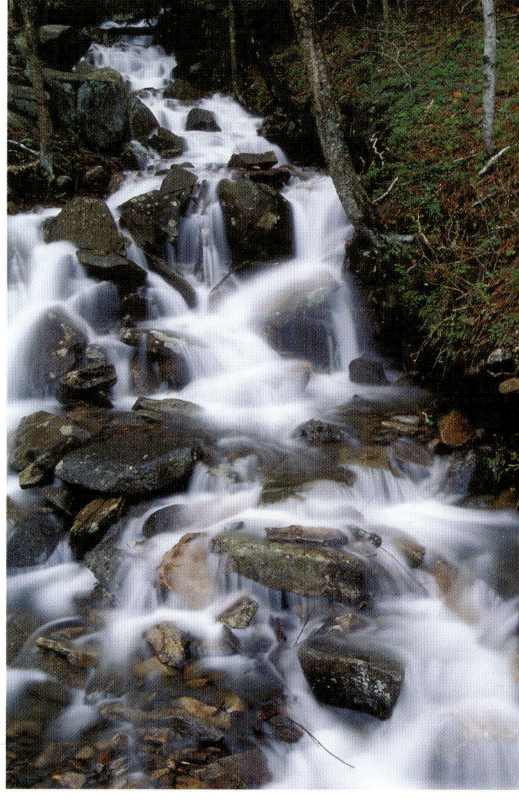

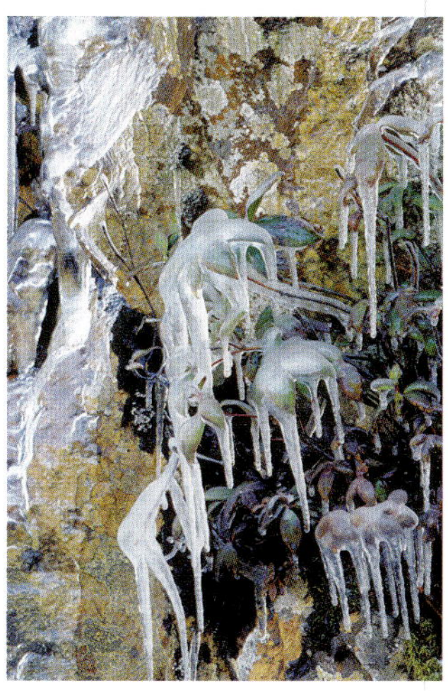

Opposite page, top left: Morton Overlook, clearing storm—The tail end of a summer thunderstorm can bring exceptional opportunities.—*NS*

Opposite page, bottom right: Heavy spring rains turn docile creeks into majestic cascades. Soft light allows slow shutter speeds necessary for silky water.—*BC*

This page: A weeping wall. Mile 10.7 becomes the "icicle wall" in winter and is a consistent location for intimate winter scenes. A Singh Ray A13 warming filter tones down the blues.—*NS*

A Weeping Wall
mile 10.7 (16.3)

The road will make a sharp turn to the right as it leaves the upper reaches of the West Prong. On the left is a seeping wall of rock, with lichen and moss, and struggling rhododendron sprouts. In the spring and summer there are beautiful lichens on the wet rocks, in shade most of the day. In winter there are beautiful icicle formations here that make wonderful intimate landscapes. Be careful that an overhead icicle doesn't detach and crash down on your head, and keep your eye on traffic—you are very close to the road. There is a similar formation a bit farther up the road in the next abrupt turn. These walls are in shade through the winter, and can pick up excessive blue in some instances. Consider using a warming filter to counter this.

Morton Overlook
mile 12.5 (16.7)

Summer sunsets at Morton are classic Smokies scenes. The sun will be on the right-hand shoulder of the mountains in early June, swing over to mid-valley in July, and start to go down behind the Chimneys in mid-August. By late August to early September, the sun is far to the left unbalancing the composition. Then it is time to move to Clingmans Dome for sunset photos if you want the sun balanced in the frame. This is a popular spot; get here early and hang out, enjoy the view, and if the clouds are right, try to catch sunbeams breaking through.

There is a phenomenon you will notice photographing the Smokies. The denser layer of air in the distance, haze, pollution, and water vapor, softens the sun's image to a red ball of varying intensity as it descends into the thicker air. Depending on weather conditions you lose the sun at varying degrees above the horizon, with variable color effects. No two days will be the same. Shooting through a clearing storm can yield spectacular images, though the potential for being disappointed is certainly great if the clouds don't cooperate. Strong images can be found here in bad weather also, so don't give up if the sun isn't out. The swirling "smoke," the Park's namesake, surrounds you when the clouds are low. Momentary breaks in the clouds reveal ridgelines and evergreen spires. Work quickly before the door closes. Don't pack up after the sun dips below the horizon either. Over the next

30 minutes the afterglow will intensify, and may be the best part of the show. Film is more sensitive to red than your eye is under conditions of low light and long shutter speeds; you may be amazed at the color you get back on your film.

Back lighted scenes are tricky, and lens flare often becomes an issue. You can usually see the patterns in the viewfinder and decide if they have artistic merit, or just detract from the image. If the sun is in the scene, try waiting until you don't have to squint to look at it directly. If you have to squint or it hurts your eyes, chances are there will be lens flare. Zooms are more prone to flare than fixed focal length lenses; macro lenses usually have the least of all.

Bracket. It may seem like a waste of film to some, but you can't always predict how film will render the scene, even with years of experience, and what pleases us in exposure may not suite you. You may have to put the different exposures side by side to pick the one you like best. Nothing is more disappointing than the discovery that you failed to capture a once in a lifetime scene the way you intended. Knowing how your film responds to different lighting conditions takes a great deal of experience; until you have gained that degree of expertise, consider taking "insurançe" images with more and less exposure than you think proper (i.e. bracket).

Time of year here is important if the setting sun is to be an element in your image. The sun travels a wide arc throughout the year, and several different balanced compositions are possible. For a few days out of the year it sets straight behind the Chimneys and

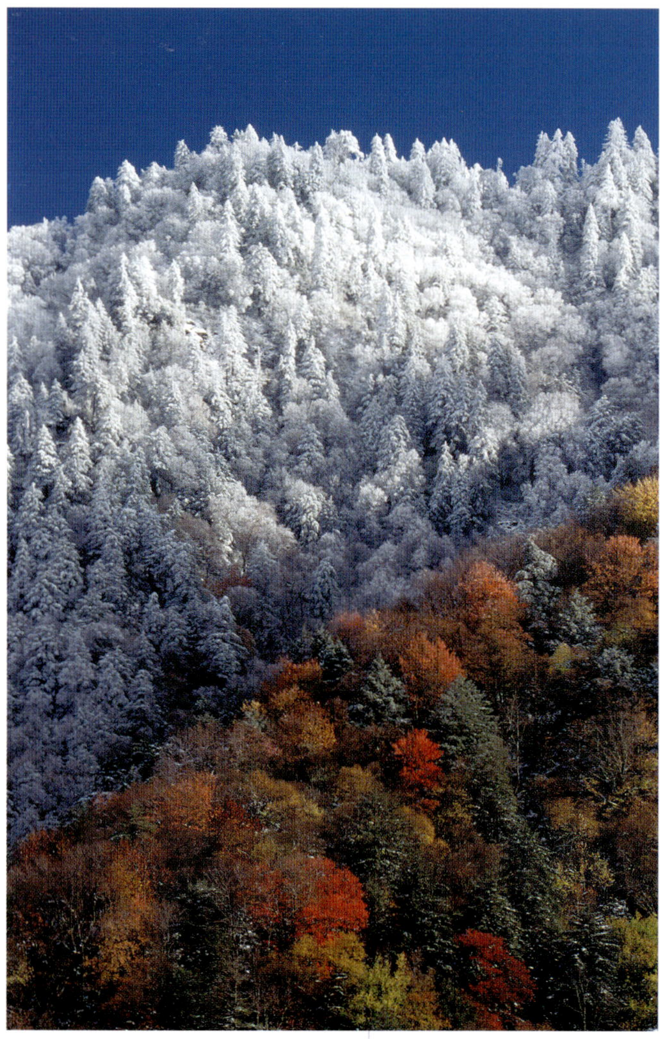

Snow combined with fall color at the Chimneys is a rare event. The flanks of the ridges held snow until the road opened in mid-afternoon.—*NS*

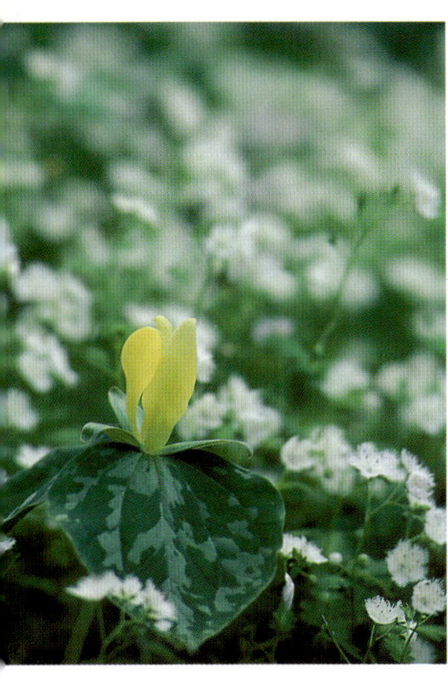

From the quiet walkways to the Chimney Tops Viewing are, these delicate white fringed phacelia can carpet the woodland floor. Adding a different species like this Yellow Trillium adds a focal point to the profusion of white.—*BC*

can be framed above it, and for a couple of days it is nestled in the gun sight notch of the mountain itself. In August, the sun is moving ever to the south as it sets. On August 17th and April 25th it will be hitting the horizon just to the right of the right peak, and on August 21st and April 22nd just to the left of the left peak. In August the arc of the setting sun carries it over the Chimneys before the 17th; in April it's after the 25th. When the sun is setting in or near the notch, try a longer telephoto composition.

When clouds are starting to clear in the afternoon down in the valleys or in Cades Cove, think of heading here or to Clingmans Dome for the chance at clearing storm images. It's a gamble, but with great rewards if it pays off.

Newfound Gap
13.2 (16) miles

This large parking lot is usually crowded, but there is lots of space to spread out. Lock your car and take valuables with you to avoid leading someone into temptation. There is water, a restroom, and the Appalachian Trail. This is also one of the most accessible sunrise locations in the park. The sun is farthest to the left, nearly out of the frame, in June, and swings into possible compositions in late summer, fall, winter, and early spring. Set up early because the best color will often be 15 to 30 minutes before actual sunrise; often the color fades as the rising sun approaches the horizon. If there is enough water vapor in the air, the sun may be a red/yellow ball above the horizon for a couple of minutes before it gets intense enough to create lens flare.

Use a longer lens to isolate portions of the landscape before you, and a wider angle to include foreground interest. Sunrise is great; mid-afternoon gives directional light "over the shoulder" for blue-sky scenics. Late afternoon thunderstorms offer a chance for a rainbow. This is a great spot at all seasons, weather cooperating. The most dramatic conditions will occur when you decided the weather was too bad to get out of bed. Watch out for vapor trails sneaking into your image after you set up your composition.

For those wanting to hike, the AT crosses here leading to Ice Water Springs Shelter, Charlies Bunion, and The Boulevard Trail, which is another route to Mount Le Conte. Spring wildflowers and the pink Catawba rhododendron are found here, as well as sand myrtle at Charlies Bunion. In some years carpets of trout lilies line the higher reaches of the trail.

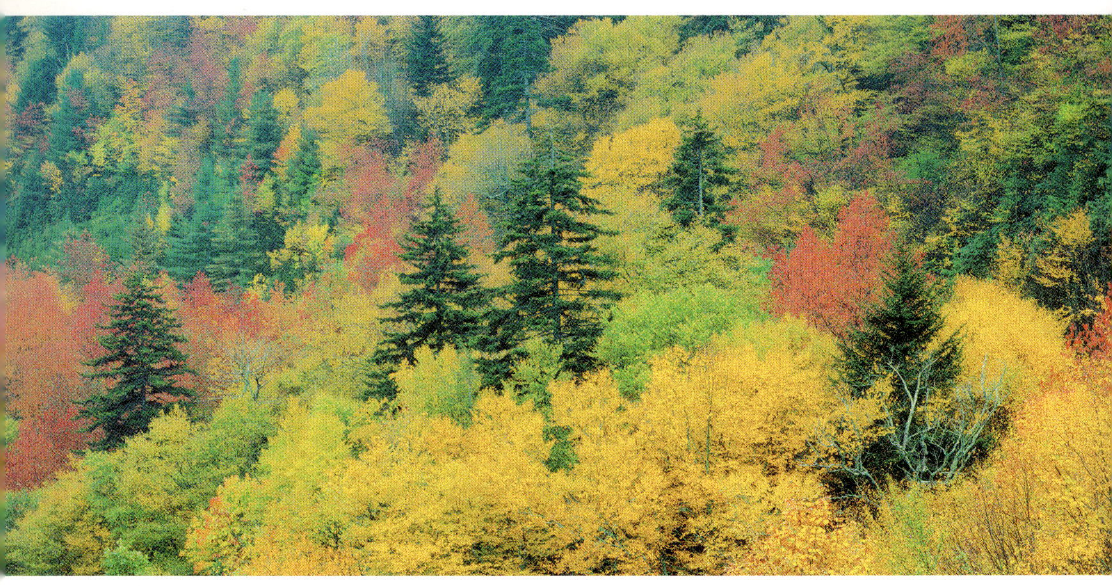

Oconaluftee Overlook sports incredible color in a good year and often peaks early in the season soon after mid-month. Shapely evergreens balance the scene.—*NS*

Oconaluftee Valley Overlook
mile 13.9 (15.3)

Sunrise alternate There is a large parking lot perhaps a half mile down on the Cherokee side of Newfound Gap that offers several different compositions. Here the sun crests the ridge sooner in spring and summer with a chance that the denser vapor laden air on the horizon will soften the sun's orb. A few degrees higher (a few minutes later) the brightness intensifies and the technical problems of flare and contrast become unmanageable. It's then time to use side lighting, either here or down the road. In fall and winter the "V" shaped valley adds interest, and you can compose without the road in your image (which can be a problem at Newfound Gap). We routinely walk across the road from the parking area to set up. In mid-October the sun is about in the middle of the "V." Use any variety of lenses for the composition of your choice. If the sun isn't soft enough to look at, try a small aperture, f:16 or smaller for a starburst effect. Be alert to contrails; you are looking towards Asheville, and early morning flights can add unwanted elements to your image. Consider using a split neutral density filter to control the contrast between light sky and darker foreground.

The starburst effect is usually accompanied by a degree of lens flare. You can sometimes bury it in the midst of other bright highlights, and sometimes you can use the line of bright highlights to "lead" the viewer to some point of interest in the frame. If there is a tree or cloudbank that's conveniently located in the composition, sometimes you can catch just the edge of the sun peeking out and get the sunburst without the flare. You'll have to experiment with it to get comfortable predicting the result. In general, meter the section of the scene that you want to hold detail in and let the starburst area fall where it will. The starburst will show best against a darker sky, which can be provided by a graduated neutral density filter.

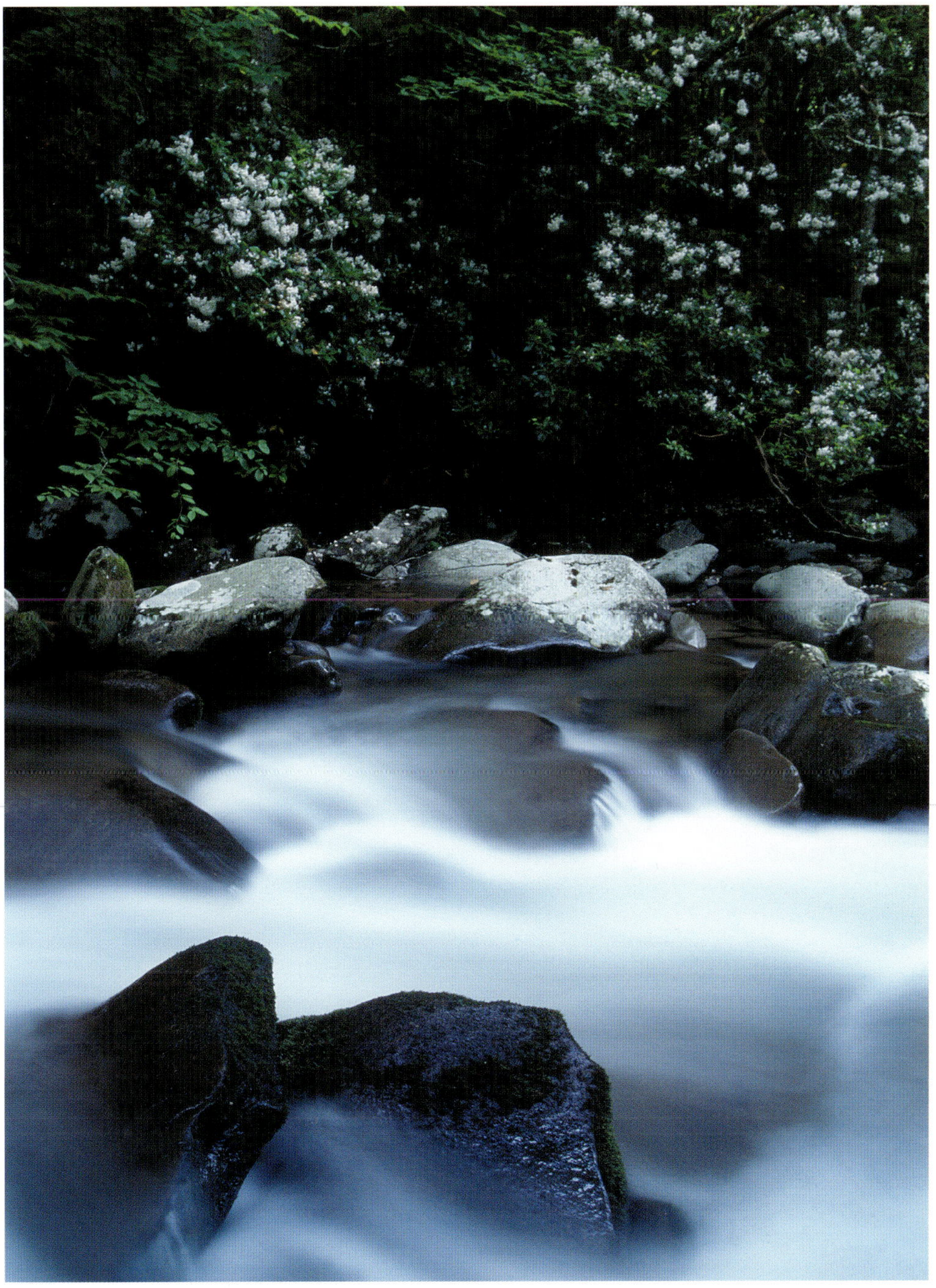

Mountain laurel blooming in early June add a pleasing accent to river scenes along the Oconaluftee River.—*NS*

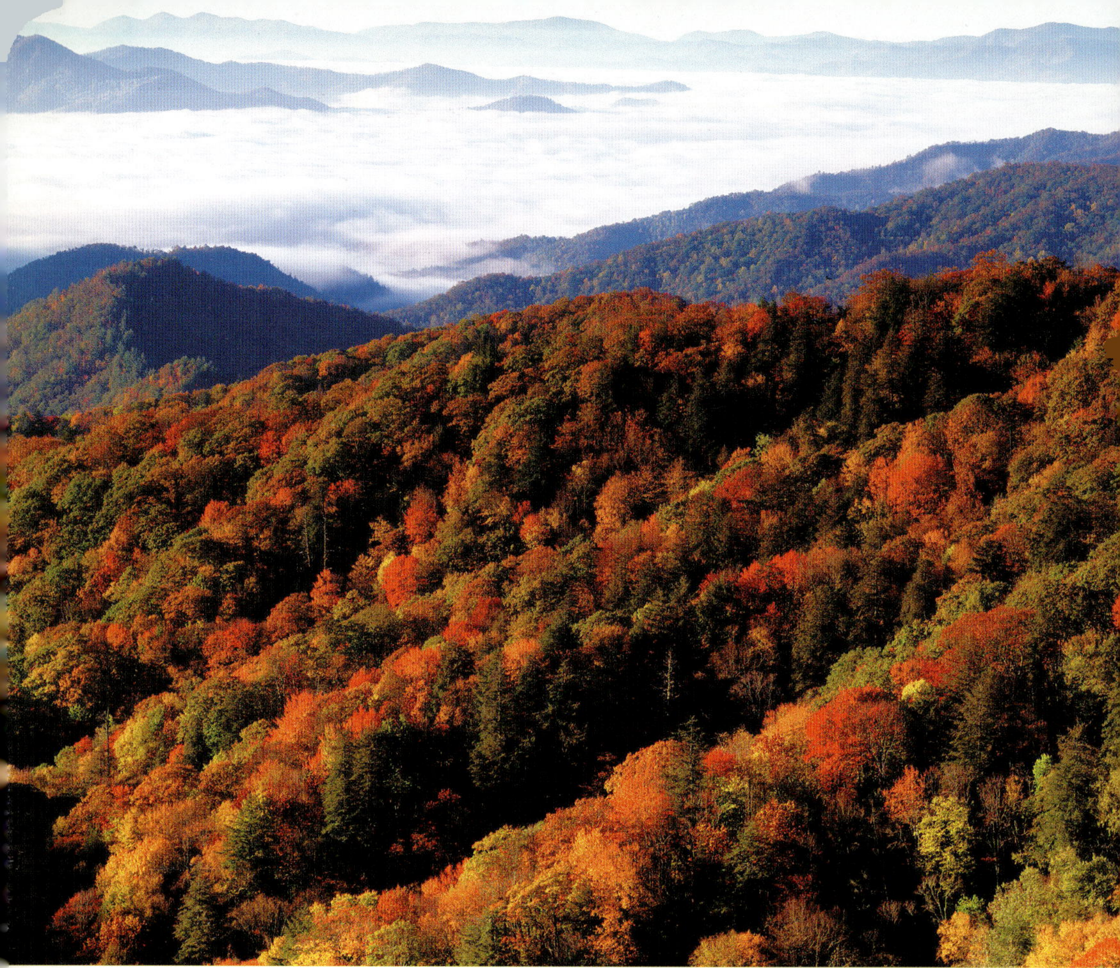

Deep Creek Overlook
mile 15.5 (13.7)

Two turnouts on the right (left if coming from Cherokee) offer excellent views of the Deep Creek drainage and Shot Beech Ridge. There is ample parking, but no signage to tell you that you are here other than the signpost # 15 keyed to the Park road guide. Spring comes late here, and nice warm light doesn't do much for delicate spring greens; this really is a fall location, though you might get lucky and find hoar frost here in just the right conditions. Fall colors are vivid here, offering one of the best grand vistas in the park. A blue sky day with a polarizer, or a stormy day all work and show different moods. A storm moving through with swirling gray clouds is especially appealing against fall color. In fall, early morning light comes in from the left, and is especially flattering. It's a great follow up scene to sunrise at Oconaluftee Valley Overlook just up the road. If the sky is blue it will polarize or you may use a graduated neutral density filter. Even on a gray day, a polarizer may be very effective in increasing color saturation and intensity.

Afternoon light is almost as nice, and you can find very nice compositions here before heading to Clingmans Dome for last light. It's a great alternative to late light from Chimneys Overlook, and you can actually set up at both locations before heading to Clingmans Dome.

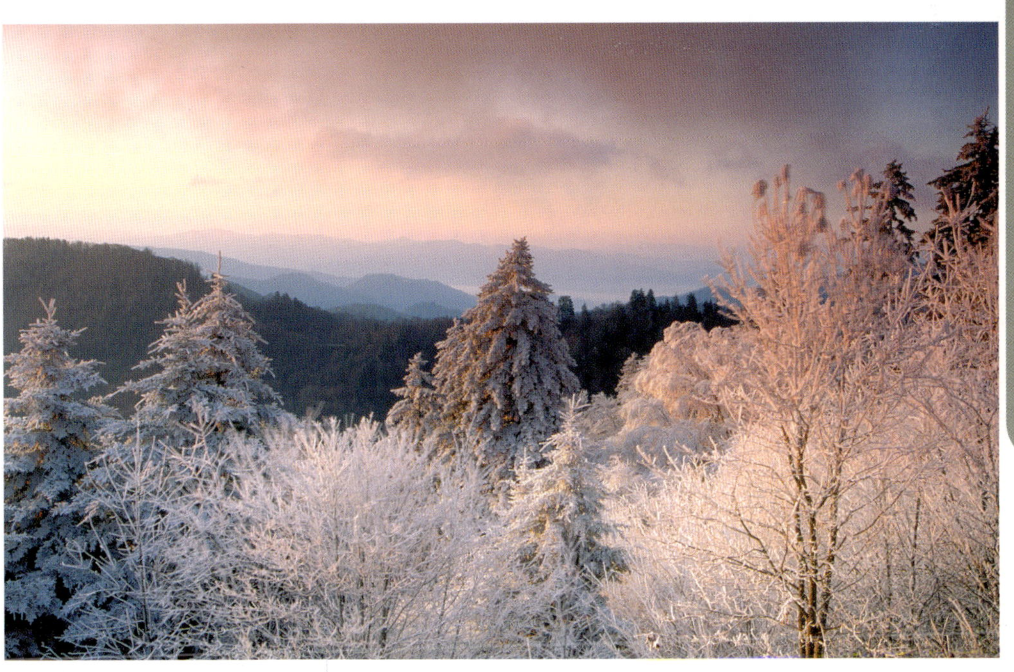

Opposite page: Shot Beech Ridge, seen from Deep Creek Overlook, often peaks shortly after mid-month. The fog settled on Lake Fontana would have blown out without a 2 stop Singh Ray grad.—*NS*

This page: A winter sunrise, Newfound Gap. Hoar frost, not snow, coats the branches of this early winter scene. A 3 stop Singh Ray graduated neutral density filter with a touch of red intensifies the morning glow.—*NS*

Unnamed Sunrise Overlook
mile 17.9 (10.8)

The road begins a large switchback here offering views to the east. There is a small parking area on the east side of the road, and the vantagepoint is just downhill, with a small gravel shoulder just beyond, in case you missed it on the way down. Here you can view sunrise with many options for composition with the sun in or out of the frame as you wish. The road is lightly traveled early in the morning, but be careful as you are very close to the road and a careless step could put you at risk of being struck by a passing car. This is the only sunrise spot on the road in early summer where you can see the sun itself come up as a pale disc—the other spots will give you a "hot" sun, far above the horizon by the time it crests the ridge.

In between Various overlooks are worth checking out for opportunities, and good images have been made from all of them; check them out and create a new classic.

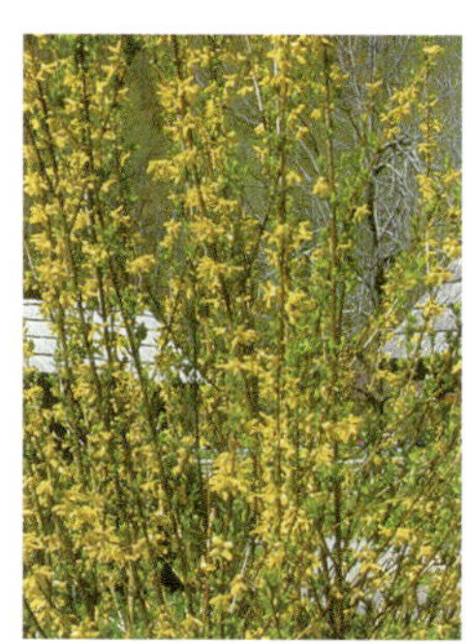

Mingus Mill
mile 28.7 (0.5)

This scenic mill operates from mid-March through December, and sells authentic stone ground cornmeal. The inner workings of the mill are visible on the self-guided tour. Photograph the mill itself from any of several vantagepoints. At the end of the sluiceway is a nice leading line to the distant mill with a wide angle. If water is spilling over the sluiceway it gives a nice accent to the boxy structure of the mill itself. It gets morning but not afternoon light. You can make soft light compositions later in the afternoon or on a cloudy day.

Mingus Mill. Late morning to early afternoon light works here on a blue sky day; a dead sky calls for a composition with minimal sky.—*NS*

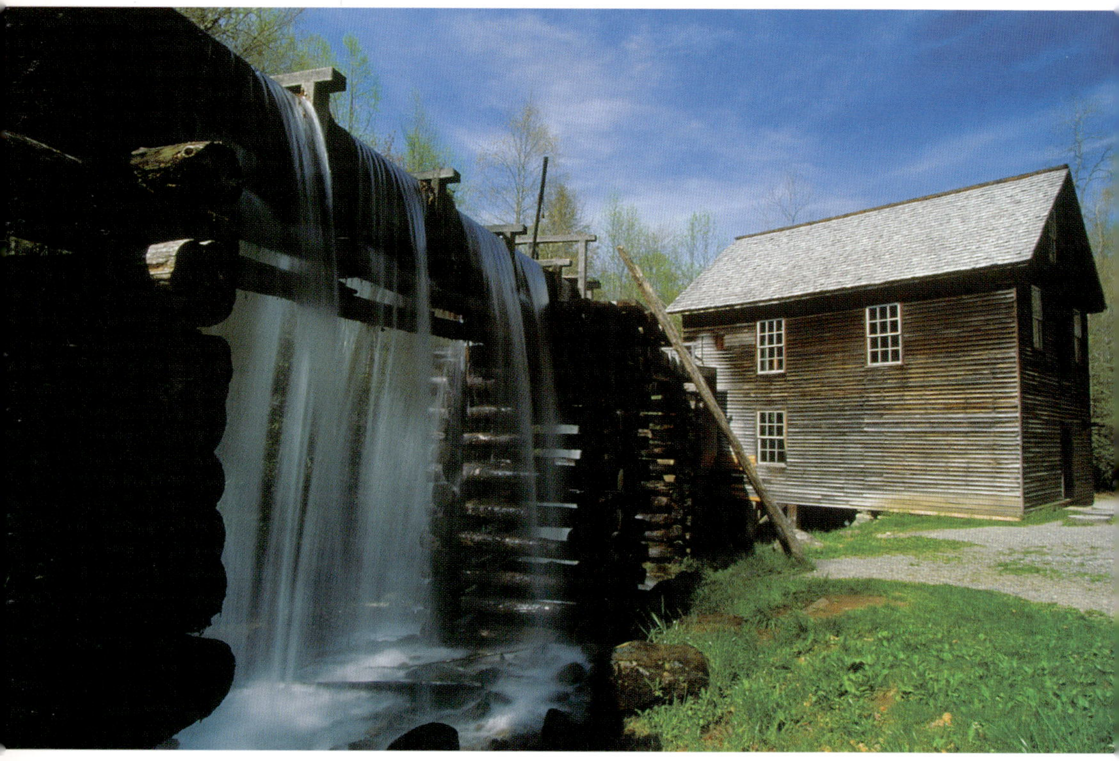

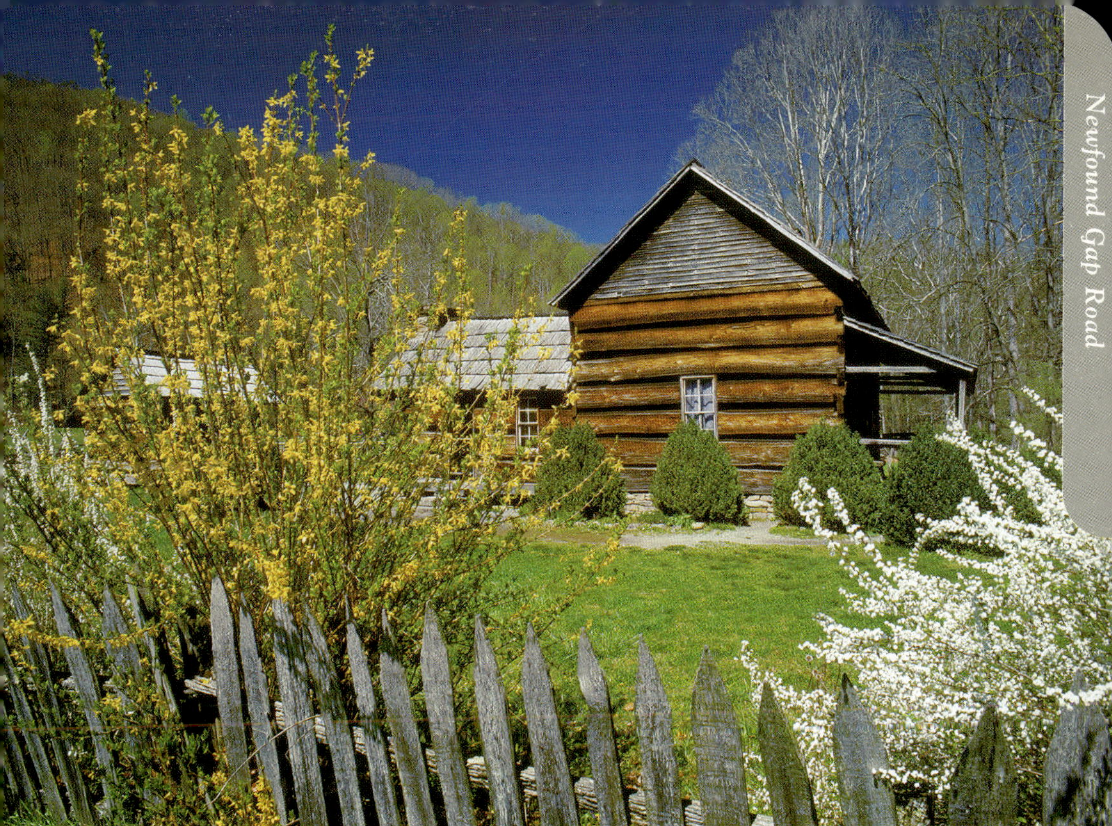

Davis House at the Mountain Farm Muaeum in early April benefits from fresh blooms, here in late morning. Singh-Ray polarizing filter.—*NS*

Mountain Farm Museum
mile 29.2 (o)

This open-air museum, complete with plowed cornrows and fences, can occupy you for hours. This is challenging photography, trying to incorporate architectural forms into a landscape. Should you show a building from the inside out, using windows to frame the scene? What about a telephoto to isolate a portion of a building? Wide angle to bring it all together! Macro for the texture in the weathered wood? The possibilities are endless. Early and late light work well here as well as soft light in all seasons

Mid-morning light on the Davis House polarizes nicely until close to noon, and other compositions work also, proving that attractive landscapes are possible towards the middle of the day. The yellow forsythia blooms early, sometimes by late March and may peak by the end of the first week of April, before other spring attractions are at their best. For current information, call the visitor center at 828-497-1900. The visitor center has restrooms, a bookstore, and a very helpful and friendly staff. You can also make backcountry reservations here.

The Blue Ridge Parkway southern terminus is just south of the Mountain Farm, leading to several high overlooks and Balsam Mountain. See chapter nine, *Other Points of Interest*. for details.

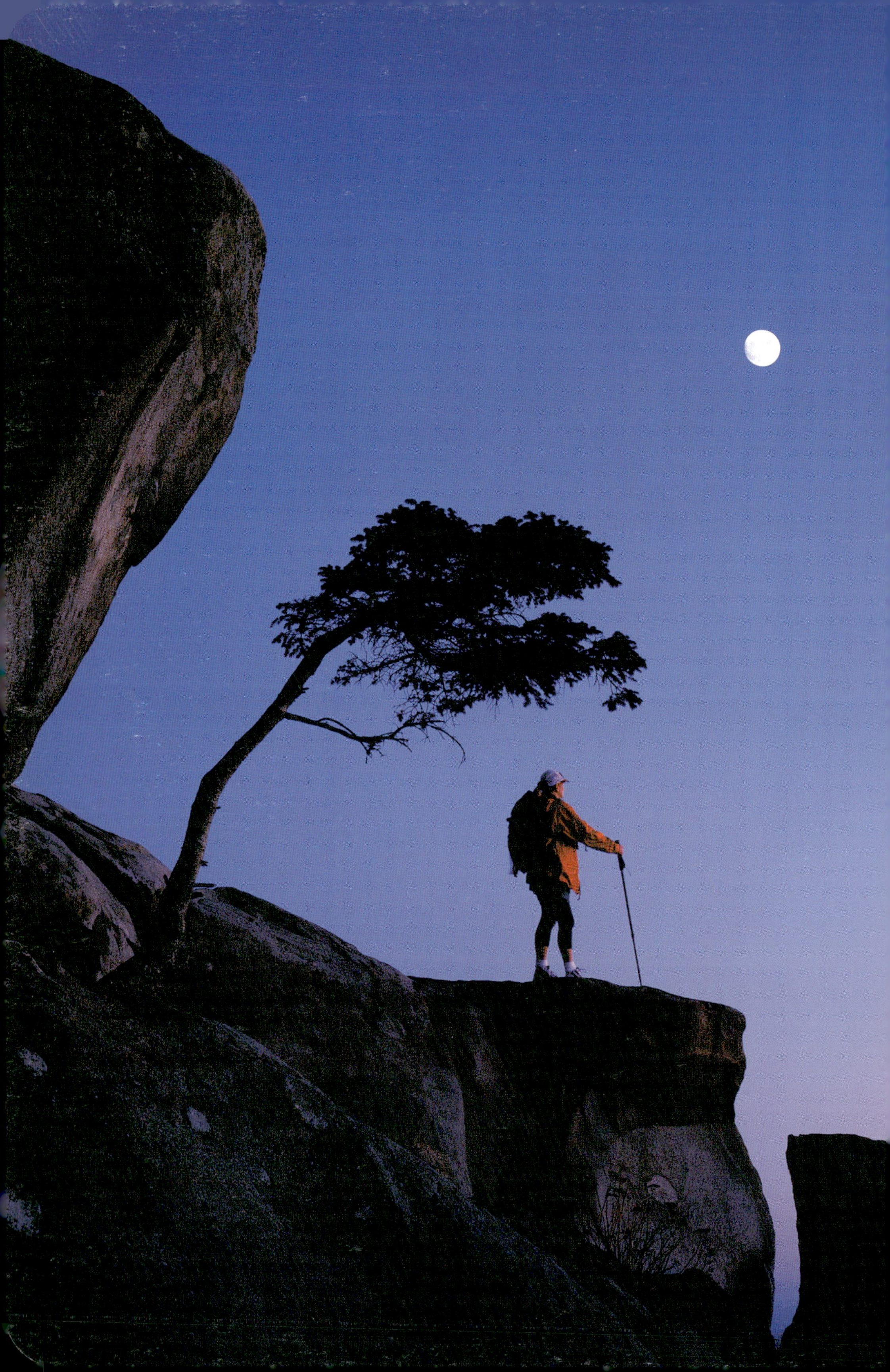

Classic Smokies landscapes

Sunrises & sunsets

Intimate landscapes

Trail head to Andrews Bald

Flame azaleas in mid-June

Appalachian Trail

Chapter Two

Clingmans Dome

Light does magical things for a few minutes after sunset. The moon is in constant motion, often apparent only when your film is processed. A few seconds is all it takes to distort its shape. A double exposure was the solution, added later when the moon was full.—*NS*

The road to Clingmans Dome leaves the Newfound Gap Road a stone's throw from the Newfound Gap parking area and follows a high ridgeline most of the way to the Clingmans Dome parking area. There are many turnouts along the way, but it's not until you get close to the end of the road that you get strong compositions for grand scenics; intimate landscapes abound, particularly in the fog. When clouds seem low from the lower elevations there is a good chance that higher elevations such as Clingmans Dome are in the clouds (fog); this can be a great photo op in bad weather.

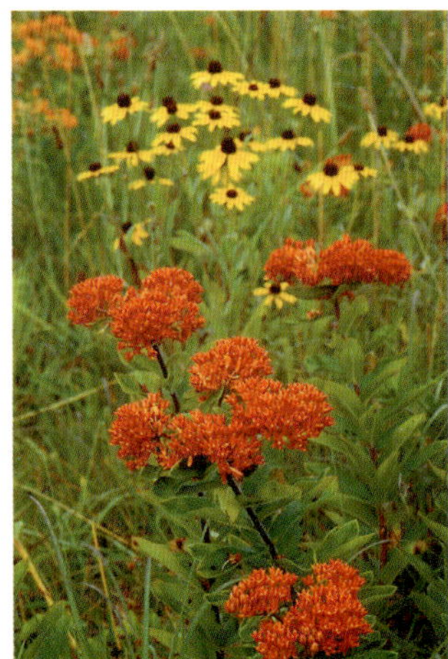

ABOVE: Butterfly weed and Black-eyed Susan make a great near/far composition. These plants are a wonderful habitat for butterflies.—*BC*

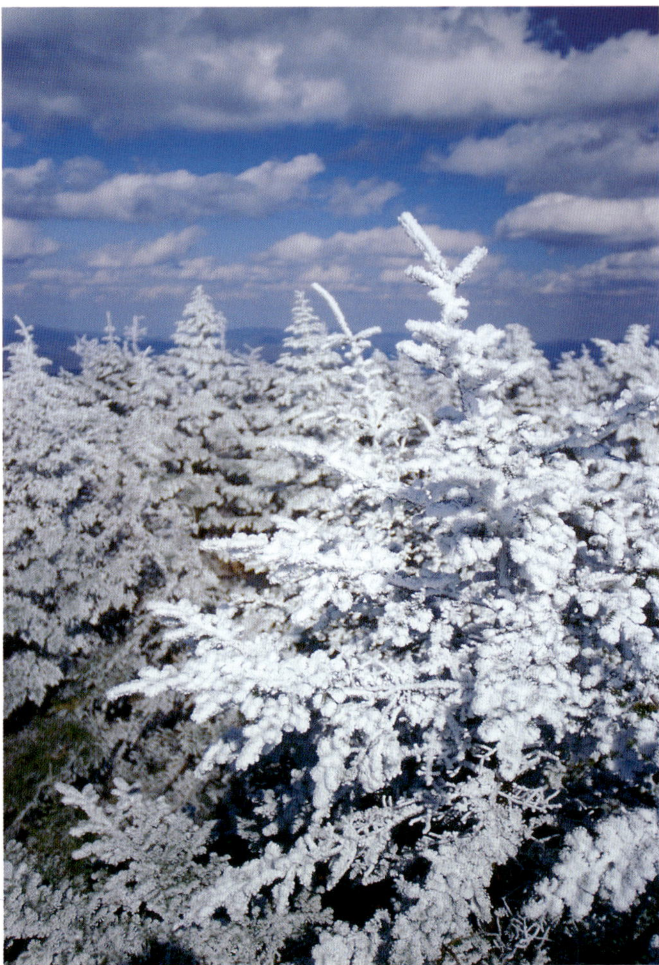

RIGHT: Spring snow storms can still sneak up and blanket the higher elevations, especially around Clingmans Dome, into the month of April.—*BC*

Mountain ash are colorful in early fall when the bright red berries add a dash of brilliance to the woods. Springs and seeps along the way offer many close-up opportunities for subjects with the "wet" look—fallen leaves, lichens, salamanders, and such. Spring wildflowers here bloom later than below, frequently lasting into late May. The main event is at the end of the road. This road closes at the end of November, and re-opens April 1, though late autumn or spring snows may force temporary closures.

CLINGMANS DOME PARKING AREA

This large parking area is frequently full and is certainly not the place to get away from the crowd. It is home to one of the classic Smokies sunset scenes, however, and no two are quite the same. Sunsets are best here in the fall; by spring the sun is far to the right and doesn't balance well in a composition that includes it. Side lighting affords variations and will put color in any clouds that are parked on the horizon. Spring is late here; the usual early spring wildflowers bloom here in mid-May. Fall colors start here in early October, but there aren't as many hardwoods on the ridge. The color is more of an accent than a broad

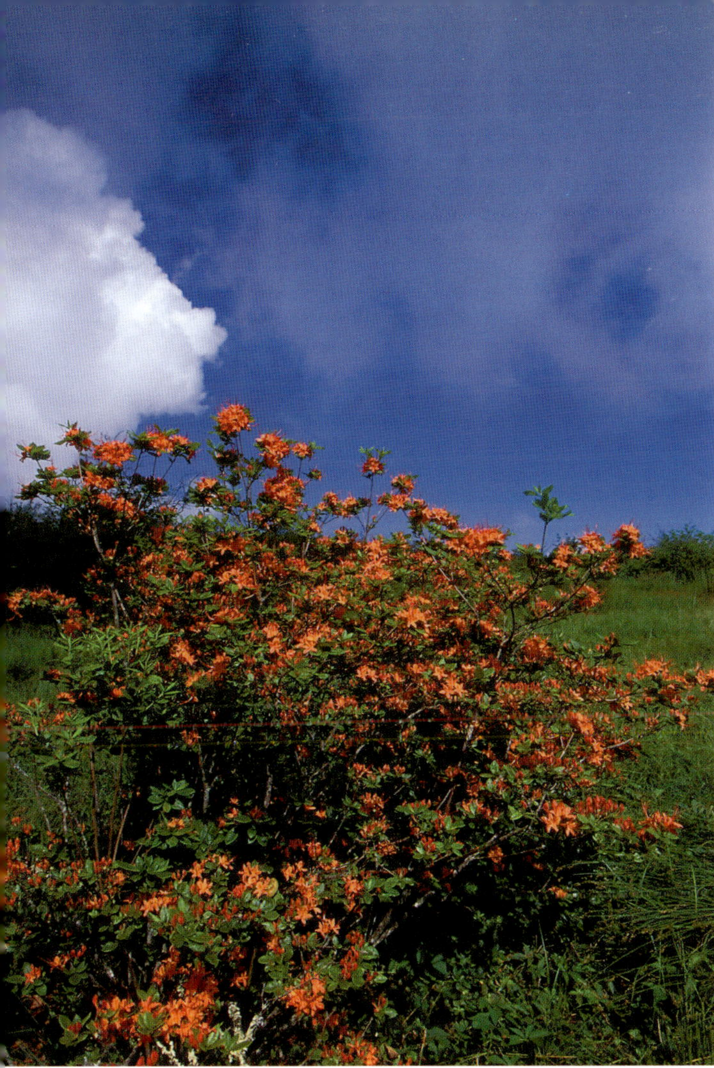

Flame azaleas peak on Andrews Bald around mid-June. Even though it is known as wild honeysuckle to locals, this flowering plant is a type of rhododendron.—*BC*

painted scenic, with the exception of the red berries of the mountain ash (which aren't in full splendor every season).

The many skeletons of dead Fraser firs that fell victim to the balsam wooly adelgid (a tiny aphid-like insect) aren't decorative but they do tell an ecological story in very graphic terms. Nature photography isn't always about pretty pictures; sometimes the most important story isn't one of unrivaled beauty. The forest is under siege by many foes; our children will likely see a very different landscape.

Sunset from this location combines a colorful red ball sun going down over layers of mountain ridges. Photograph sunset here after Morton Overlook plays out toward the end of August, but it is best from mid-October to the end of November. Longer focal lengths here exclude the treetops of the dead firs in the foreground. A 200+mm seems nicely balanced; more or less may suit you better. The rock outcropping at the right hand side of the west end of the parking area gives a good vantage point, and you can compose over the tops of the dead trees with a long enough lens from anywhere along the west side of the loop. There is a well-worn trail from the right hand side near the

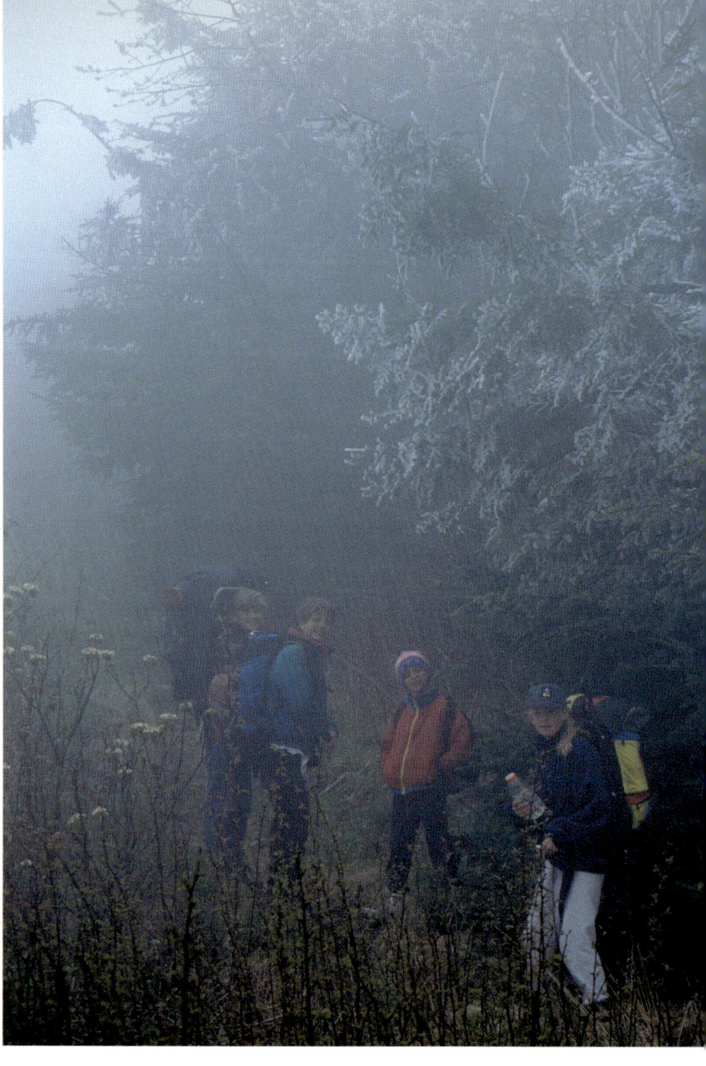

Hikers in the mist on the AT. Kids, colors, fog, frost on the AT near Clingmans—what more could you ask for?—*NS*

end of the parking area which is safer than climbing up the rocks.

Sunset here is a very exciting time for the photographer as the sun seems to pick up speed and sprint the last few degrees to the horizon. Set up at least 30 minutes before to avoid getting flustered in the last minute rush. Frequently it doesn't soften in intensity enough to kill lens flare until it touches the horizon which leaves you very little time indeed in which to refigure exposure, bracket, change composition (because there is no one "best" composition), check to see that your horizon lines are kept level, make sure you don't bump your tripod or the person next to you, and make sure the sometimes howling wind doesn't cause too much vibration—and before you know it, it is all over.

Sunrise from here is not very popular because it is a long haul from where you can spend the night, but we have made some of our all-time favorite images here in mid-August when the flowers were prime; the fringe of wildflowers can give the illusion that you are in a meadow filled with glory. You can find good summer compositions at the last few pullouts just before the parking lot, and at the East End of the parking area (end of the return loop). Fall compositions are all along the east

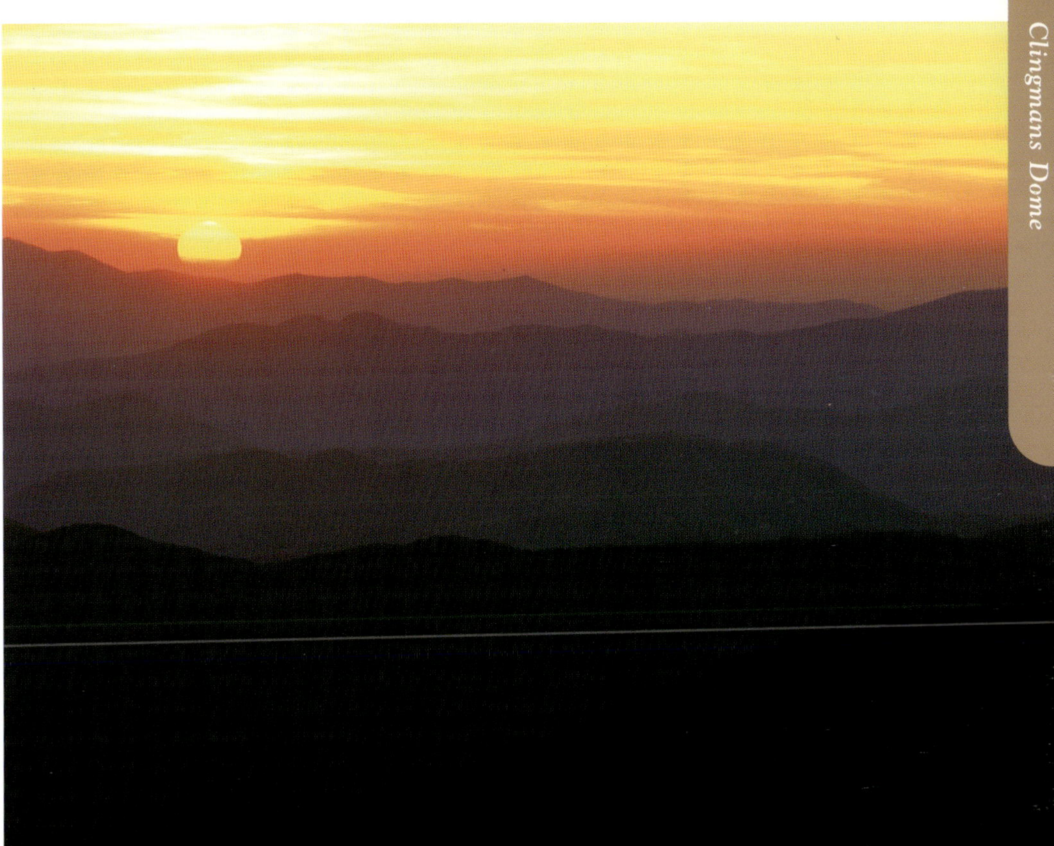

The classic Smokies scene. Wait for the sun to soften as it reaches thick air on the horizon; a 3 stop Singh Ray grad helped balance sky and ridges—*NS*

and south end; back, side, or front lighted.

Occasionally this high elevation will be in cloud, obscuring the view, while Newfound Gap below is clear, with a ceiling above and a clear horizon. That fact and the extra 15 minute drive (30 minutes round-trip if conditions are bad) to Clingmans Dome combine to discourage sunrise photos form here. When the peaks are in cloud, try moody compositions in the fog.

Alpenglow occurs before sunrise and after sunset respectively and here shows as a magenta band above azure blue where the reddish rays of the sun nestle above the blue shadow cast by the earth. Clouds will enhance the effect. Many photographers miss this effect while they pack up just after sunset or arrive too late prior to sunrise. The colored wash of pre dawn and post sunset light is so attractive looking towards the sun, and the anticipation of the sun cresting or disappearing is so strong, that many folks never see this happening behind them.

Moonrise and moonset give you more options and combine well with alpen-

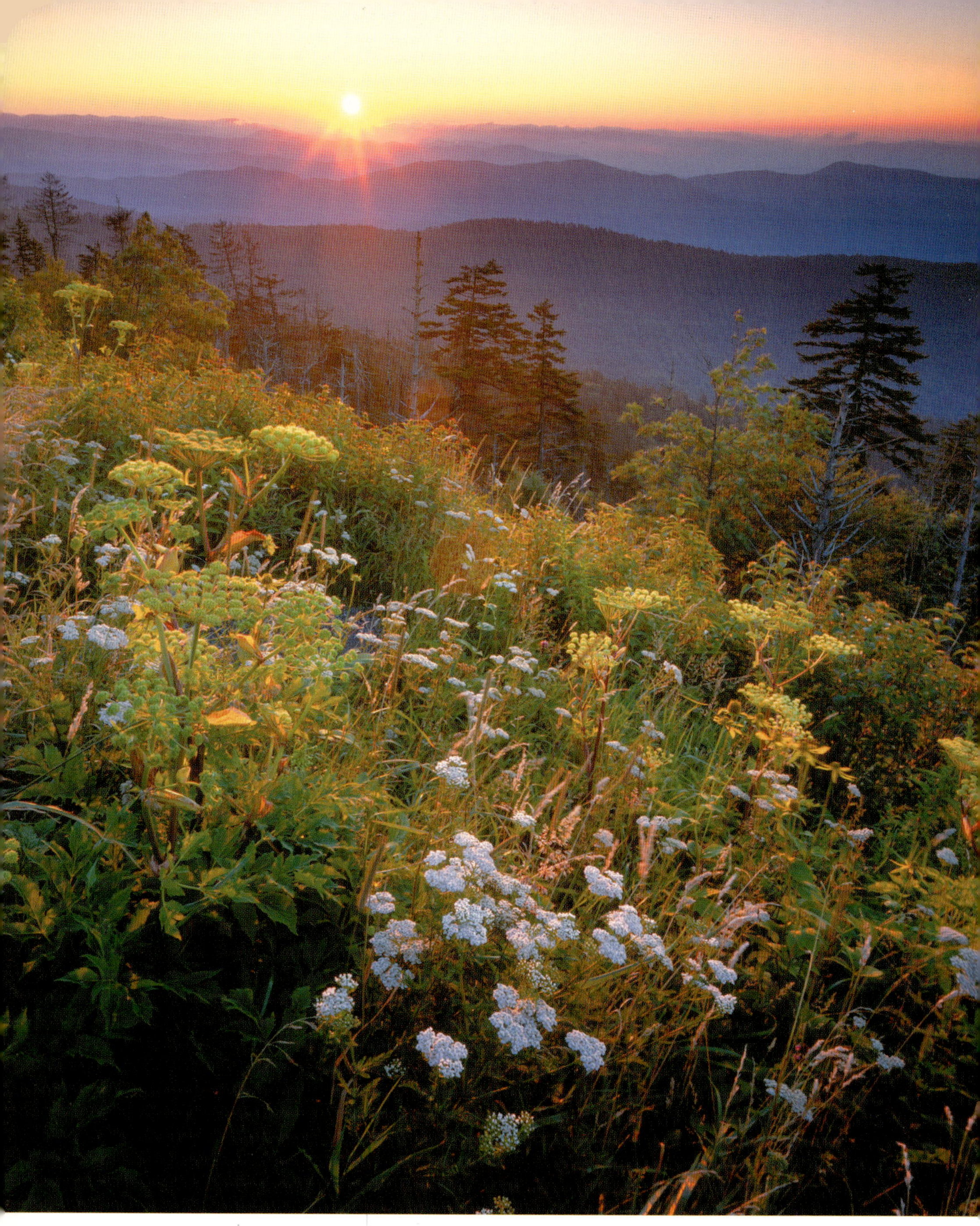

The sun has just the right "snap" to it for only a minute or so as it climbs throught the early morning mist. Earlier, it is too pale; soon after it is too bright and flare is a problem. 3 stop Singh Ray grad.—*NS*

glow (see above); remember to look over your shoulder when making sunrise and sunset images. On the day of the full moon, the moon rises at the same time that the sun sets, give or take a few minutes. The moon rises and sets about 40 minutes earlier and later for each day before and after full moon. If its not a crystal clear day, the moon will appear dirty looking until it climbs to cleaner air a bit higher above the horizon. Your images will probably be more satisfying 1 or 2 days before full moon. Bracket, especially towards the under exposed side to prevent the moon's detail from washing out. You may have to combine images in Photoshop to get what your eye sees if you want detail in the moon and the foreground; a graduated neutral density filter also helps. After the sun sets, the moon brightens quickly relative to the land below, and the contrast range exceeds films ability to record both extremes. Either you'll get a moon with detail in a black frame, or a white blank circle in the scene depending on how you bias your exposure. The moon is constantly moving; a longer exposure of a few seconds will produce an egg shaped disc. Longer focal lengths accentuate this. Double exposing the moon into your chosen composition may be the only way to record on film what you see before you. Keeping the focal length used for the moon no more than twice that used on the landscape will keep proportions realistic, but the effects are a matter of taste. The lookout tower atop Clingmans Dome is about a 10-15 minute fairly steep uphill walk from the parking area, and gives you views of the surrounding mountains. The view is becoming more obstructed as the trees that were cleared years ago are taking over. Most people prefer the compositions from the parking lot, which is also less work.

The Appalachian Trail

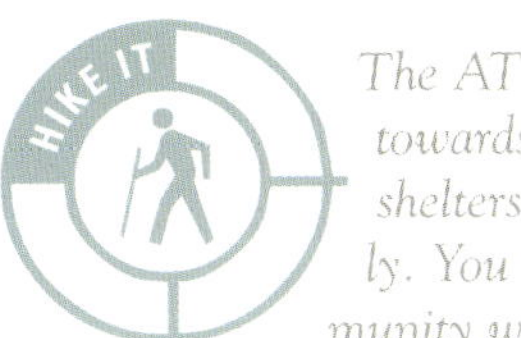

The AT crosses here and proceeds along a ridge towards Double Springs Gap and Silers Bald shelters at about 2.6 and 4.5 miles respectively. You will find a typical spruce-fir forest community with a few views, and at Silers, the remains of open bald being reclaimed by the forest. Andrews and Gregory balds are maintained as open balds to preserve their character, others such as Silers are left to nature's natural processes. The origin of the balds is unclear; native Americans, grazing wildlife, and early settlers may have maintained them if they were ever natural in origin. The AT here is more of a hike than a photo op.

Andrews Bald

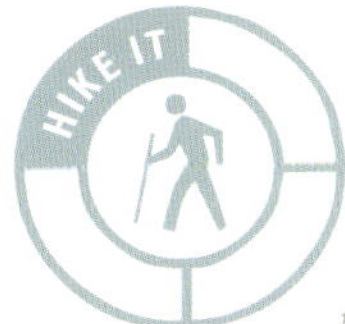

This hike is a 1.7 mile mostly downhill walk on the Forney Ridge Trail from the head of the parking area to one of the two best locations for flame azaleas in the Park. They tend to be in peak about a week to 10 days earlier than on Gregory Bald, often by mid-June. Catawba rhododendrons grow here, as do blueberries; the rhododendron peak a few days before the azaleas.

For first light, you will have to hike some in the dark. If you turn off your flashlight to let your eyes get adjusted to the dark, the predawn sky will give you just enough light to navigate by. You can be on the bald for sunrise or shortly thereafter. Likewise you can hike back in twilight if you chose afternoon light. After a little over a mile, the Forney Creek trail branches off to your right, giving you an opportunity to make a wrong turn and get lost. Take a map and compass.

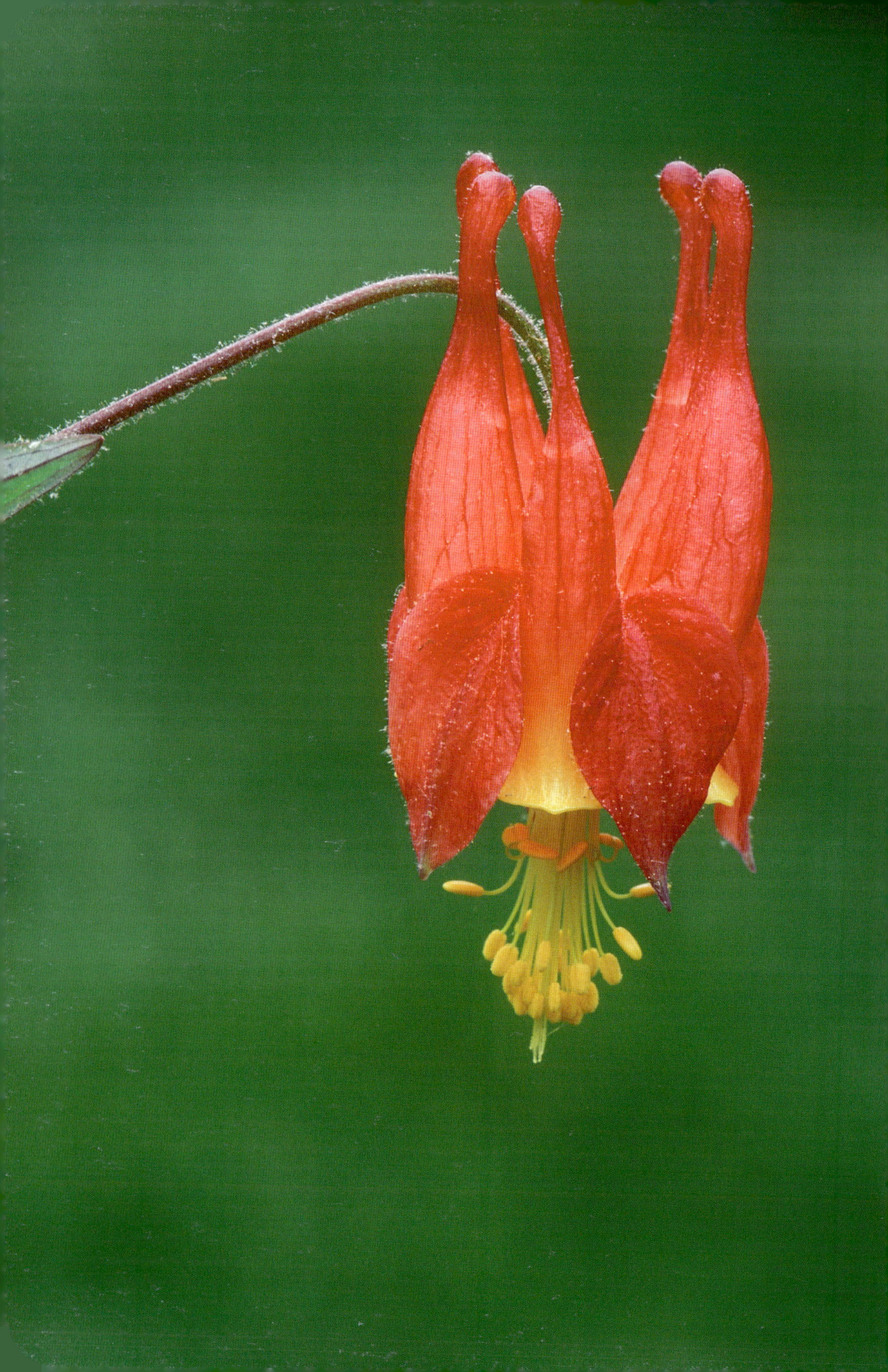

Waterfalls

Streams

Spring wildflowers

Trailhead to Laurel Falls

Intimate landscapes

Action/adventure subjects

Chapter Three

Little River Road

Wild Columbine.
—*BC*

Follow the meandering Little River Road from the "Y" at Townsend to Sugarlands Visitor Center for one of the most photogenic drives in the Smokies. Driving 17 miles would take about 45 minutes for most visitors, but photographers will find that a minimum of several hours to half a day is more the norm when the light is good. The diversity runs from wildflower macros and stream/waterfalls images to people in canoes and kayaks negotiating the adventurous water of Little River. Of note is the fact that there are gates

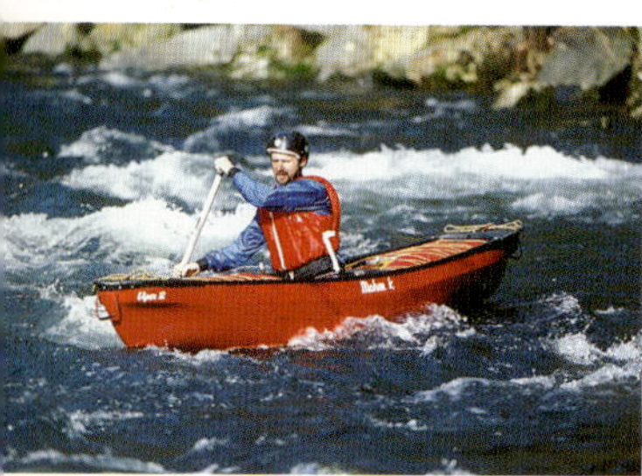

Above: Paddlers favor the higher water found after heavy spring rains. Set up in one spot and pre focus on an area that they will paddle through.—*BC*

Right: Little River road is one of the best places to find fire pink in mid to late April; it may last to late May at the highest elevations.—*NS*

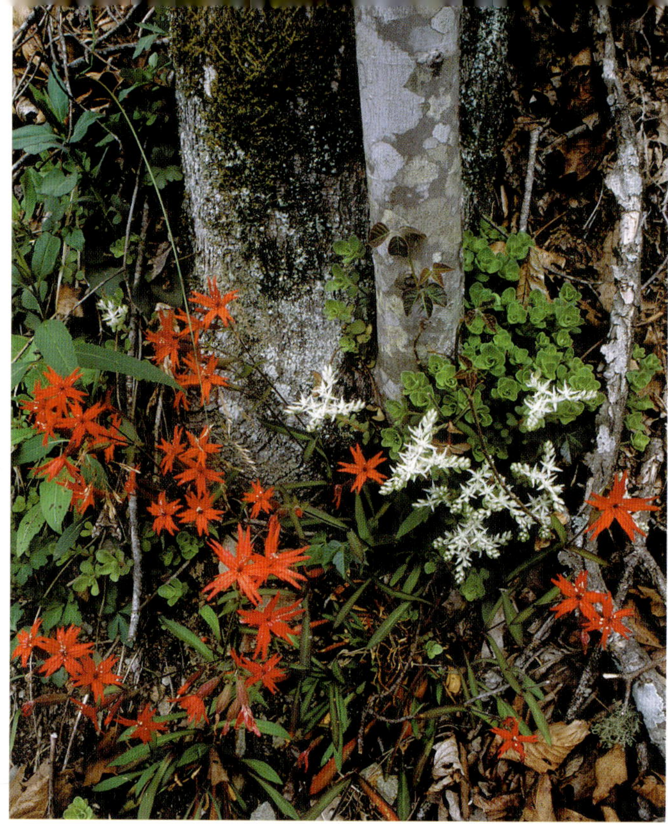

on the road at the "Y" and at Elkmont and the road is closed at these gates for inclement weather such as snow, ice and flash floods.

Before you start on your journey down this road, pull off in the ***parking area at the "Y"*** and explore the landscape between the parking area and the river. This is a great place for wildflowers in the spring and the Chestnut Top Trail, which begins on the other side of the road, is a premier wildflower trail in early spring. The first half mile of trail will keep most photographers busy for an entire morning with overcast skies or using a diffuser as the sun starts hitting here midmorning. This is one trail that you can find trailing arbutus, a delicate early spring flower. The confluence of rivers at the "Y" makes for a great place to watch boaters and fishermen and any other number of people enjoying the refreshing cataracts found here. Before setting off down the road of exploration, set your odometer to zero. (Mileage in parentheses is taken from Sugarlands Visitor Center.) Just remember to reverse the right and left directions if taking the route from the opposite direction.

A word of advice: this road is narrow with abundant traffic, so pull off into marked parking and walk if needed. Be careful if you set up near the road, as vibration and wind from traffic can affect your tripod and camera or blow that dainty little flower all over the place. The only "facilities" along this road are found at Metcalf Bottoms Picnic area, so plan your coffee usage accordingly.

The first place to pull off and work is ***0.6 (16.1 from Sugarlands) miles from the "Y"***. There is a small cascade on the right with a parking area on the left next to the river. This cascade is a great spring find, especially after a rain. There are numerous vantage points, but the most productive seem to be the

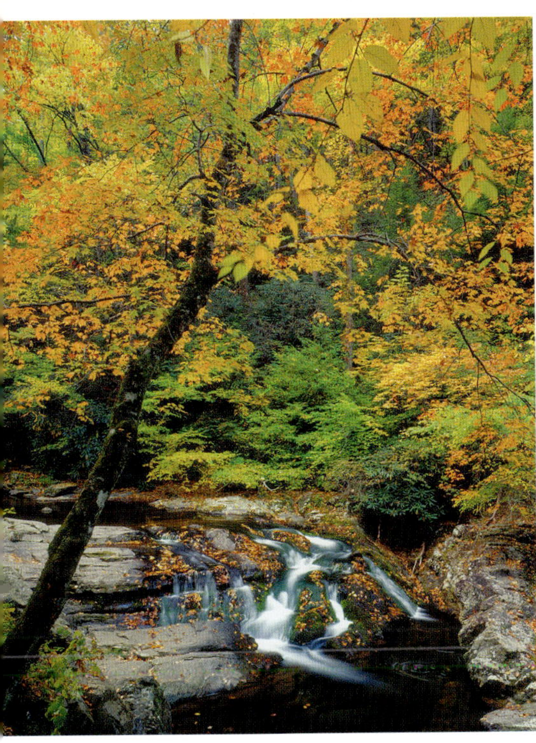

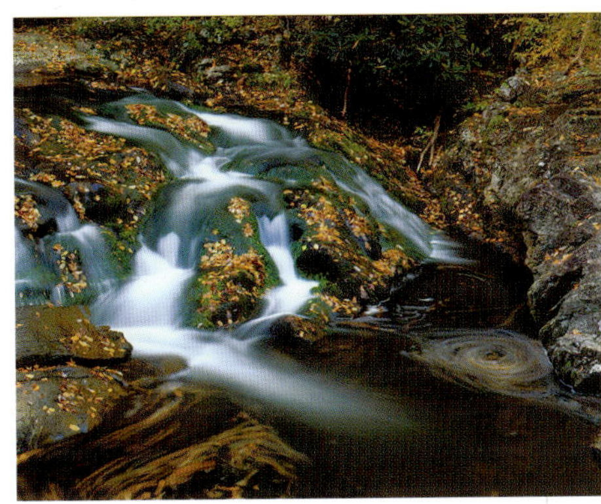

ABOVE AND LEFT: A scene within a scene—find this gem about 1/2 mile past the "Y;" a closer view (on a different day) gives swirls of color in the eddies below the cascade. Many locations can yield multiple interesting compositions; slow your pace and let the scene speak to you.—*NS*

trails along the right and left sides of the stream. This spot works well on overcast days, especially after rain has dampened all the rocks. Most stream shots along this route will work best with wet rocks as the dry rocks tend to be too light (hot spots) to record well on film and compete in significance with the white of the water. Don't forget to check out the Little River side of the road, especially for passing boaters. Summer time is good, but the right hand side of the cascade is grown up and difficult to hike up to achieve different vantage points. Try the left side in summer.

From this point to mile 3.0 there are a number of pull offs right next to the river. Many of these are adjacent to small rapids that make for great white water action images.

There are several vernal waterfalls (present only when enough rain causes more than a trickle of water over the rocks) along this road and one of the favorites is at ***mile 2.4 (14.4 from Sugarlands).*** There is enough parking for 3-4 vehicles with the waterfall located across the river from the road. Be careful as you look for your best vantage point as the rocks and bank can be treacherous. Early spring with the light green early foliage helps add to the delicate nature of this waterfall. Don't forget to explore the vantage point from stream side.

Riversides full of rosebay rhododendrons can be found from mile 2.4 to 2.8 in mid to late June. Just pick your favorite location and park in the most convenient spot.

Cross the bridge at mile 4.0 (12.8 from Sugarlands) and park. There are several sets of steps leading from the parking area toward the river. This section of the stream offers nice rapids and even a shot from the parking area through the trees in early spring can make for a pleasing image.

Right: Long exposures after or before sunset pick up color casts both from reflected sky light and color shifts due to long exposures and reciprocity failure.—*NS*

Below, left: Partial polarization lets the rocks show through while retaining surface texture. Full polarization would have eliminated all but the brightest highlights.—*NS*

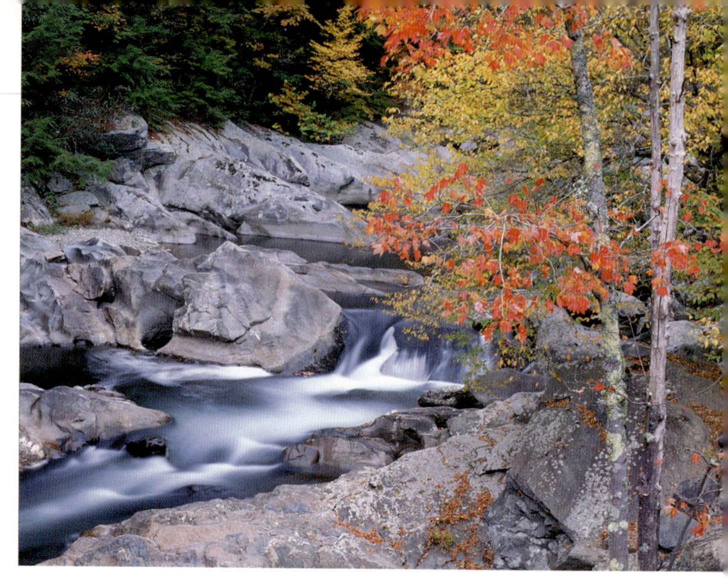

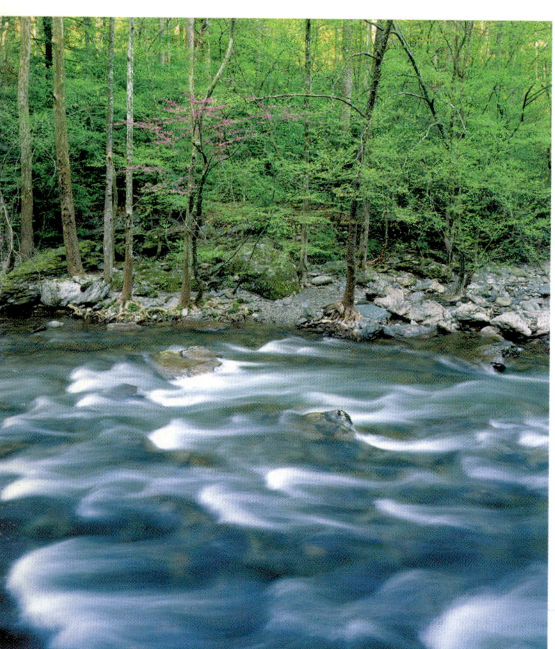

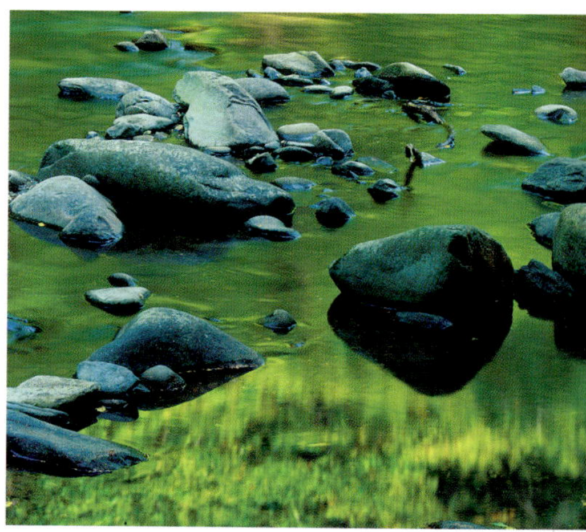

Above: Green summer reflections can turn neon with highlights taking on a yellowish autumn like tint.—*NS*

Meigs Falls

mile 4.6
(12.1 from Sugarlands)

The next significant waterfall is Meigs Falls. There has been significant overgrowth of trees, which partially obscures the view now, but an adventurous soul can cross the river during a low flow and gain a vantage point for photographs that most visitors will never see, except in your image. This image is actually better in the winter, especially with snow when the vegetation has thinned out.

The Sinks

mile 5.7
(11.1 from Sugarlands)

A series of falls that pass from one side of the road to the other under a bridge presents an extreme challenge to whitewater enthusiasts and abundant oppor-

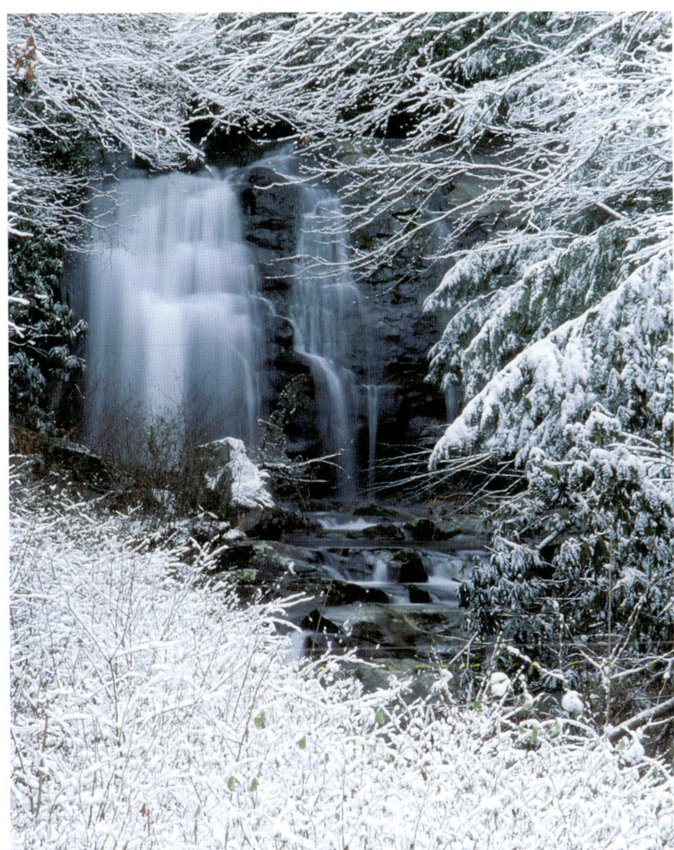

LEFT: Meigs Falls can be accessible after a snowfall if the road is open. Use a telephoto lens to zoom in and isolate the falls and snow covered foliage.—*BC*

BELOW: Many vernal waterfalls are appreciated only in early spring. Without heavy rains, they are but a trickle of water, and after the trees leaf out, they are well-hidden. —*BC*

tunities for the intrepid photographer. Pull into the parking area and begin scouting with the overlooks looking downriver. This perspective looks magical with a coating of snow. Explore the trail to the right as it gives a different aerial perspective of the river. The trail into the forest at the left of the parking lot, ***Meigs Creek Trail***, is worth exploring for wildflowers, insects and mushrooms. Venture across the road (remember to mind your mother and look both ways first) and you will find wonderful compositions of river and cataracts and if you look down, you may even find some "holes" washed in the rock that collect rain and provide wonderful possibilities with foreground elements or reflections. Please explore this location with extreme caution. It seems that hardly a year passed without a death from drowning at this location. Watch where you walk along the riverside.

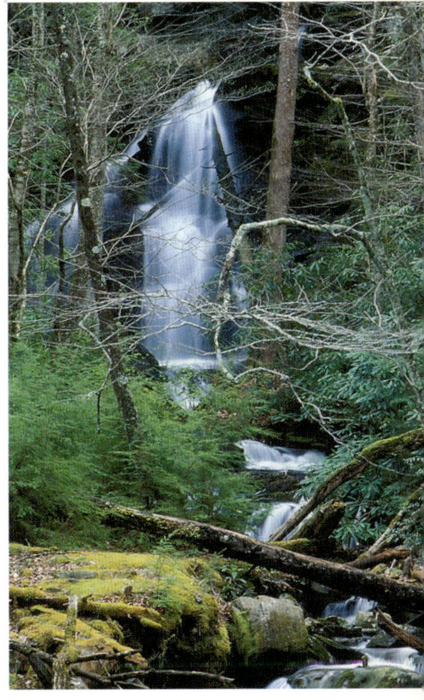

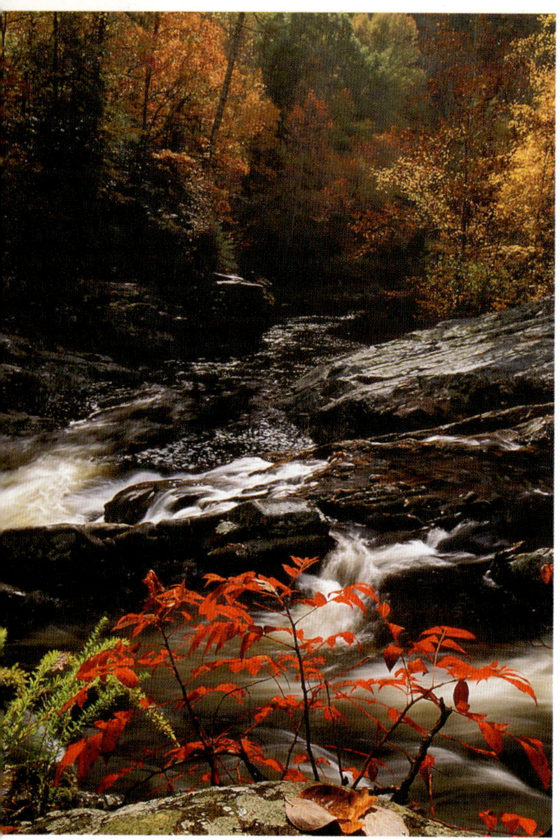

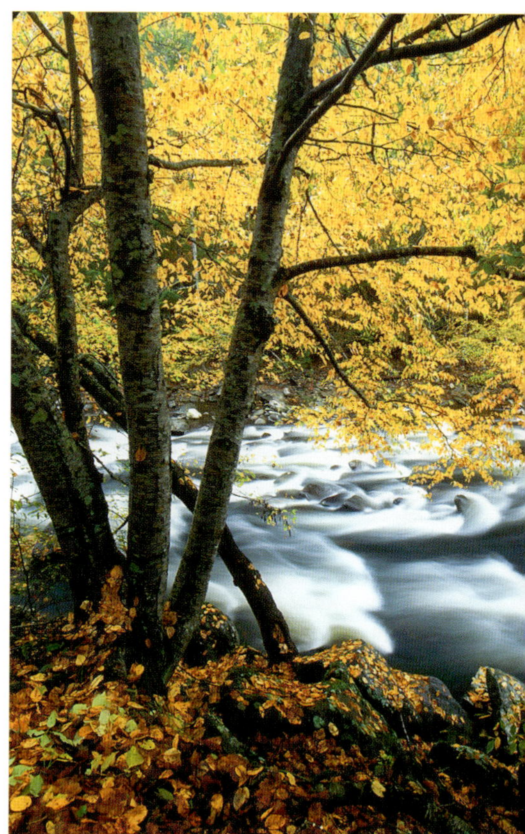

Metcalf Bottoms Picnic Area
mile 7.4
(9.5 from Sugarlands)

This is a good place to relax, eat lunch and plan the rest of the day. Stop in the parking area furthermost to the left and walk to the road and look across to the embankment. If you time your trip right (mid-April or so) you may get the opportunity to see one of the most splendid wildflowers in the Smokies, the Yellow Lady Slipper. These orchids do not individually bloom every year and, unfortunately, beautiful plants like these are subject to poaching. If you are fortunate to see these beauties, please photograph them from a distance and don't disturb the area around them. Report anyone you see removing these plants to the nearest ranger. It is a federal crime to purposely damage any plants or wildlife in the park and they are protected so we all have a chance to enjoy their beauty in a natural surrounding.

The ***next 5 miles*** out of Metcalf Bottoms towards Elkmont Road are strewn with quiet parking areas and easy access to the river. Fishermen frequent this area, so action images which include wading fishermen can be taken here. This is also a great area in the summer to kick off your shoes and wade along the stream. Be careful of the slipperiness of the rocks, especially if you are carrying your equipment. Wet and dented cameras don't take very good images. One particularly good site is at mile 12.1 (4.8 from Sugarlands). Parking is off the road and enough room for about six cars. Rhododendrons are accessible from the parking lot for mid-June adventurers.

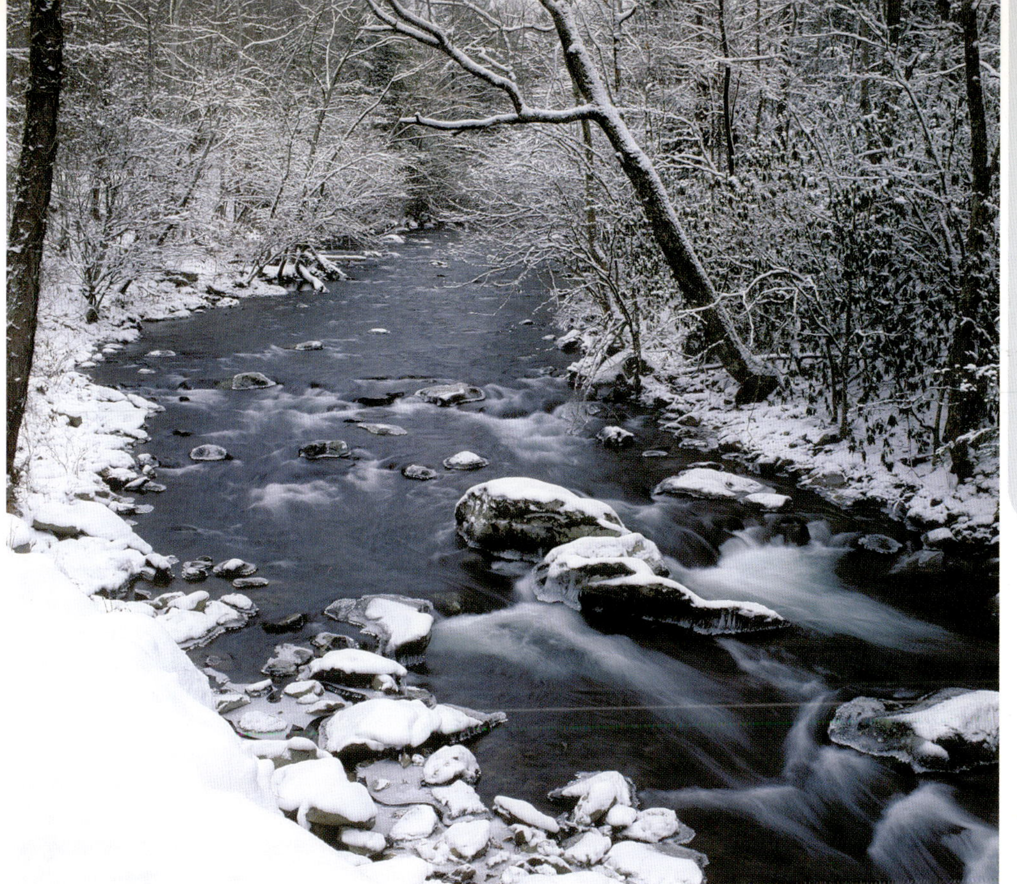

Elkmont Road
mile 12.4
(4.5 from Sugarlands)

Elkmont Road to the right ends Little River's meandering along the road, but you can drive up this road and continue along the river for another mile. If you turn left at the campground, you can continue to the gate at Little River Trail, passing the Elkmont nature trail 1.8 miles from Little River Road. River scenics at the beginning of the road and forest quiet areas further up are worth exploration, especially if you want a short hike with more solitude. The campground here is probably the best place to stay if you are camping, as the access to Cades Cove is not that far, Little River Road is at your feet and Highway 441 up to the top is just around the corner. You may also get a site next to the stream and be lulled to sleep each night by the constant gurgle. Late June and into July is the time to watch for the synchronized firefly show. These little luminescent insects blink in unison here and this is one of the few places of this occurrence in North America.

Above: Little River near Elkmont is often accessible after a snow. On an overcast day, meter the snow and open 2 stops (+2). Medium tones are hard to find in such scenes. Brighter snow loses detail, and darker snow makes for a dark overall scene.—*NS*

Opposite page, left: The Sinks provides a spectacular backdrop for backlit red sumac leaves. This breaks the overcast and soft light rule for stream photography—photographic rules are not absolutes.—*BC*

Opposite page, right: Little River just below the "Y" offers an ethereal feeling to this intimate landscape. Bright overcast light is essential for this feeling from the water.—*BC*

Laurel Falls

mile 13.5 (3.4 from Sugarlands)

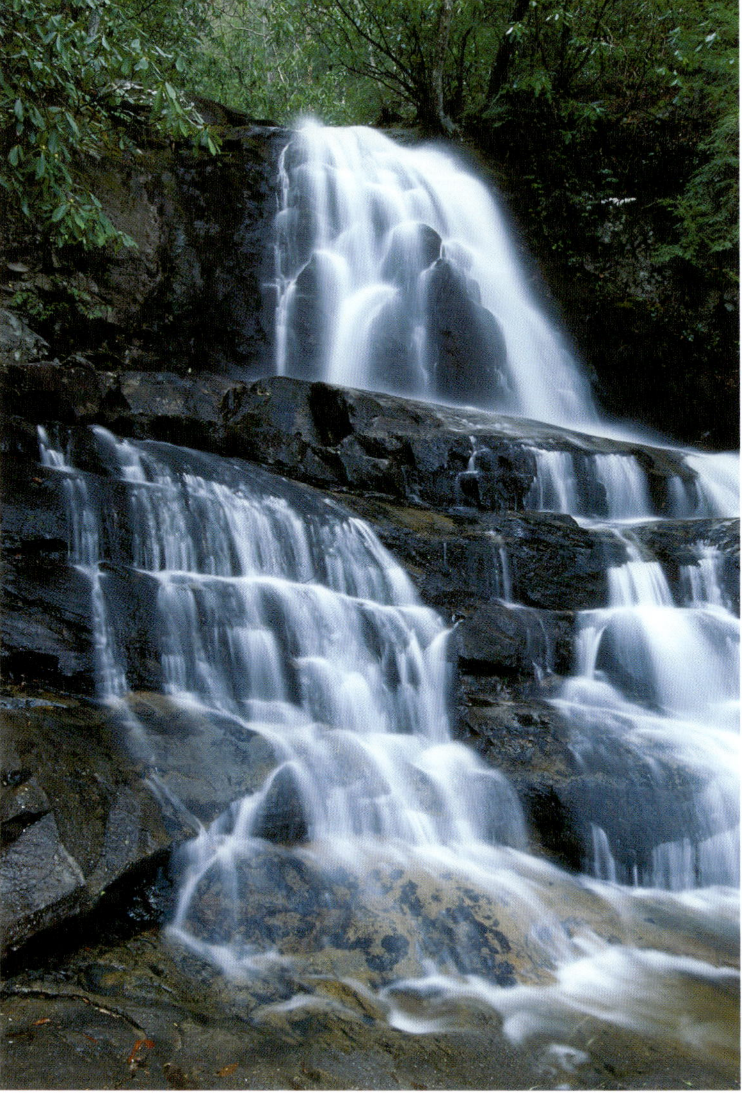

This is one of the most accessible and prettiest waterfalls in the Smokies. The hike up the 1.3 mile paved trail and is well worth the effort. Get to the parking lot early (before 9 a.m.), as it fills up quickly and that means lots of people around the falls. Strategies for non human populated images include early morning forays and trips during "stormy" weather. Just after a rain is the ideal time as the rocks are all wet and the less adventuresome have not come back into the park from shopping in Gatlinburg and Pigeon Forge. This is another place to experiment with extreme wide angle lenses and very slow shutter speeds. This is usually accessible in winter, even after a snow storm. Beware of slick rocks at all times and don't climb on the falls.

From Laurel Falls the road descends 3.4 miles to Sugarlands Visitor Center. There are several overlooks to stop at, but at some the trees in the foreground have grown to such a height to limit the usefulness of these areas for grand mountain landscapes.

At the end of the road lies the Sugarlands Visitor Center. The largest and most visited information center in the park, Sugarlands contains the majority of administrative offices as well as an interpretive center and excellent bookstore. Rangers and volunteers here are more than happy to help you with any aspect of your visit.

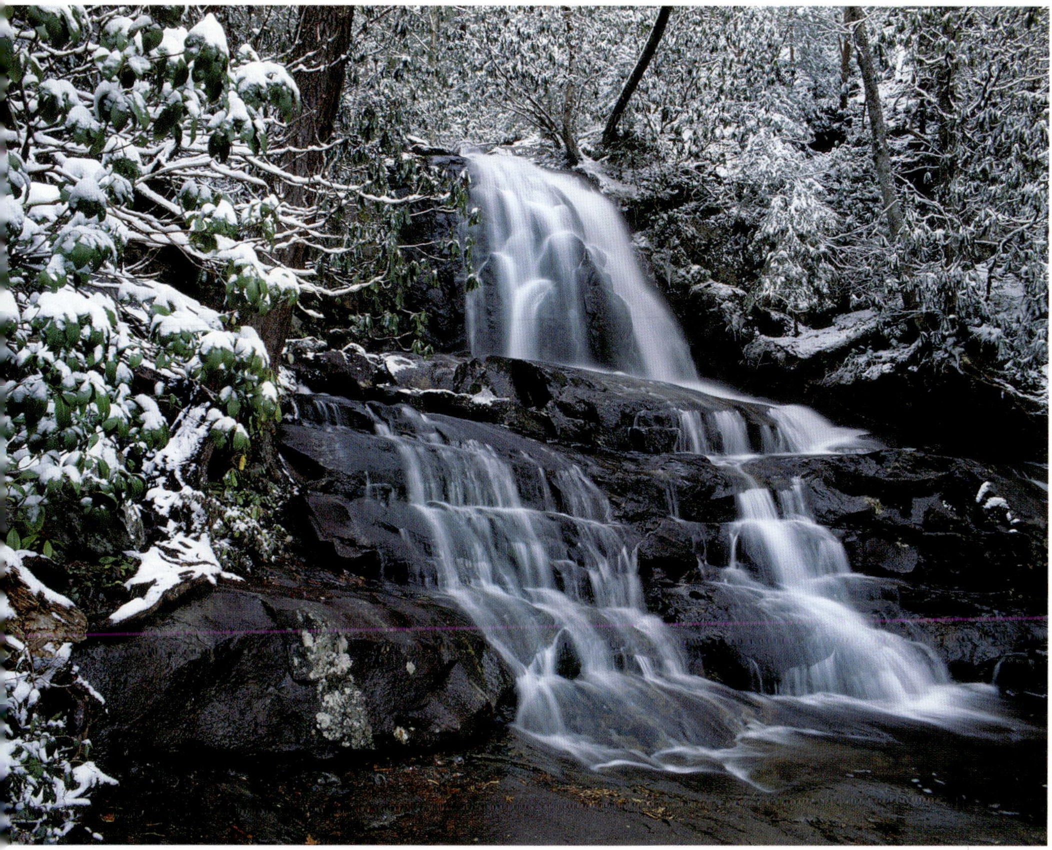

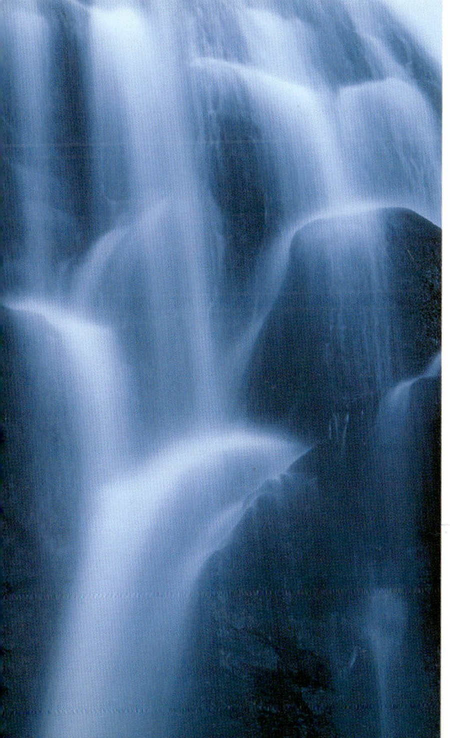

OPPOSITE PAGE: Laurel Falls is well worth the easy hike up the paved trail in springtime.—*BC*

THIS PAGE, TOP: A couple of inches of fresh snow is all it takes to dress this winter scene at Laurel Falls.—*NS*

THIS PAGE, BOTTOM: While at the falls, take time to experiment with sections of water. These tight images of water and rocks can look very relaxing.—*BC*

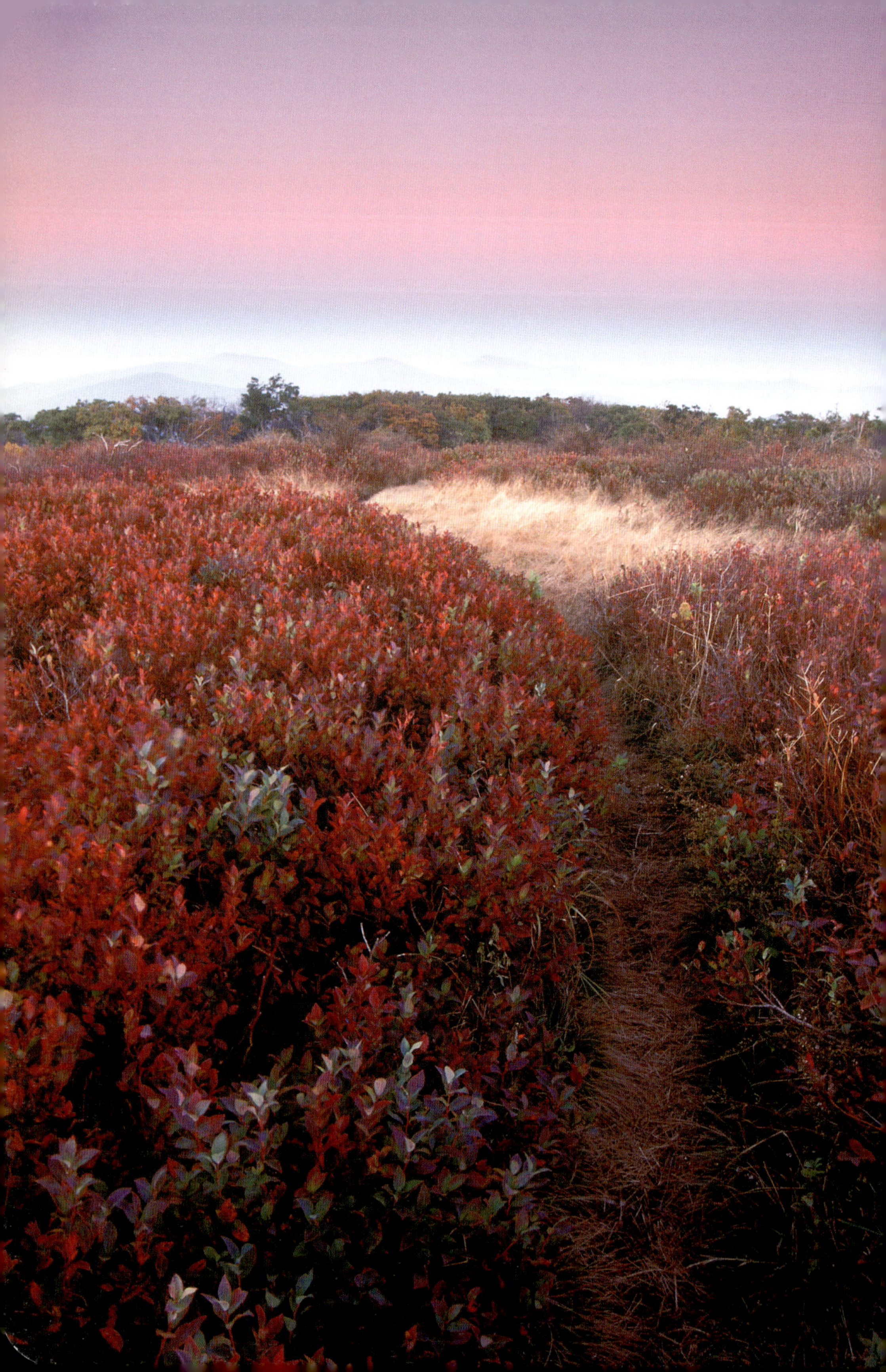

Wildlife

19th Century structures

Smokies landscapes

Wildflowers

Hikes to Gregory Bald and Abrams Falls

Chapter Four

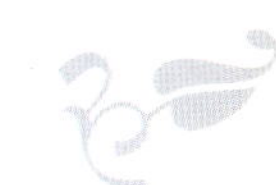

Cades Cove

Gregory Bald, famous for flame azaleas in late June and early July, is also vibrant with the color of wild blueberries in autumn. The predawn sky color is faithfully recorded by using a two stop Singh Ray graduated neutral density filter. *—BC*

CADES COVE, one of the most popular destinations in the park, provides a wealth of opportunities for the photographer. On any given day, you are likely to see a professional photographer from anywhere in the world taking advantage of the diversity offered in the Cove. Within striking distance of its eleven mile paved road are examples of 19th century architecture, grand vistas and landscapes, abundant wildlife and wondrous displays of wildflowers.

This 6 mile long cove, surrounded by mountain crests, bears marks of a long history of human habitation. A glimpse of early mountain life, with activity dating back to 1821, can be seen in the preserved churches, cabins, barns and the grist mill. A quiet walk through any of the church cemeteries reveals the struggle of man against nature in this pastoral area of Appalachia.

To get to Cades Cove, turn right at the "Y" when coming from Townsend or travel straight on Little River Road from Sugarlands Visitor Center. At 0.4 miles from the Townsend "Y," you will see a parking area large enough for 8-10 cars. The series of rapids here is the most photogenic place until you reach the Cove itself. As you enter the cove, there is a picnic area to the left that has bathroom facilities and newly reconstructed picnic sites. Down this same road is the ranger station and a small concessions store that has great ice cream. The gate to the one way loop is back on the main road past the information pavilion. All mileages are from the entrance gate to Cades Cove, which is only open from sunrise to sunset.

From mid-May to mid-September every year, the Loop is closed to cars on Wednesdays and Saturdays until 10 a.m. This gives bicyclists and runners an open road to travel without the concerns of automotive traffic. Tips on traveling the Loop: once past the gate, traffic is one-way except on Sparks Lane, Hyatt Lane and Forge Creek Road; travel slowly and watch for wildlife; use pullouts if stopping; travel early in the morning and late in the evening to avoid traffic congestion; use Rich Mountain Road as an exit possibility during peak traffic times.

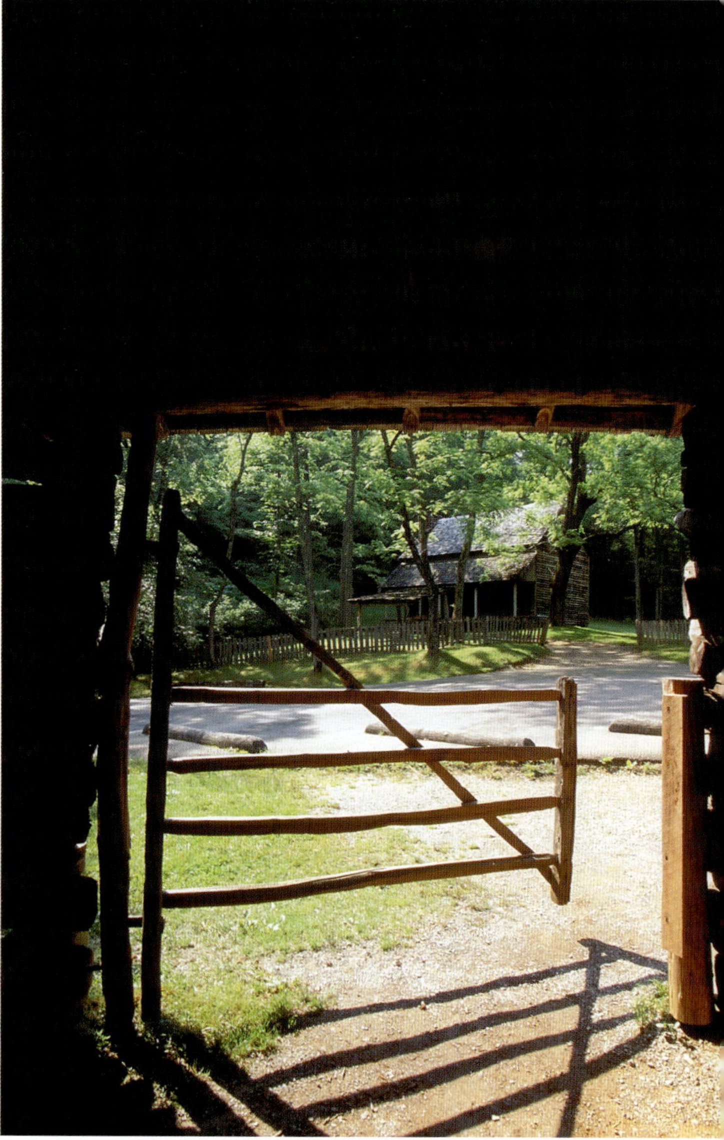

Doors and windows can be used to frame a view of the world outside.—*BC*

TOP: Without the deer, this composition would lack foreground interest. Without the sun it is just another deer; this image needs both elements to succeed. The mist was dense enough not to need a grad; a few minutes later it had burned off.—*NS*

BOTTOM LEFT: The Red Eft is a juvenile form of the Red Spotted Newt. After two years, this terrestrial form morphs into the aquatic adult.—*BC*

BOTTOM RIGHT: Monarch butterflies migrate through the park in the fall on the way to winter in Mexico.—*BC*

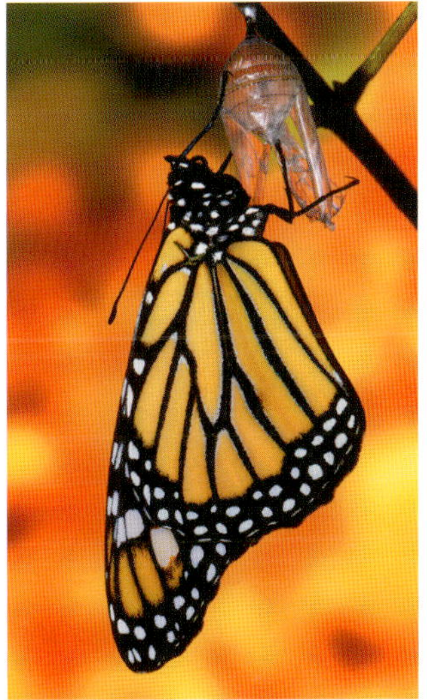

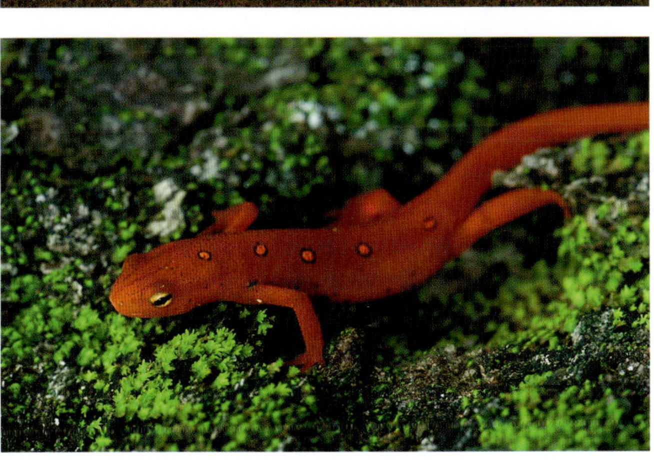

Photographic Opportunities

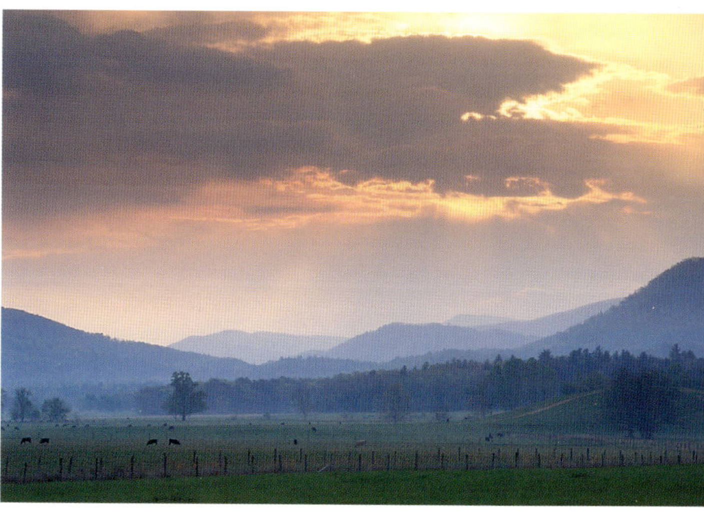

Hyatt Lane offers many opportunities for the grand landscape.—*BC*

ARCHITECTURE

For the history buff or those interested in mountain life, Cades Cove is a treasure trove of preserved buildings. From the churches and their adjacent cemeteries to the working grist mill, photographers will find plentiful opportunities.

Historic sites provide the opportunity to pursue various types of images, all in one area. The different homes offer opportunities to shoot the entire cabin in a general scenic composition. Once you have a nice shot of the cabin, look around for a very interesting foreground element (maybe a group of flowers) and use a wide angle lens to include the cabin in the background to provide character that says Great Smoky Mountains. These cabins have wildflowers and a number of domestic flowers that the original families planted. You can even see large stands of daffodils in the early spring in certain areas that mark the location of a previous homestead.

Cabins provide the chance to shoot detail work of log construction, doors, windows, steps, porches, and chimneys. Reflections in the window glass also make for interesting images, especially catching the very early green of spring in the trees or reds

Structures to visit and their mileage from the beginning of the loop

Historic Structure	Distance from start of loop road	
John Oliver Place	0.9 miles	0.2 mile hike out to cabin on right
Primitive Baptist Church	2.1 miles	Down side road to the left
Methodist Church	2.3 miles	Roadside
Missionary Baptist Church	2.7 miles	On left, just past Hyatt Lane
Elijah Oliver Place	4.2 miles	0.5 mile hike from parking area
Cable Mill Visitor Center	5.1 miles	Multiple structures
Henry Whitehead Place	5.9 miles	0.5 mile down Forge Creek Road
Dan Lawson Place	6.4 miles	Roadside
Tipton Place	6.9 miles	Roadside
Carter Shields Cabin	7.8 miles	Roadside

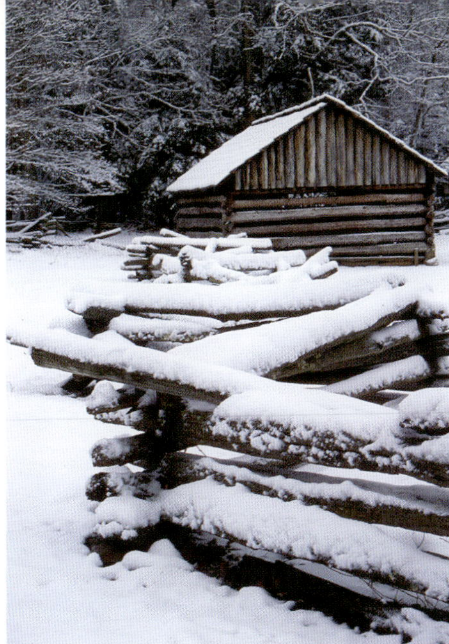

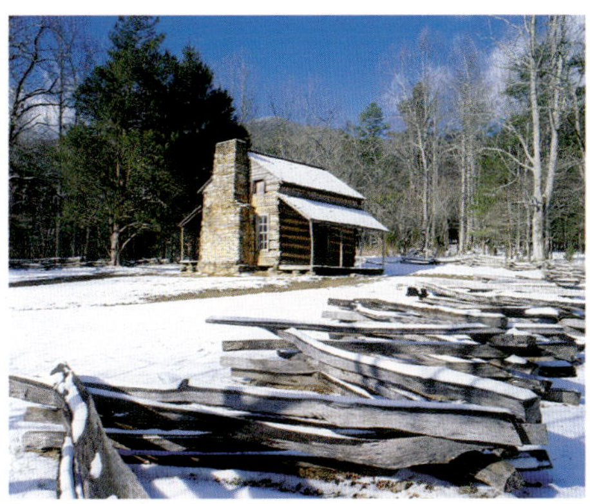

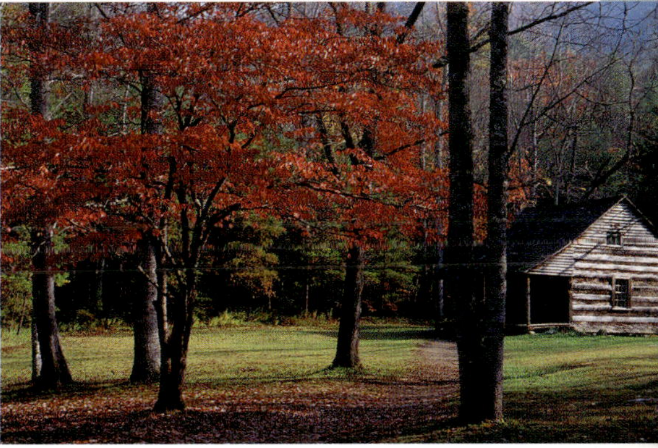

Top left: Cades Cove is potentially more accessible during winter snows than other areas of the park. Remember that snow may need a little more exposure on dark, overcast days due to the reflected gray from the skies.—*BC*

Top right: John Oliver Cabin is within easy walking distance, about 15 minutes from the entrance. Little River/Laurel Creek road may be open to the Cove, even if the loop road itself is closed due to ice.—*NS*

Above: At the Carter Shields cabin, oblique afternoon side lighting adds luminance to the dogwood leaves without the flare and contrast problems associated with strong back lighting.—*NS*

and yellows of fall foliage. A winter snow storm can provide a feeling of the past by covering up most traces of the present. Cabin interiors tend to be very dark, but shooting out of a window, (using the window as a frame), can make for interesting images. Using a flash to fill in the window frame can also give the wood texture and color.

Churches give some recorded history that you can photograph just by walking through the cemeteries. Some engraving on the stones belies there age, but side lighting will help highlight faint writing and make for interesting compositions. Interiors are easier to photograph as there is more light from larger windows. Fog adds a mysterious feeling that can work well with the different churches, especially shooting grave markers in the cemeteries with just an outline of the church in the fog.

The Visitor Center is a focal point of activity. Besides information, the store provides opportunity to purchase books, film, and various gift items, the most important (besides this book) being fresh corn meal. Fresh corn meal is the most important ingredient for homemade corn bread, a staple of mountain folk diets and also a continuing

TOP: Rich Mountain Road Overlook develops distracting shadows in the scene by late afternoon. A Singh-Ray Color Intensifier Polarizer reduced reflections on the foliage and added punch to the colors.—*NS*

BOTTOM: Check to see when period re–enactors are giving demonstrations—they make great subjects. Fill flash balanced the smith with the background light.—*NS*

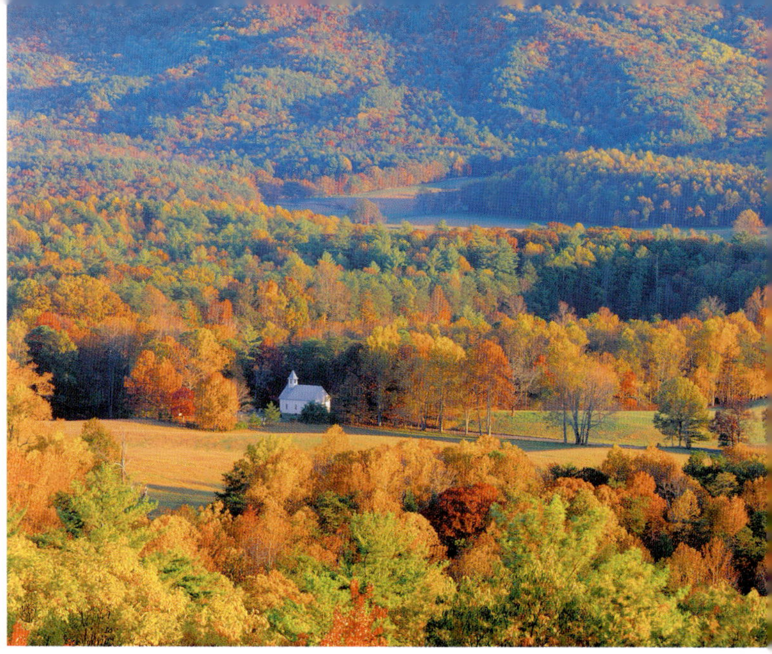

Southern delicacy. The grist mill where the corn is ground into corn meal is an interesting subject for any photograph. The barns and other structures, including old farming implements, make it difficult to think about going anywhere else to photograph.

JOHN OLIVER PLACE

A short hike across the field leads to this picturesque cabin set away from the road. Numerous angles to shoot from and white-tailed deer can frequently be found grazing in the meadow before reaching the cabin. Wonderful rail fence makes for interesting compositions alone and with the cabin in the background.

If you have been exploring Sparks Lane, there are parking places on the right about 200 yards further down the loop road. Park here and walk across the meadow.

PRIMITIVE BAPTIST CHURCH

Quaint church down a gravel side road to the left. Occasionally a wedding ceremony is performed at the church when the Park Service allows a couple to celebrate their nuptials in the majestic surroundings of the Smoky Mountains. The cemetery warrants a stroll through.

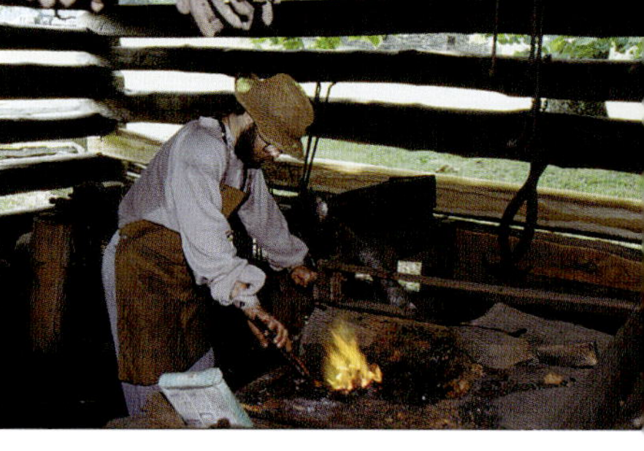

METHODIST CHURCH

Nice white church sitting up on a small hill off the road. Unique front with two separate doors. Spring is a great time to shoot this church, surrounded with dogwoods, especially on a blue sky day in the morning. This church can also be seen from the Rich Mountain Road Overlook, which looks great in the fall or with fog.

MISSIONARY BAPTIST CHURCH

Just past Hyatt Lane, this structure seems to be less visited. Back lighting occurs in the morning, which could be great if there is the right density of fog. Front lighting occurs in the afternoon, so this church may be on your afternoon list of subjects. Deer and bear frequent the area, so look around while you are exploring.

A horse-drawn buggy in cantilever barn at Tipton Place. Isolate elements after you've taken the big scene.—*BC*

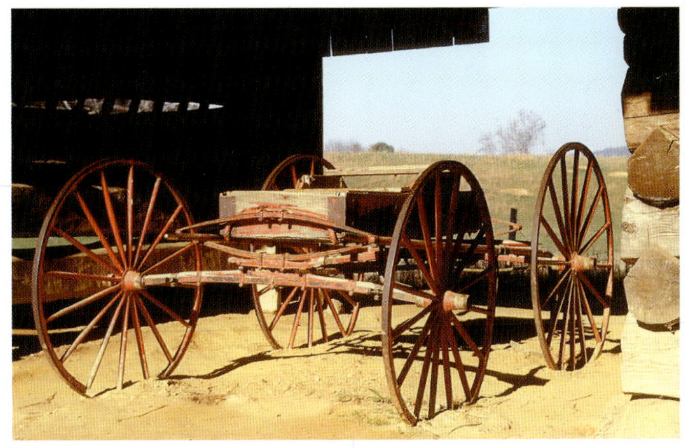

ELIJAH OLIVER PLACE
Group of cabins that is a short 0.5 mile hike from the parking lot. You can also hike 0.5 miles from the Abrams Falls trailhead to get to the cabins. There are several historic structures besides the home, some with great reflections in the windows.

CADES COVE VISITOR CENTER AND CABLE HISTORIC AREA
Good place to break for mid-morning or lunch. Modern bathroom facilities (no shovels needed). Blacksmithing, molasses-making, and other interpretive programs periodically presented, so it's a great opportunity to film living history activities. Various homes and types of barns and out structures have been restored, so take time to walk around and explore early Appalachian life.

HENRY WHITEHEAD PLACE
3/4 mile down Forge Creek Road features some of the best log construction of the era. The roof was replaced in 1998, but now is aging well and has the appearance of an older roof.

DAN LAWSON PLACE
Just past the intersection with Hyatt Lane, this log house offers a variety of angles to shoot from. Early morning fog seems to drape around the cabin with the right conditions.

TIPTON PLACE
House on the right with a replica cantilever barn on the left. Barn was built in 1968 to replace the original. A horse drawn buggy is parked in the center of the barn and greatly adds to the yesteryear feel of the place.

CARTER SHIELDS CABIN
One of the most photogenic cabins in the Smokies. Set back in a small clearing with dogwoods in the yard, this cabin has the potential of being in a calendar for the Smokies year after year. Early morning light or fog or light rain enhances the mood of the scene.

Tips for Architectural Images

- **Try to keep vertical angles straight up** or least symmetrically by not tilting the buildings.
- **Polarizers** can help cut glare off of windows and wet walls, but use them sparingly when trying to capture reflections in window glass.
- **Interesting foreground elements** always add dimension and character to any architectural image.
- **A slow shutter speed during rain or snow** will add a dynamic dimension to the mood of the image.
- **Including wildlife or people** gives a sense of scale to any picture.
- **Fog always decreases the clutter of the background** when taking images that include the surroundings. Exposure for fog is relatively easy by spot metering the fog and opening up one stop when shooting in manual mode or compensating at +0.3 or +0.7 using a Matrix or Evaluative meter setting.

Look for bears in the cherry trees towards the back of the loop when they ripen in late summer.—*NS*

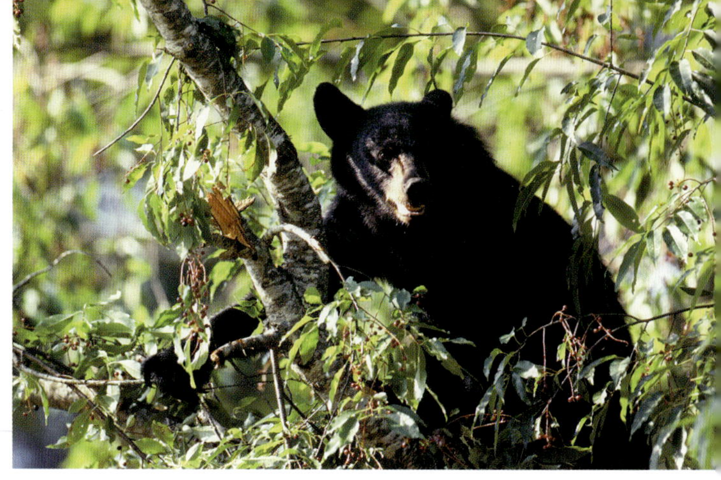

Vistas and Landscapes

Cades Cove abounds with opportunities for images of pastoral landscapes and breath taking vistas. Since grand landscapes need clear atmospheric conditions to be able to include distant mountains sharply, early spring and late fall and periods after a clearing storm are best for attempting the grand landscape. Cades Cove is noted for its wonderful foggy early mornings which work well with intimate landscapes, especially in combination with wildlife or buildings.

Sparks Lane
(0.8 miles)
Hyatt Lane
(2.7 miles)

Some of the best places for landscapes are Sparks Lane and Hyatt Lane. Both two-way roads have fences, solitary trees and wildlife that can be added as an interesting foreground element. The meadows used to be grazed by cattle, but when the last permanent inhabitant of Cades Cove died in 1998, his cattle herd was removed and the meadows are being managed back into a state the Park thinks is consistent with the early to mid-1800's appearance. Controlled burns were used for several years and a cycle of frequent mowing has now been started in hopes of bringing back native flora and fauna and preserving the historic scene.

Several ***overlooks (mile 3.4 and 3.8)*** offer views of both the meadows below and the mountains that define the cove to the southeast. Early morning light, especially in the spring and fall, paints the scene in subtle hues from a heavenly paintbrush. Rapidly changing light means it is imperative to find your spot early and set up and wait. Familiarity with your equipment will allow you to adjust quickly to changes in light without having to fumble with setting you camera or lens.

Rich Mountain Road
(mile 2.9)

This one-way trek out of the Cove offers a wonderful overlook of the meadows and a chance to frame up the Methodist Church in more of an aerial perspective set against the trees and meadows. This image works well with thin, drifting fog in the spring or fall color in autumn. Once committed to this one-way road, there is no turning back to get into the Cove. This can be an alternative way to leave in the morning if you have already made the loop and think conditions are right to shoot the church. This road eventually leads back to U.S. 321 at the west end of Townsend.

Wildlife Opportunities

Considered one of the most productive areas within the Smokies for wildlife, you can see and photograph anything from bear and

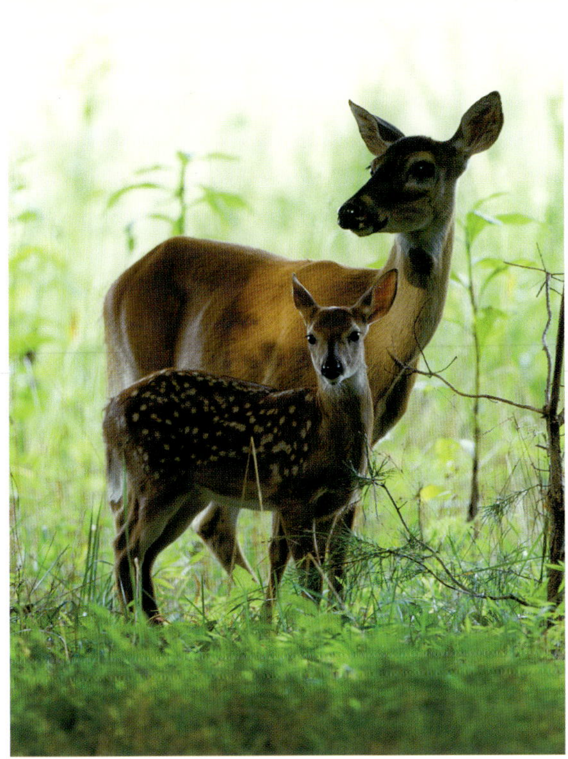

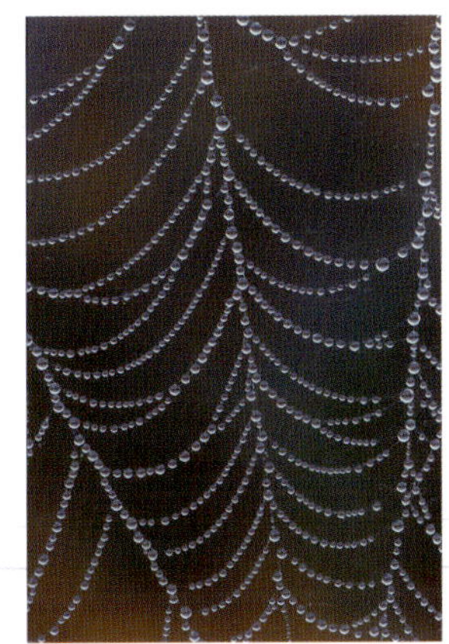

ABOVE: Dew-covered spider webs can be challenging. Keep you camera back parallel to the web to keep it all in focus with a shallow depth of field.—*BC*

LEFT: As in fashion photography, the look makes the scene; the fawn made eye contact for one frame before turning his head…no time to bracket. Learn to get it right the first time.—*NS*

deer to amphibians to insects. The Cove is considered by many nature photographers to be the easiest and best place to photograph white-tailed deer in the United States. Wildlife photography will vary from season to season, depending on the species.

White-tailed deer can be found just about any day somewhere within the meadows of the Cove. Spring is the least photogenic time for deer, especially if there was a hard winter, as their bodies are not full and coats look somewhat ragged. Early summer starting in June could present the chance to photograph fawns with their mothers. Mid to late summer, before the "rut," is a good time to find bucks with antlers in velvet. Fall (October to early December) is the peak for great images of bucks in their crowned glory. Groups of bucks will tend to congregate and an occasional rattling of antlers against antlers will be heard as the joust for leadership (actually the right to a certain area or group of females) ensues. This age-old behavior usually leaves nothing harmed but the male ego of the loser. The best way to find deer is to drive the loop slowly, stopping occasionally to glass the fields with binoculars. A long lens, 300- 500 mm in a 35mm system, will allow an adequate image while keeping a non threatening distance. Don't expect to get magazine or calendar quality images with a point and shoot camera. You may get lucky and have a deer stand close enough to your vehicle as you drive by to open the window and get a great head shot.

Bears are best found in the late summer or early fall as they forage for food to store up for their long winter's nap. The area starting at Hyatt Lane and proceeding on the loop road to the other end of Hyatt Lane seems to have the highest concentration

Photographing Wildlife

Ethical wildlife photography is not walking up to a wild animal and snapping a portrait of Smokey the Bear. Consideration should be made not to ever stress a wild animal. This means not moving or touching any animal. Getting too close can stress many of the creatures we photograph and that is why you will see very large lenses in the hands of professional and advanced amateur photographers. This allows the up close and personal look of the animal without intruding into their zone of fear.

The National Park System has laws against wildlife harassment. Harassment can include getting too close, coming between a mother and baby, cutting off the route of escape to a safer area, and feeding the animals. Feeding the animals, especially bears, is extremely detrimental to the point that the common phrase is "a fed bear is a dead bear" because bears then approach people for handouts and become targeted for relocation or euthanasia. Park rangers and professional nature photographers take a dim view of anyone who does not respect the natural resources that we have been entrusted to protect.

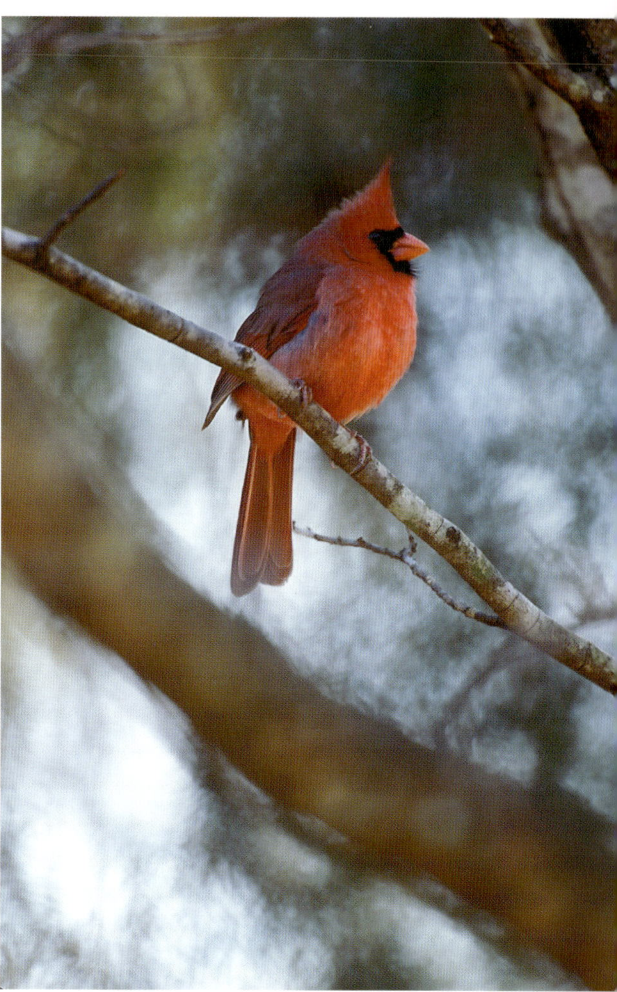

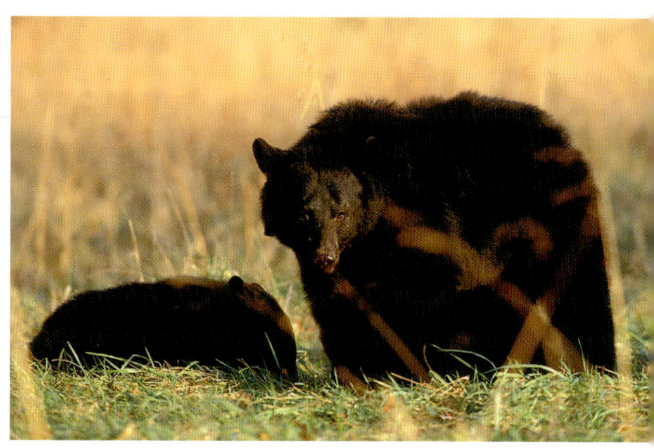

TOP: Northern Cardinals add a wonderful red accent to a snowy winter day. Use a 300mm + lens to isolate the bird.—*BC*

BOTTOM: Bears are extremely dark; it is best to spot meter the black coat and place this value at -1 to -1.5, otherwise you will loose detail in the fur.

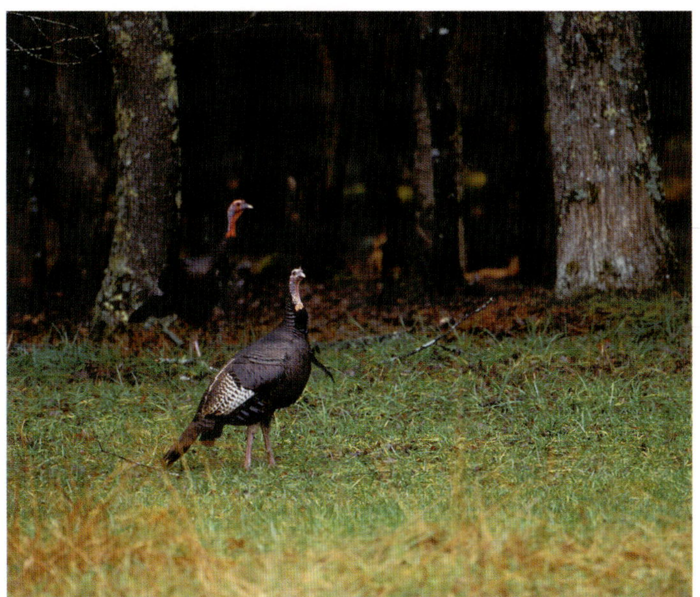

Wild turkeys are extremely wary and difficult to photograph. Use your car as a blind and have your camera ready to shoot.—*BC*

of visible bears in the Cove. The walnut trees on the right side of the loop road, just past Hyatt Lane, seem to be a favorite foraging place. Sitting 100 hundred yards away and hearing the distinctive crunch of whole nuts being ground up by a sow and her cubs is a distinct possibility here. Also look for bears in the trees where Abrams Creek follows the road. There are wild cherry trees along here that provide desert for an ambitious bear.

Spring, while not optimal for mammals, is great for finding ***amphibians*** such as frogs and salamanders. Vernal ponds which spring up from incessant rains provide great opportunities for viewing frogs and frog behavior. Just listen for the melodic croak and follow to the source. Since frogs like wet conditions, make sure your footwear is waterproof or you have a dry set of shoes in the car. Salamanders can be found in the small creeks and along the creeks within the Cove. They too like a damp environment, so be prepared. A telephoto lens will be optimal to photograph these animals without disturbing them.

Birds can be seen anywhere around the loop, any time of the year. Wild Turkeys are very wary and will need much patience and a very long lens to get good images. Owls, hawks, woodpeckers and a variety of migratory birds can be seen around the Cove. Look up in the denser areas of trees, especially at dawn and dusk to find owls. Woodpeckers, especially Pileated Woodpeckers, frequent standing dead trees to feast on the insects collecting there. Blue birds can be seen flitting around the meadows, especially fence lines and solitary trees at fence lines.

Wildflowers

Cades Cove isn't the first place that people will talk about when discussing the colored gems scattered in the Smokies, but there are enough flowers around to make any photographer with a botanical bent happy.

Early spring finds small flowers bursting out along the various trail and side roads. Abrams Falls Trail is a great place to find Trailing Arbutus, Hepatica and several varieties of violets. Cross the bridge and follow

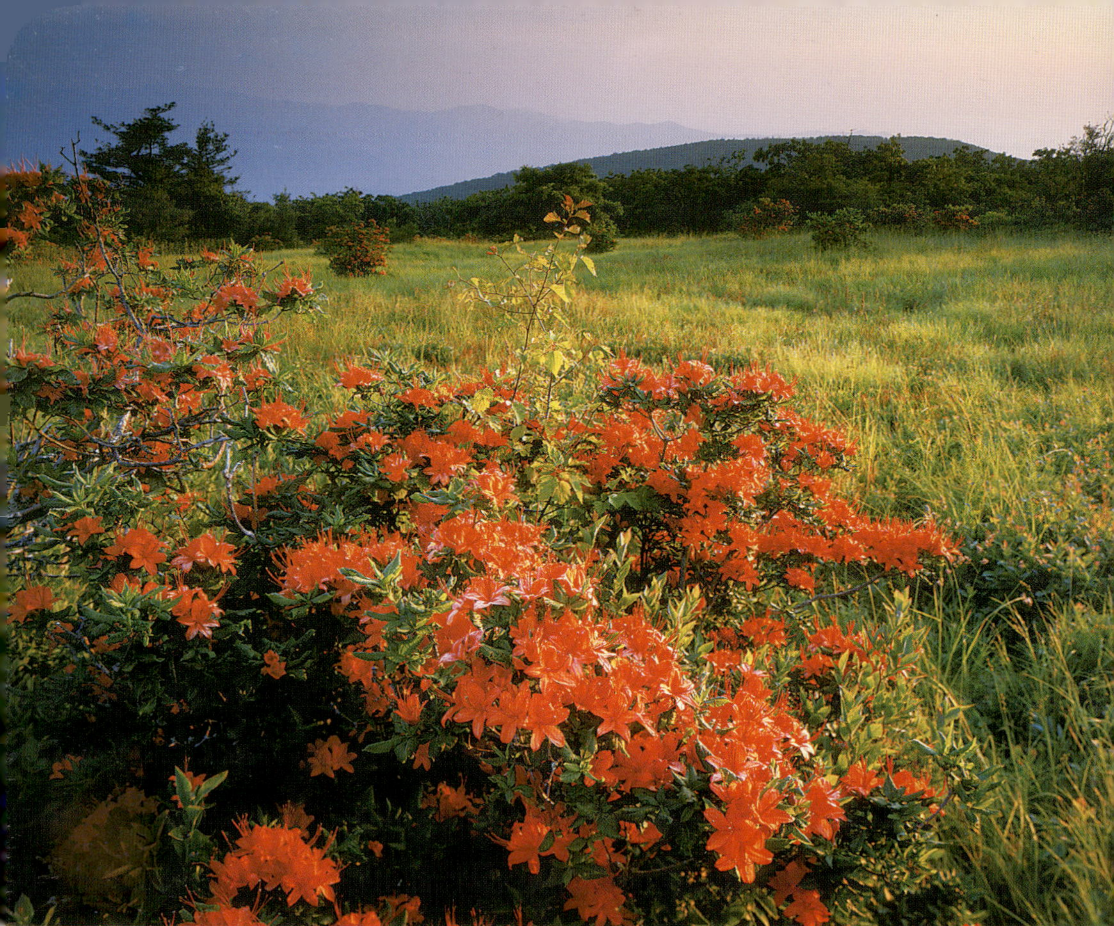

Flame azaleas at Gregory Bald usually peak in the 4th week of June. Oblique side light adds a glow to flowers and leaves. A 3 stop Singh Ray grad keeps the sky from blowing out. Notice the gradient in the sky from right to left, a compromise that day.—*NS*

the trail along Abrams Creek, looking on the hillside away from the creek. A great proliferation can be found within the first mile of the trail. One of the best kept secrets for wildflowers in this area is the ***Rich Mountain Road***. The road climbs up and out of the cove and once you crest the mountain and head down towards Townsend, you will see some of the best displays of Bloodroot, Hepatica, violets, Star Chickweed, trillium and Squaw-root. You may have to pull over and walk back to some of the flowers as the road is not extremely wide at some of the best displays. Be careful about cars coming the wrong way, as this has happened on more than one occasion.

Mid-summer is a good time to look for different flowers in the meadows. As the meadows are reclaimed from the non-native fescue and native grasses and meadow wildflowers replenish the open areas, we will see more of the meadow type flowers that used to inhabit this area. The narrow leaved sunflower is one such flower. The meadows on either side of the road down Sparks and Hyatt lanes are great for these open area flowers. Rosebay rhododendrons (white blooms) can be found on Laurel Creek

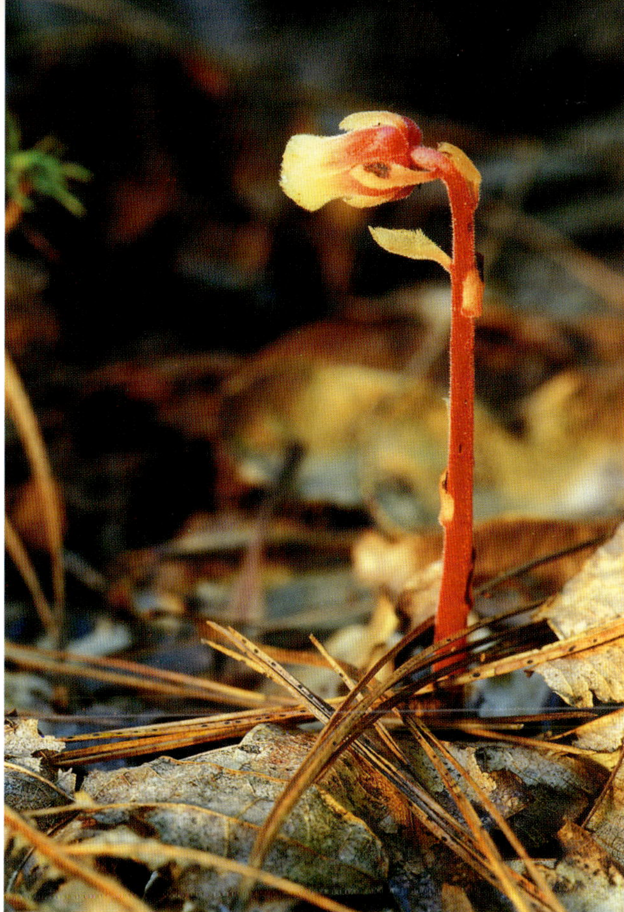

Pinesap is a parasitic plant without chlorophyll. It can be found in the forests along Forge Creek Road.—*BC*

Road and also on the back side of the loop road from The Tipton Place out to the ranger station area. If you are adventurous enough for a long hike and/or overnight stay, Gregory Bald explodes with color from hybrid Flame Azaleas in late June and early July. The colors vary from white to red and everything in between.

Fall finds a profusion of Joe Pye Weed in the meadows. These make great stopping places for butterflies migrating through in the fall. The Pine Oak areas, such as around the Missionary Baptist Church, are the natural habitat for atypical flowers such as Indian Pipe. This flower contains no chlorophyll and lives by extracting nourishment for roots of pine and oak trees. It is also called Ghost Plant because of the lack of color.

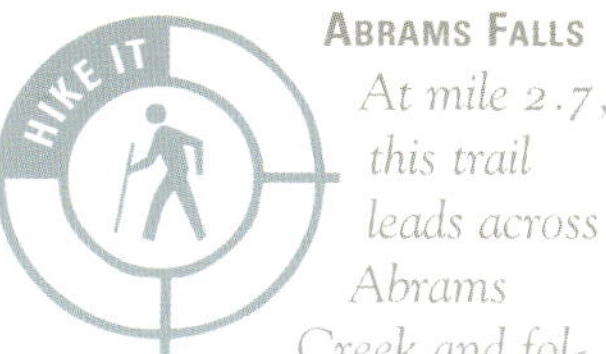

Abrams Falls

At mile 2.7, this trail leads across Abrams Creek and follows the creek for a decent part of the gentle 2.5 mile hike to the falls. Spring hikes present great wildflower opportunities and the falls are usually full from the abundant spring rains. Early summer through late July sees mountain laurel or rhododendron blooming along the creek. Fall hikes in October present the chance of great color around the waterfall.

Gregory Bald

A strenuous hike from the trailhead at the end of Forge Creek Road. The alternative hike originates from Parson Branch Road. Climbing 3000 vertical feet over 5.7 miles, this is not for the faint of heart or the unconditioned photographer. The rewards of this hike are extremely high in June, for this is the location of the famed flame azaleas. The azaleas are hybrids that bloom in multiple colors from white to dark red and almost any color in between. Campsite 13 is a short 0.5 mile hike from the Bald, if you want to pack in camping gear also. This area works best very early in the morning or very late in the evening. Fall on the Bald is resplendent with colorful blueberry plants and autumn foliage.

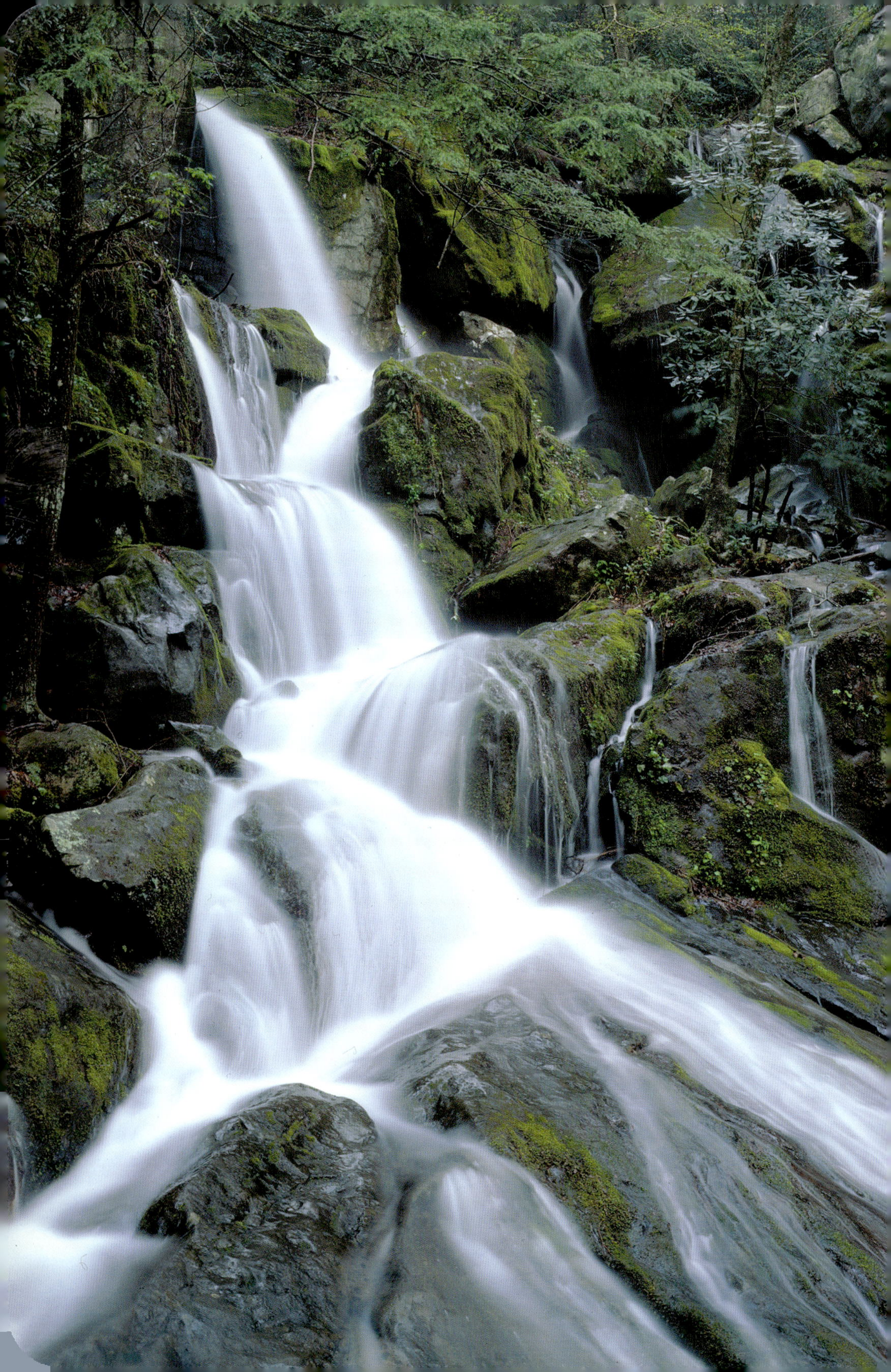

Waterfalls

Historic structures

Wildflowers

Opposite page: Place of 1000 drips: best when it is wet, this tiered waterfall all but dries up in dry periods. It goes into shade in the early evening.—*NS*

Chapter Five

Roaring Fork

Below: Coral type fungus is one of many fungi found within the parks. Don't pick or eat any mushrooms as several varieties can be deadly.—*BC*

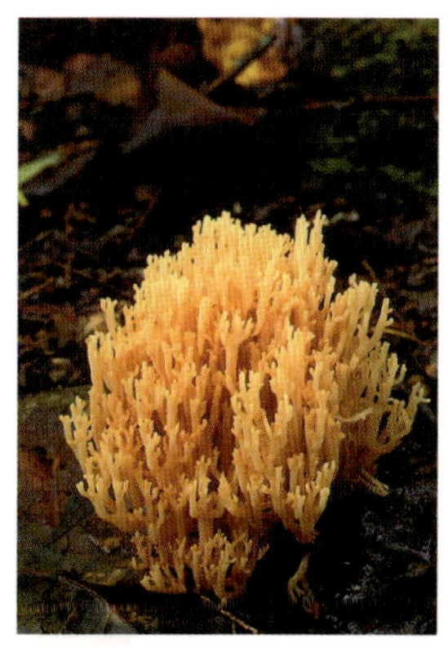

Six miles of natural bliss and only minutes away from downtown Gatlinburg—this is Roaring Fork Motor Nature Trail. Lying at the end of Airport Road (turn at traffic light #8), this paved one way road leads you to wildflower wonderland in the spring and fabulous foliage in the fall. Babbling brooks, and roaring streams and dripping springs keep this area moist and green. You can even get a glimpse or two of 19th Century farm life in the preserved architecture of several farms. Just remember that this road closes in the winter, usually after the first major snow. Yes, the southern Appalachians do get snow and sometimes in abundance.

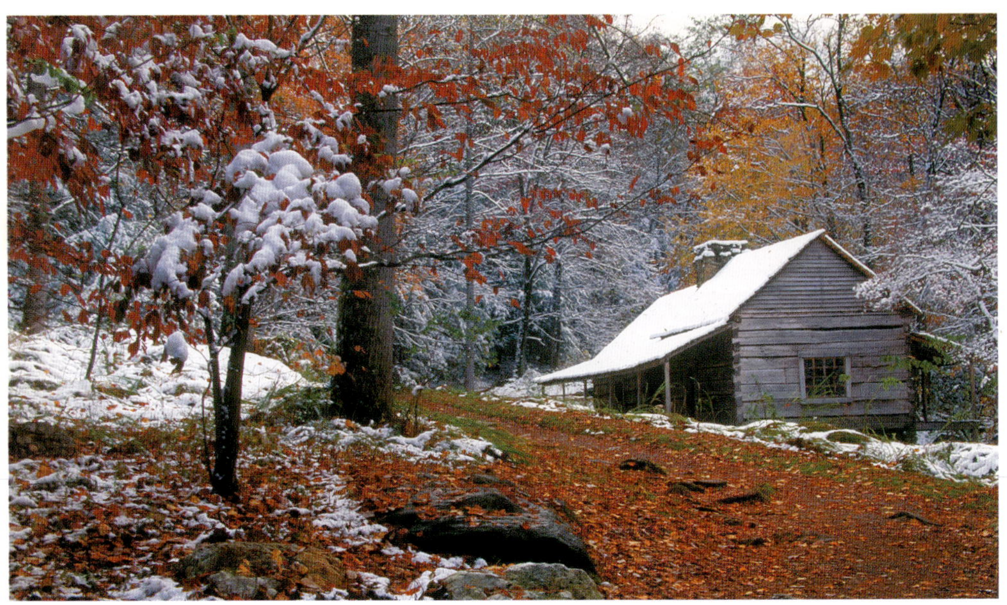

Noah "Bud" Ogle farm
2.6 miles from Light #8 in downtown Gatlinburg

The first stop on Cherokee Orchard Road, it's worth a long stop and exploration. This is technically not part of the Motor Nature Trail, but a visit here is definitely worth a stop. You may not have time to continue the Motor Nature Trail after you have explored this area fully. The farm now consists of a log house and a barn set away from the house. You can shoot from the inside framing up flowers or dogwoods through the old windows or doors or shoot from the outside and get wildflowers in the foreground of the cabin. Walk around with your wide angle lens or short telephoto and set up when the scene strikes you. This image works well on a foggy day that reduces the clutter of the surrounding forest and gives a mysterious feeling to your images. Most of the Motor Nature Trail is difficult to shoot on a sunny day. Get there early before the fog burns off.

Now set your odometer to zero as you leave the parking lot. All mileage is from this area. Within several hundred yards the road will become a one way loop. The Motor Nature Trail comes off this loop at 1.0 miles. If you have run out of time and want to come back later, stay on the loop and it will bring you back around to Ogle's cabin and you will be headed back down Cherokee Orchard Road, to Gatlinburg.

The Noah "Bud" Ogle Nature Trail

HIKE IT

This path wanders off to the right from the cabin. You will cross a stream within several hundred feet and from there on is wildflower heaven in the spring time. If you walk far enough (about 0.5 mile) you will come to a stream and remnants of an old tub mill and the sluice way. There are so many different images to shoot here, you might have to come back a different day to do the rest of the Motor Nature Trail. This area is one of the best places to find showy orchis in the Smokies.

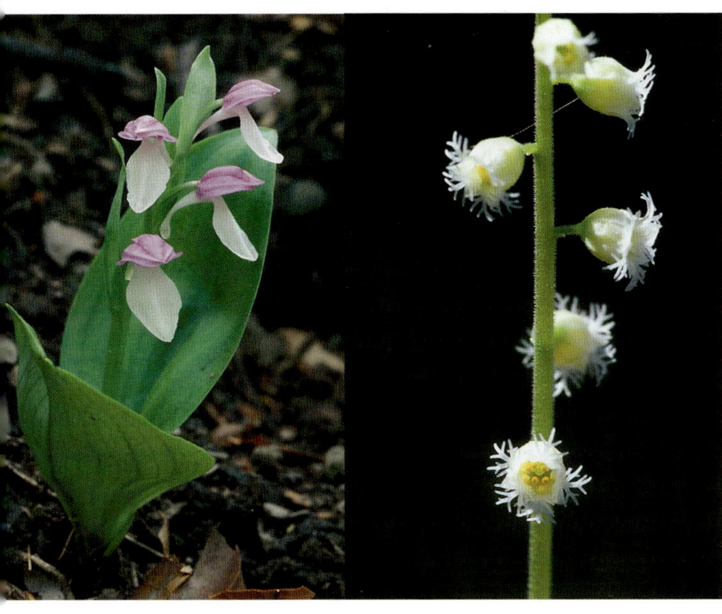

Opposite page: Snow readily shows color casts. A Singh-Ray Color Intensifier pumped up the reds and yellows with relatively little crossover into the highlights.—*NS*

This page, left: Showy Orchis is one of the over 30 orchids found within the Smokies.—*BC*

Right: Miterwort (Bishops Cap) has an extremely small flower measuring 4 mm across. Here you can appreciate the delicate lace edges.—*BC*

Rainbow Falls
mile 0.7

This is one of the five routes up Mt. Le Conte. It is a pretty hike, but strenuous if you want to go to the falls and back (5- 6 miles round trip), especially with camera gear. Walk to Grotto Falls if you want to hike to a waterfall.

Turn right and go uphill at mile 1.0 on the small, winding Motor Nature Trail. Go slow as there are blind curves and trees that like to take up space abutting the road. More than a few of these trees bear the scars of collisions with cars. They do have the right of way. The first few miles until you reach the trail to Grotto Falls is not as productive as the latter section. From about Mile 2.5, you will be going downhill, so remember to use your lower gear unless you want to test your bumper out on a large tree when your brakes fail.

Grotto Falls Trail Head
mile 2.6

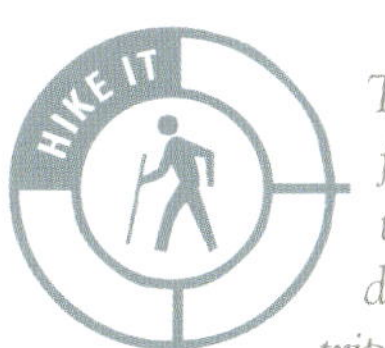

This begins a short 1.2 mile hike to a quaint falls that actually is undercut and allows you to walk behind the falls. The approach looking directly at the falls is a good place to set up a tripod and practice long exposures of water for that silky effect. A polarizer helps cut down on the reflections from both the water and the foliage

Mile 3.4 to 3.6 (marker #9) is great for small creek work and wildflowers. This area is especially productive during the month of April when wildflowers are plentiful. You will find bishops cap, trillium, dwarf ginseng, foamflower, solomon's-seal, Jack-in-the-pulpit, and multiple violets in this area. If you go all the way to marker #9 and park on the left, you can take an unmarked trail just uphill from the parking area. This leads to a confluence of Roaring Fork with one of its branches. This cascade is a wealth of photographic opportunity.

Jim Bales Place
mile 3.8 (marker #10)

This is just across the bridge from the parking area on the left. There is a cabin, corn

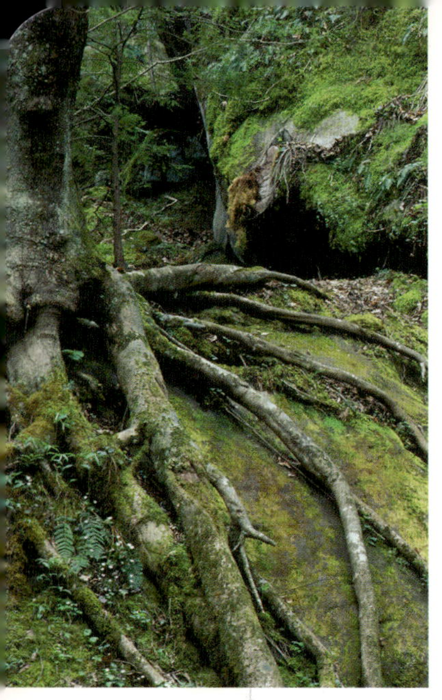

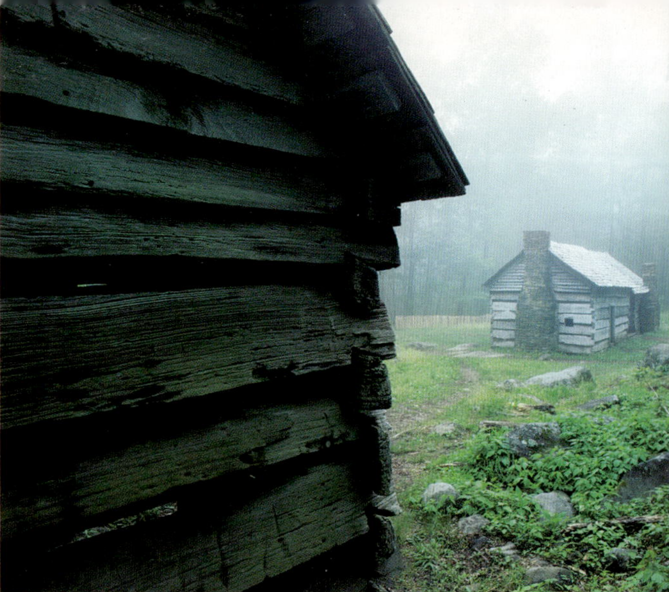

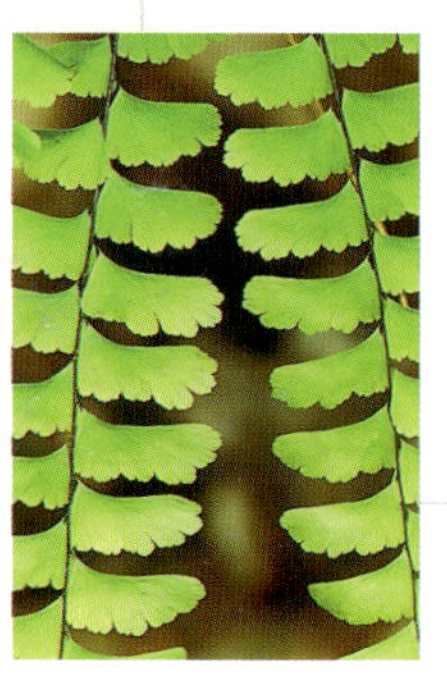

Top left: This tree has taken root atop a boulder in the Place of a Thousand Drips. Roots are visible coursing over the rock surface in search of nourishment.—*BC*

Top right: Blue late evening light is very "cold;" make an insurance image with a warming filter. The colder color balance may better convey the mood of the moment or may just be "too blue."—*NS*

crib and barn located here. All are very photogenic with several dogwoods located just adjacent to the cabin for lots of work with just dogwoods in forest and dogwoods with the cabin. If you traipse up the trail past the barn, you will see an old stone wall and a rhododendron behind the right end of the wall. This rhodie blooms in mid-June and makes for a nice setting of old structure and nature.

For a nice perspective of the stream, walk to the stream edge from the wall and then meander downstream about 100 feet and you will find a nice overlook that is about 15 feet above the stream and presents a wonderful vantage point looking back upstream. On a foggy day, this is a stream image that is hard to beat.

From Jim Bales Place to Ephraim Bales Place (mile 4.1) you will find several solitary pullouts. This area is one of the resplendent areas in the spring for wildflowers. The same type of flowers found early around marker #9, but sometimes even denser in population.

Ephraim Bales Place
mile 4.1 (marker #11)

This is an original home site with cabin, corn crib, barn and hog pen. Explore the area with a wide angle lens or back up a bit and use a short telephoto. The stream is also close by if you haven't exhausted you quota of stream shots yet.

Alfred Reagan Place
mile 4.6

This unique structure strikes you as immediately different, even from the road. It is painted. Seems the Reagan family wanted to spruce up their little bit of mountain paradise and used "all three colors from the Sears catalog". The tub mill down by the road was also the work of Mr. Reagan and presents many chances to record a glimpse of history.

Stream Pull offs (mile 4.9 and 5.1) are both to the right and offer easy accessibility and nice views of Roaring Fork.

Place of a Thousand Drips
mile 5.7

Not your typical waterfall, here it cascades to trickles, depending on the season and the most recent rainfall. When full, the stream cascades in sweeping flows down the rock face. It times of lesser flow, the water follows very distinct channels that it has cut into the bedrock. A wide angle can be used to demonstrate the multitude of rivulets and a telephoto can zoom in on individual flows. There isn't much extra room to set up, so be careful not to block traffic or get hit by a car. This is our last stop, so take your time and enjoy the solitude before you head back through the congestion and traffic that is Gatlinburg.

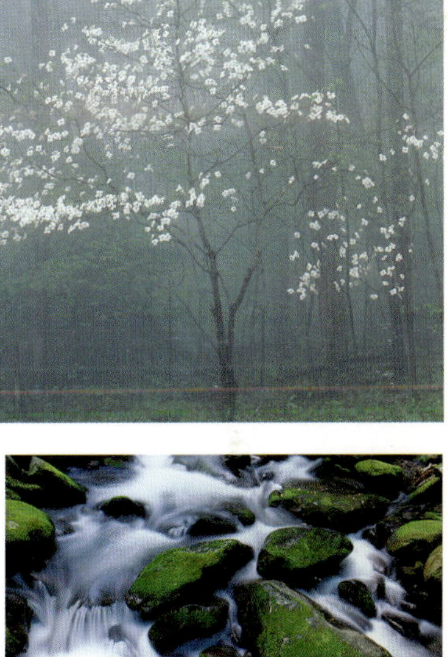

Top: Dogwoods bloom in April and a foggy day like this is perfect to set the mood.—*BC*

Middle: The Roaring Fork has some of the best moss covered rocks in the park, with several bridges offering a convenient aerial perspective. Best early in the day before traffic becomes a problem.—*NS*

Bottom: Rosebay rhododendron bloom here in late June and July. Wading out to a midstream perch fills the foreground with graceful cotton candy water at shutter speeds over 1 second.—*NS*

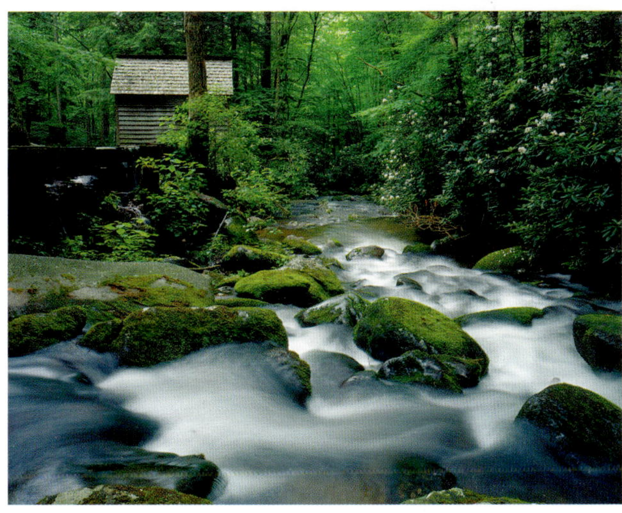

Wildflowers
in the Smokies

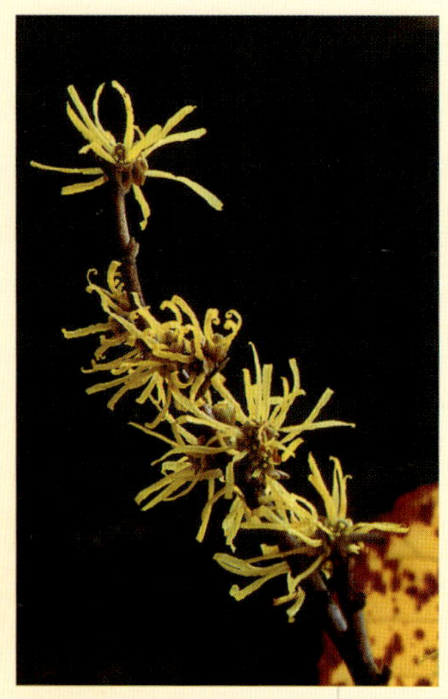

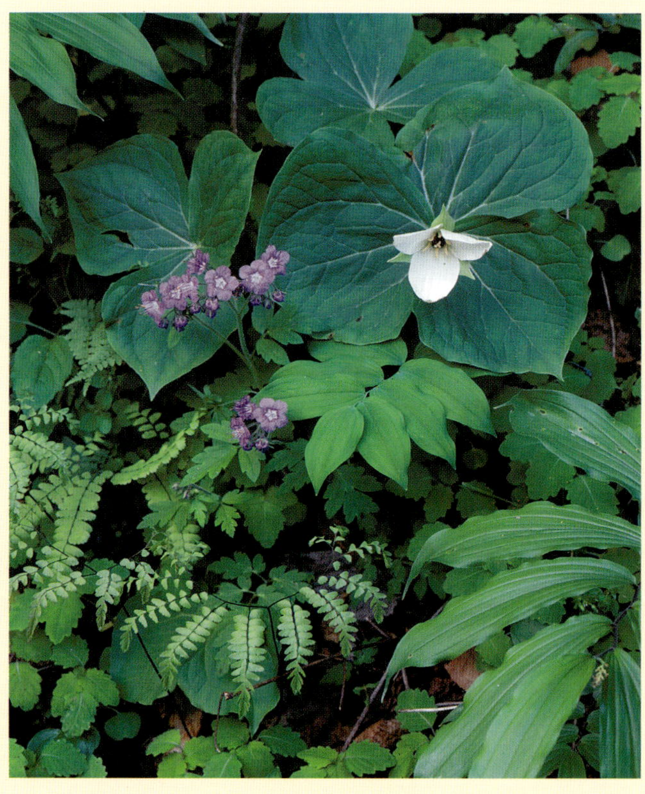

Left: Witch hazel flowers are found blooming in November and December on a shrub that can grow as large as a very small tree.—*BC*

Right: Chestnut Top Trail and the steep bank below it are prime wildflower locations in mid-April.—*NS*

Every year *millions of people flock to the Smokies to enjoy one of the grandest shows of wildflowers in the world. Wildflower viewing is so popular, there are numerous events dedicated to the annual spring beauty pageant. Both Gatlinburg and Townsend have separate wildflower pilgrimages during the peak month of April. From the streams at the lowest elevations to the highest peaks, you can find radiant blossoms. They vary in size from just several millimeters across (Miterwort) to much larger than this book* you are holding (umbrella magnolia). Shades of white, red, pink, yellow, purple, blue, green, and brown can be found throughout the Smokies.

The advantage of chasing wildflowers in the Smokies is the extreme elevation change. Newfound Gap Road (U.S. 441) rises 3,500 feet to Newfound Gap and Clingmans Dome Road then another 1,250 toward the Dome, so if you miss a flower because it was prime several days ago, just drive up several hundred feet in elevation and you will likely find it in prime condition there. There is an ongoing bloom of flowers starting in March in the lowest elevations and continuing to November.

Wildflower Photography Hints

Flower photography is not that difficult if you have the right equipment and lots of patience. In fact, given how close the compact digital cameras can focus, you don't need special macro equipment. But, you still need patience. First, find a bloom or blooms that look fresh without brown spots or insect holes or tatters from the wind. Then walk around the area (careful not to trample any other plants or flowers) and find the viewpoint you like. Consider doing a group shot first and then move in for the single portraits later.

Weather is an important factor in flower photography. Dry sunny days in the Smokies are not the best time to photograph botanical blossoms in the forest. You need even lighting that comes from an overcast day or a diffuser. Light rain helps as it cleans the flower up and intensifies the color. Waiting for the rain to stop is one of those patience lessons. Remember good rain pants and waterproof boots, these will keep you more comfortable and a comfortable photographer is a productive photographer.

Equipment for macro photography depends on how close you want to get and how much money you want to spend. The bare minimum is a camera with a lens that will give you one half life size image on film (if you look directly at your film, the image is 50% size of real life). Most compact digital cameras will achieve this easily. The next item on your list will be a tripod. Remember the patience lesson. Cameras get really heavy when holding them in one place waiting for rain, wind, and light to cooperate. Look for one in your budget that weighs enough to hold your camera steady even in wind but not so heavy that you never want to pick it up. Ball heads for the top of the tripod are the most useful for photography in the field.

Filters are needed for specific effects and the most used filter is the polarizer. This reduces reflections from the rain you just waited for as well as reflections from the waxy leaves in the background. The rhododendrons and laurel have shiny leaves and are very prolific in the Smokies. A warming filter will help on those overcast days when the light appears cool. Exposures will get even longer with filters with polarizers using 1-2 stops of light and most warming filters using 1/3-1/2 stops of light. This just means slower shutter speeds for a correct exposure, hence the need for the tripod.

Modifying light is a way to set your image apart from all the others of the same flower. You will see people using diffusion discs (transparent white material on a metal loop) that will act as an "instant cloud" if it happens to be sunny, but everything else about the day is great. Along with the diffusers, you will see reflecting discs. These reflectors are gold or silver or white and sunlight can be reflected back into an area that would normally be very dark. All these discs fold up to 1/3 their open size and will fit in many photo backpacks. This method is highly preferred over using a flash to add more light to the subject. The preferred light is a bright overcast light which gives diffused, even light to your subject. All modifications to light are attempting to achieve what Mother Nature sometimes gives to us free.

Favorite Spring Wildflower Areas

1 Cove Hardwood Nature Trail

Located behind the amphitheater area in the Chimney's Picnic Area on Newfound Gap Road (U.S. 441), this is an extremely productive trail for wildflowers. A sea of white fringed phacelia will accost your vision just before you turn into the parking area. Park and walk back to the road and up to capture this carpet of white. When you have finished with these dainty blossoms, carefully walk back to the parking area and up to the trail. Early April finds phacelia, spring-beauty, rue anemone and violets in profusion. Later, these give way to large-flowered trillium, yellow trillium, Jack-in-the-pulpit, bishop's cap, Solomon's-seal, and great chickweed. Look to the left along the hillside as you enter the trail to see the delicate yellow mandarin, a member of the Lily family. The hike around the loop is approximately 1 mile and it is best to get here early in the morning as the sun starts to encroach on this area by 9 a.m. in spring and the wind seems to pick up about the same time. This still gives you a couple of hours to work the area. On a still, overcast day you can shoot all day long. Even a light mist won't interfere and can make for some great opportunities.

2 Tremont

The gravel road past the Great Smoky Mountains Institute at Tremont is resplendent with wildflower opportunities in the spring. Starting with violets for early flowers and progressing to Jack-in-the-pulpit, showy orchis, Solomon's-seal, false Solomon's-seal, bishop's cap, foamflower and the ever magnificent dogwood blossoms. This is one of the best places to do stream scenics which include dogwoods in bloom. Fraser sedge can be found at the edge of several of the vernal waterfalls to the right, but catching the blooms at their peak is difficult as they last only a couple of days. You will find yellow trillium here, but for large groups of trillium look at the Cove Hardwoods Trail. The area around the parking at the end of the road is most prolific for various wildflowers, including dwarf crested iris and little brown jug. Streamside shots with bluets are also possible.

3 Greenbrier

The road into Greenbrier follows the Little Pigeon River and offers many vantage points for stream photography, some with blooming dogwoods, but the best wildflowers are at the end of the road. You will see numerous patches of wildflowers along the hillsides, but explore these on your way back out as the largest concentrations lie ahead. Continue to the end of the road, park and start walking up Porters Creek Trail. The next mile will offer some of the most diverse collections of wildflowers in the spring. Look for violets, Jack-in-the-pulpit, painted trillium, bishop's cap, foamflower, spring-beauty and perhaps a chance to see a yellow lady's slipper. Continue on Porters Creek Trail to the left for a short hike that contains an abundance of flowers. On your way out, turn right and cross the bridge towards Ramsey Cascade and park anywhere along the road. Along here you will encounter some of the nicest groups of dwarf crested iris, little brown jug and wild ginger. At the end of this road is the trailhead to Ramsey Cascade, a hike well worth taking for the flowers and the waterfall at the end. This hike is described on page 98.

4 Roaring Fork

This hidden oasis is located so close to Gatlinburg, you would think it would be overrun by visitors, but solitude can be found here. The first place to explore for wildflowers is the Noah "Bud" Ogle Cabin area. Walk the trail that runs behind the cabin and for the next 1/2 mile you will encounter a variety of flowers. Violets, Jack-in-the-pulpit, sweet shrub, bluets, Vasey's trillium and Catesby's trillium and possibly yellow lady's slippers. Explore the two side trails for several hundred yards for different perspectives of the same flowers. This trail makes a loop and it is well worth exploring the area all the way around. If you are on a tight schedule, you can turn around once you have reached the tub mill by the stream. Roaring Fork Motor Trail, starting at mile 3.4, offers similar flowers in a slightly different setting, as some are grouped around historic structures and some are in close proximity to the streams. Miterwort and foamflower and dwarf ginseng seem to carpet the sides of the road around mid-April with trilliums appearing as little islands in the sea of white.

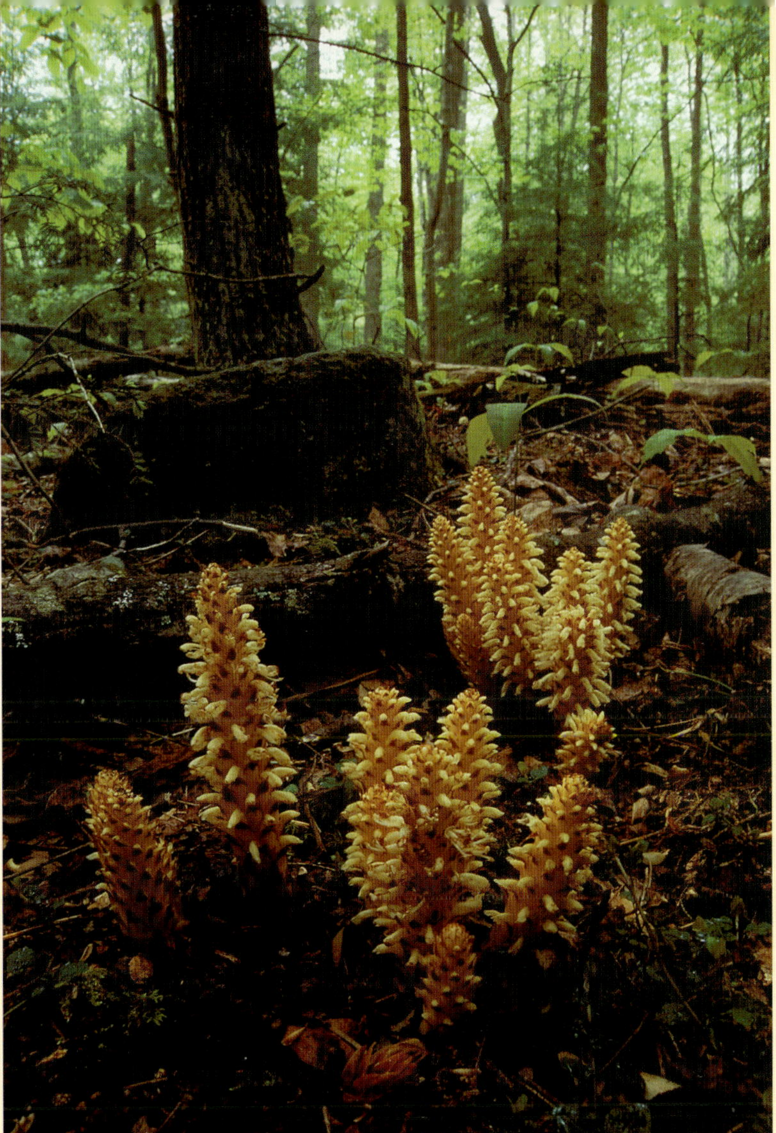

Squaw-root is parasitic on oak roots. Look for this non chlorophyll containing plant in April and May.—*BC*

5 Rich Mountain Road

Few people go to Cades Cove for the wildflowers, so this exit road is a well kept secret to those wildflower enthusiasts that brave this one way road out of the Cove. For the first mile or so the road climbs up Cades Cove Mountain and the majority of the wildflower opportunities are after you crest the top of the mountain and start your journey downward. Most flowers are on the hillside on your right and parking is not always easy. Leave plenty of room for another car to pass. You won't have to look hard to find bloodroot, spring-beauty, Dutchman's breeches, squirrel corn, yellow trillium, bishop's cap, foamflower and a plethora of violets. The mountainside shades the flowers until later in the morning, so this drive works well even on sunny days.

Several other areas worth mentioning are described in other sections. *Flat Creek Falls Trail* in the Heintooga Ridge/Balsam Mountain area is at a higher altitude and is a wonderful place to find early spring flowers that bloom earlier on the Tennessee side. If you find that you have just missed peak flowers along Tremont or Cove Hardwoods, a trip to Flat Creek Falls Trail might find the ones you missed. (This trail is discussed further on page 103.) The *Chestnut Top Trail* (described in chapter three, *Little River Road*) at the "Y" in Townsend is a great place to start before heading into Tremont.

RIGHT: Trout lilies. Always look for nice groupings of flowers. Look at the leaves to see why it is called "Trout lily."—*BC*

BELOW: Painted Trillium. Fill the frame with your subject. Don't center it in the frame and remember to give it some room at the edges.—*BC*

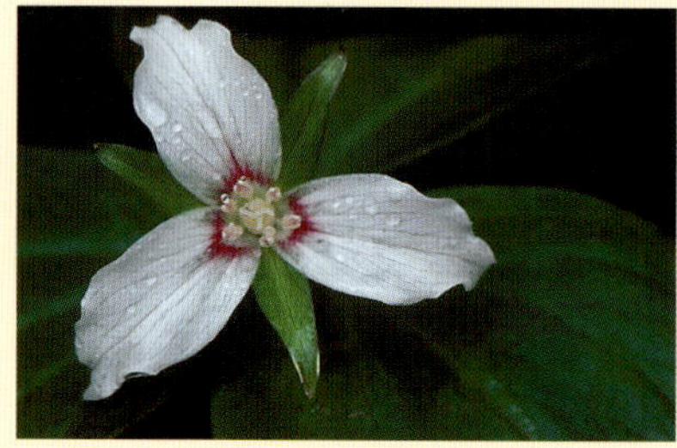

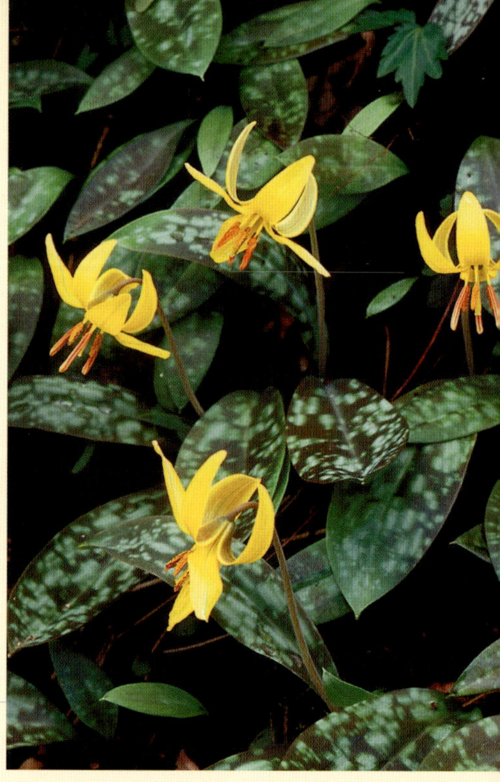

Wildflower Image Tips

• **Isolation** *Find a single blossom and use a large aperture (shallow depth of field) to make the background blurred and appear less cluttered. Work around the blossom and look for the view that gives a solid background or a dark background if your flower is well lit. This separates the flower from the background and draws attention to what you find most appealing.*

• **Extreme macro** *Get as close as possible and photograph elements of a solitary flower; pistil, stamens, sepal, petal, dew drop on petal. This can be achieved with a macro lens or extension tubes or close up diopters or with a digital camera that focuses very closely.*

• **Diffused Light** *Use a diffuser on days when the sun is shining directly on the flower you wish to photograph. Use one big enough that the background can be shaded too. Or use your shirt or jacket to shade the background. Carrying a large piece of black plastic can help by draping it to shade a large portion of background. If you don't shade the background, it will be much brighter than your flower and detract from the overall image.*

• **Reflected light** *A muted gold reflector works best, but a gold, silver or white reflector can also work to add light into areas that may be a little dark. This especially works well if you have to use a diffuser to shade your flower. You can set up multiple reflectors. One advantage of a reflector over flash is that you can see the results before the image is made. Another advantage is that the color of light is much more natural than electronic light from a flash.*

• **Stabilize** *A simple stick propping a flower stem can stop it from swaying in the breeze. A more elaborate tool is the Wimberly Plamp, which can encompass a stem without crushing it and hold it very steady in a gentle breeze. Rubber bands, Velcro strips and simple string can also help stabilize things that go swish in the breeze. If it is too windy, put on your artistic cap and think of how to make some abstract images of flowers moving around. This technique can be quite stunning and give an impressionistic effect. Don't ever let a little wind stop your creative muse.*

• **Think in groups** *Many flowers look very nice in groups instead of solitary portraits. Look for shapes formed by groups. Remember to give the group some breathing room at the edges.*

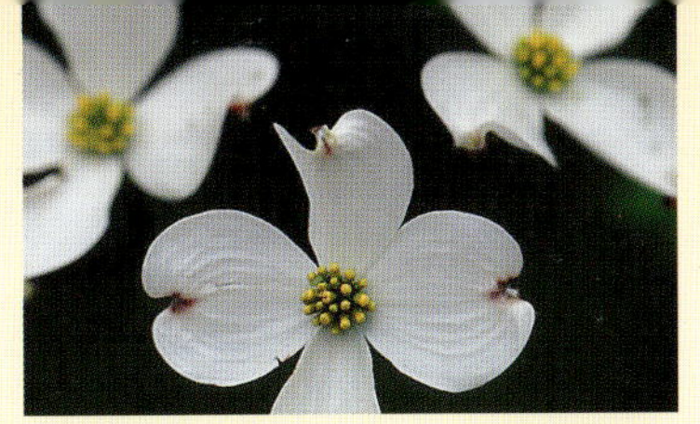

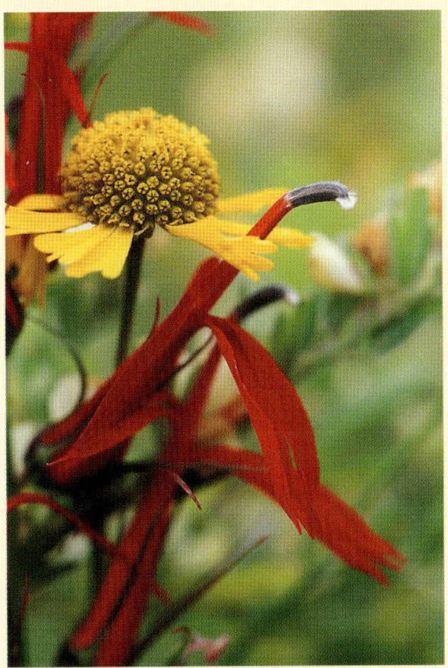

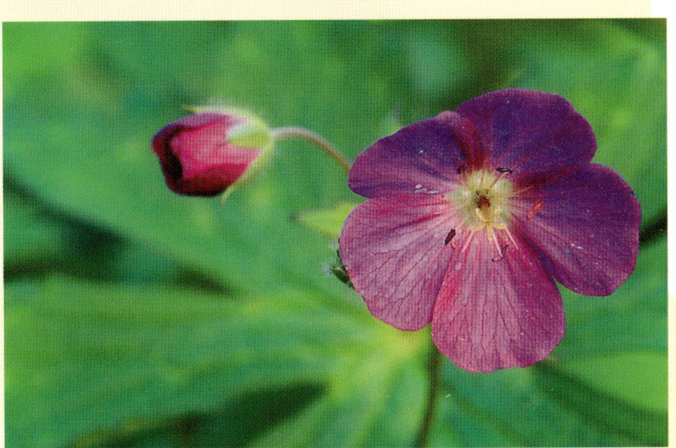

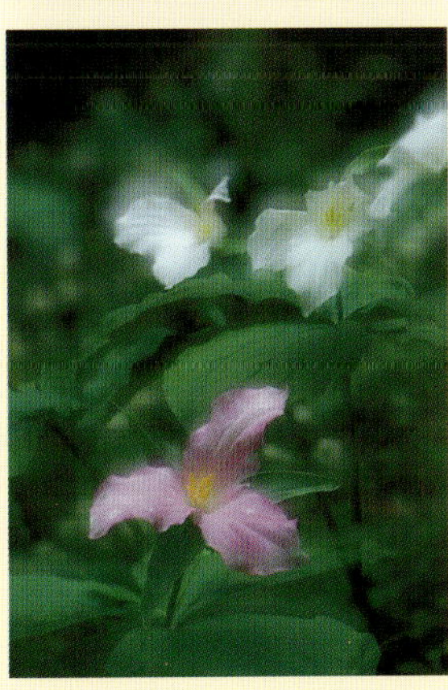

TOP LEFT: Telephoto isolation picks out this eclectic mix of Cardinal flower and Sneezeweed TOP RIGHT: Flowering dogwood blooms positioned to form a V-shape. Note that none of the blooms merge together (touch each other.) ABOVE: A diffuser saved the day when the sun was beating down on this wild geranium. LEFT: Trilliums using a double exposure technique to give an ethereal feel.—*BC*

- **Telephoto** *300-500 mm lenses make for great flower portraits, especially if you can use an extension tube to get a little closer. This helps in isolation and gives a very soft and uniform background and also helps with flowers that are too high on a cliff or too deep in a bunch to access by normal means.*
- **Wide Angle closeup** *Using a small (8 mm) extension tube with a 17-24 mm wide angle allows you to get very close to a flower but portray the flower within its natural setting. This gives a wide angle view of the forest but with the ability to have a large flower in the foreground for emphasis.*
- **View from below** *Using a wide angle lens allows a view of tall flowers from ground level. Putting the blossoms against a blue sky from a very low vantage point is a much different view than normally seen. This is combat photography because you usually end up on your belly trying to get the camera in the correct spot. A right angle viewfinder on a SLR helps with this technique, but a digital camera with a rotating view screen makes this much easier.*
- **Ethereal image** *Using a double exposure technique can lend a delicate glow around your flowers. Set your camera to double exposure mode, take the first image at a smaller aperture (larger depth of field) with sharp focus at one stop underexposed. For the second image of the double exposure, use a large aperture (shallow depth of field), and focus in closer (making the fuzzy image larger than its sharp counterpart) and remember to under expose the second image by one stop. This takes some practice to get the exact results you like, but playing with this is extremely rewarding for those photographers who want to explore advanced creative techniques.*

Blooming Calendar

January	February	March	April	May	June
Nothing yet; may find some Witch Hazel or Hearts-a-bustin' still around.	*Still early, but during mild winters the Trailing Arbitus might start to bloom late in the month.*	*Spicebush, Spring Beauty, Hepatica, Trout-lily, Bloodroot, Sweet white Violet, Round Leaved Violet, Bird's foot Violet, Fraser's Sedge, Serviceberry.*	*Many flowers below 2500 feet elevation reach their peak around the third week. Trilliums (Yellow bloom earliest), Jack-in-the-pulpit, Dutchman's Britches, Squirrel Corn, White Fringed Phacelia, Dogwood, Silver Bell, Bishop's Cap, Foamflower, Crested dwarf Iris, Yellow Mandarin, Smooth yellow Violet, Canadian Violet, Solomon's Seal, Rue-anemone, Dwarf Ginseng, Columbine, Showy Orchis, Pink Lady's slipper, Fire Pink.*	*May-apple, Bleeding Heart, Yellow Lady's slipper, Star Grass, Little Brown Jugs, Wild Ginger, Squawroot, Indian Cucumber, Sweet Shrub, Partridge berry, Wood-sorrel, Indian Pink, Galax.*	*Indian Pipe, Canada Mayflower, Cardinal Flower, Pipsissewa, Mountain Laurel, Yellow Bead Lily, Catawba Rhododendron (purple), Rosebay Rododendron (white), Sand Myrtle, Trumpet Honeysuckle, Flame Azalea.*

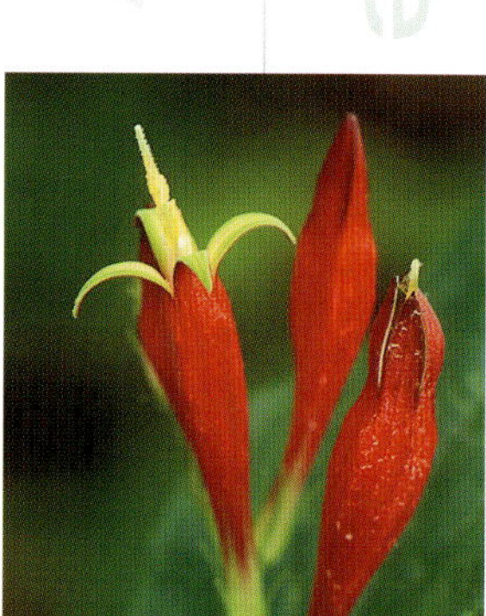

Below: Yellow ladyslippers. Two gold reflectors were used to control the lighting on the flowers in deep shade.—*BC*

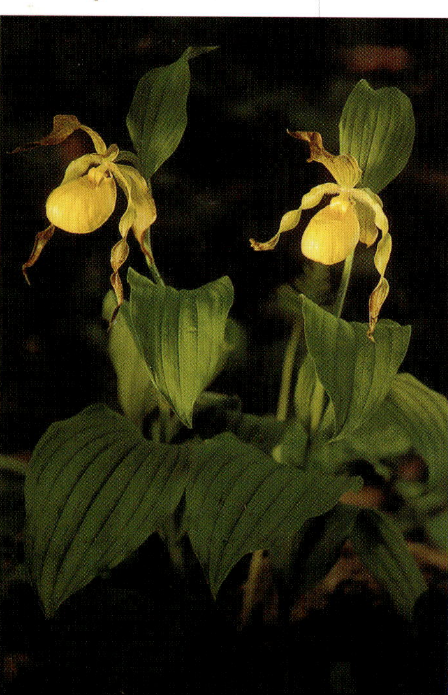

for the Smokies

All are start dates and usually occur at the lower elevations of a flower's range.

July	August	September	October	November	December
Thyme-leaved Bluets, Pine-sap, Sundrops, Clingmans Hedge-nettle, Purple-fringed Orchid, Queen Anne's Lace, Grass-pink, Touch-me-not, Crimson Bee-balm, Turk's cap Lily, Yellow-fringed Orchid.	*Closed Gentian, Monks Hood, Stiff Gentian, Great Lobelia, Tall Ironweed, Goldenrod, Sweet Joe-Pye-weed, Grass-of-Parnassus, fruits of Trillium, Doll's Eyes, Yellow Bead Lily, Jack-in-the-pulpit.*	*Black-eyed Susan, Mountain Gentian, Nodding Ladies' Tresses, Pink Turtlehead.*	*Continuation of Mountain Gentian, Nodding Ladies' Tresses, Coneflower and some Asters, Fruits of Mountain Ash.*	*A few Nodding Ladies' Tresses remain, fruit of Hearts-a-bustin'.*	*Brilliant yellow filaments of Witch Hazel.*

Opposite page, top: Indian pink can be found along Rich Mountain Road in May and June.—*BC*

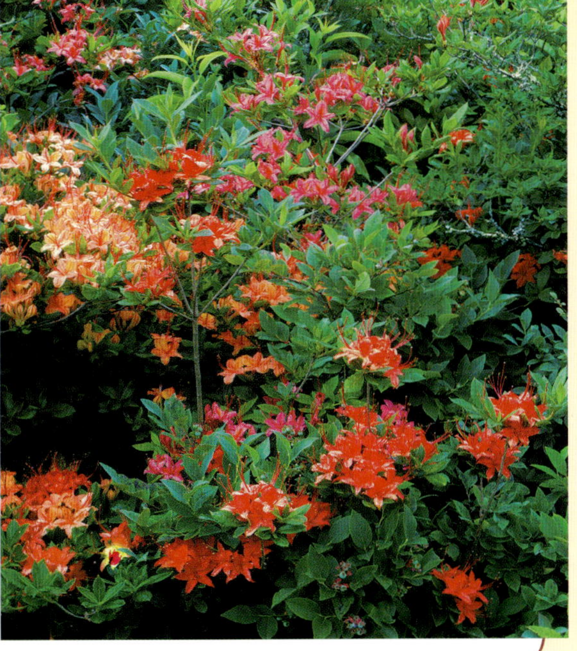

Right: Multicolored flame azaleas are a prime attraction on Gregory Bald in the fourth week of June.—*NS*

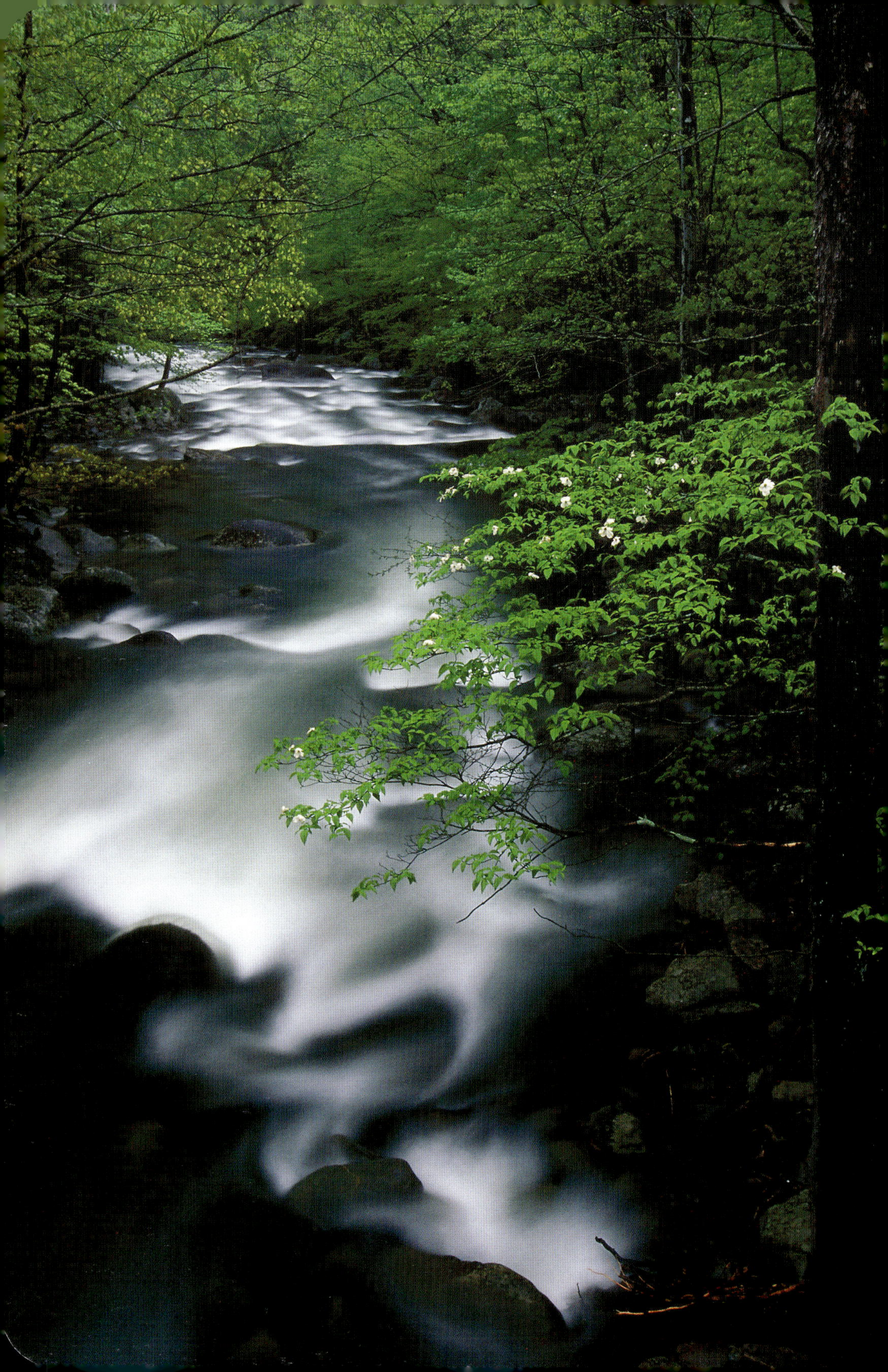

Stream scenes

Intimate landscapes

Wildflowers

Photo hikes to waterfalls

Chapter Six

Tremont

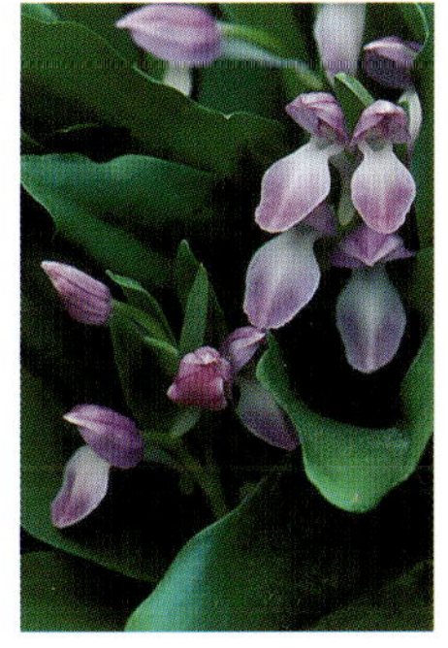

Above: Showy orchis grows very close to the road in several areas, making it easier to locate when it is in bloom.—*BC*

Left: Towards the end of the road in Tremont is a bridge that offers wonderful aerial perspectives of Middle Prong in both directions.—*BC*

Perhaps a quarter of a mile from the Townsend "Y" is the turnoff to one of our favorite areas in the Smokies, the Tremont region. The mass of visitors ignore the side road and keep going to Cades Cove, leaving this area in relative solitude. The road follows the Middle Prong of the Little River past the Great Smoky Mountains Institute, ending at a turnaround and the Lynn Camp Prong trailhead. The Middle Prong offers exquisite stream scenes, and a short hike from the trailhead at the end of the road leads to Lynn Camp Prong falls. Potential compositions begin immediately, and just get better after the pavement ends at the Institute two miles in, reaching a crescendo in the final mile.

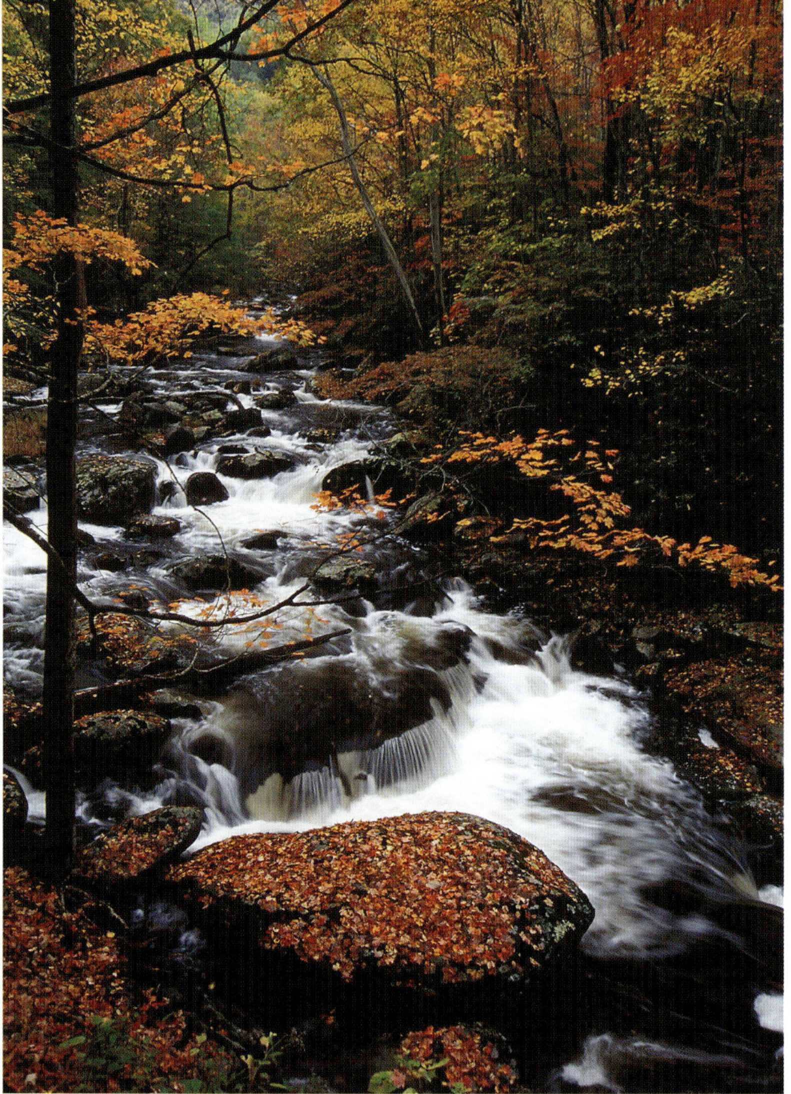

Never give up on fall foliage just because leaves are falling. This image was probably taken about a week after the image on page 83. Some images flow better as verticals, some as horizontals; a great scene works well both ways.—*BC*

This three mile stretch of gravel road can occupy a whole day when conditions are right. Stream scenes (usually) work better in soft light. An overcast day is good, drizzle or intermittent showers are prime; you get that priceless "wet look," and you can work from your vehicle. The high ridges shade the main scenes in early morning and late evening, giving low contrast conditions that flatter stream scenes; good reflections can be had at various times and various bends in the river when there is more light. If you jog or bike, this is a great secluded road for both.

The entire road is one endless photo opportunity. As it follows the river you will frequently need to park to investigate possible compositions at the water's edge, or (cautiously) wade or hop rocks out to midstream. Lower Spruce Flats Falls is visible from the road, and several nice compositions can be had here; each bend in the river offers something new. Remember to look over your shoulder frequently to see what the light is doing behind you.

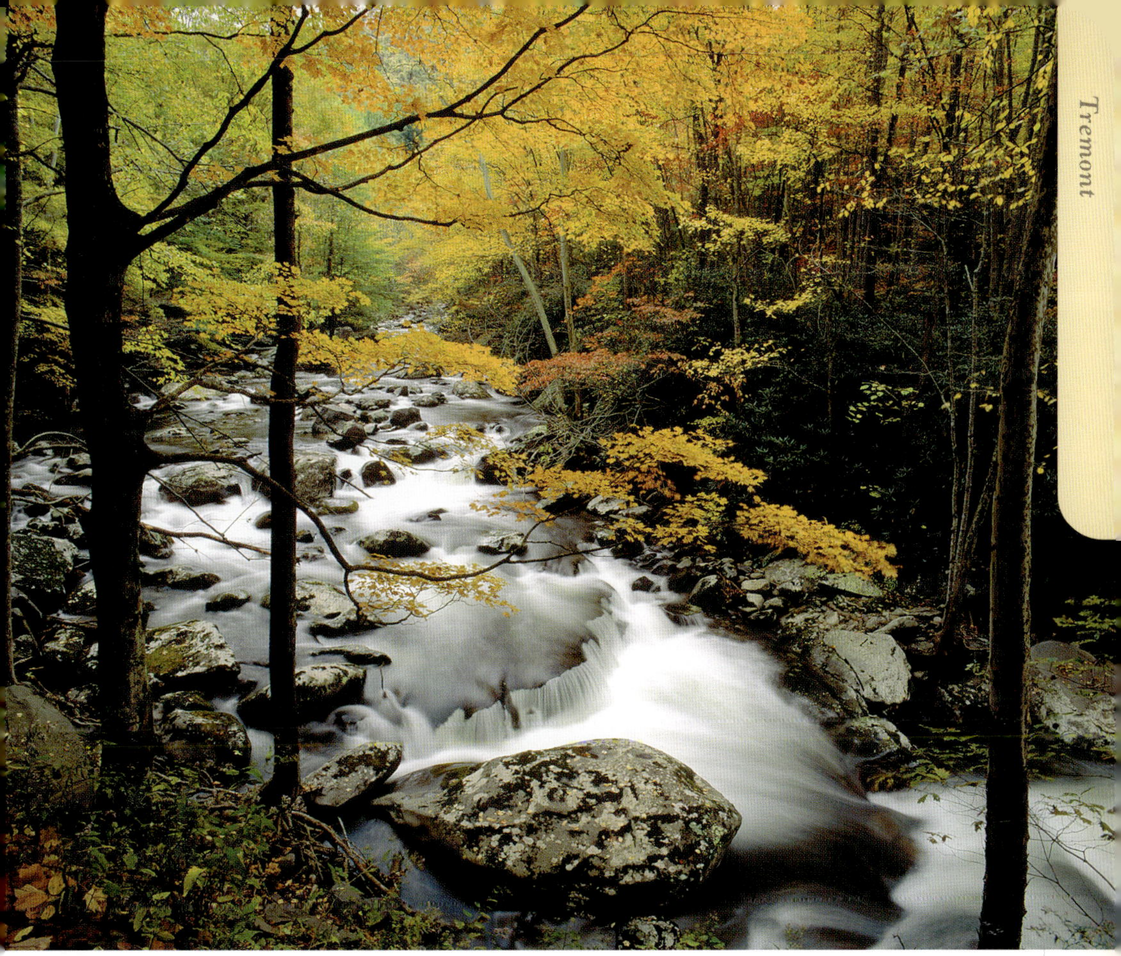

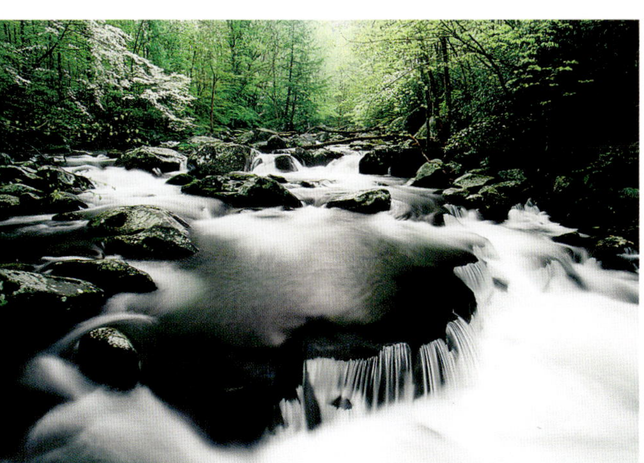

ABOVE: Here at the last bend in the river you have another uncluttered aerial perspective. It's at its best when the river is full, following a substantial wet period or storm, but not flooded. If the water is too high, give it 24-48 hours. Another composition awaits from the flat rock below you. A Singh-Ray polarizing filter controlled the degree of reflection in these wide angle compositions. Partial polarization often gives the most pleasing effect.—*NS*

LEFT: Similar to snow, the white water should be about +2 on a cloudy day, selectively meter it and opon up 2 stops. *NS*

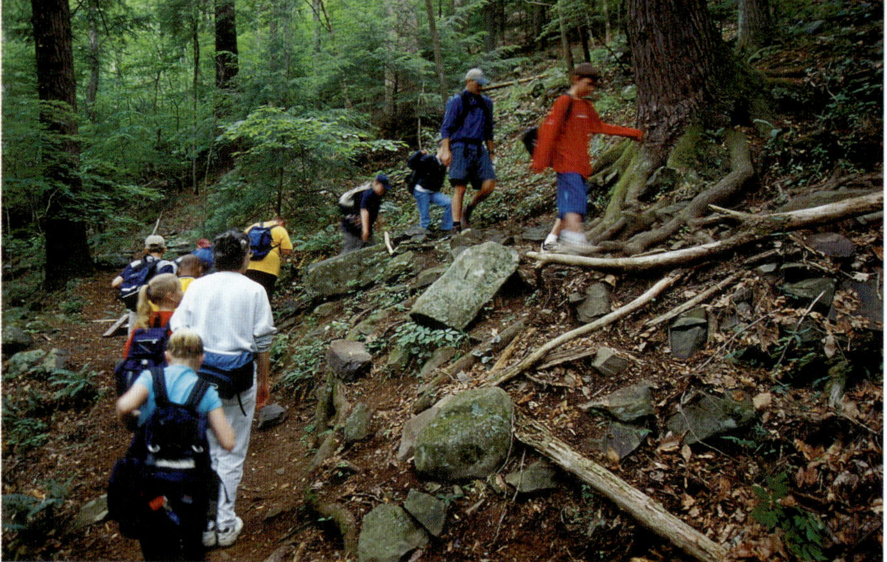

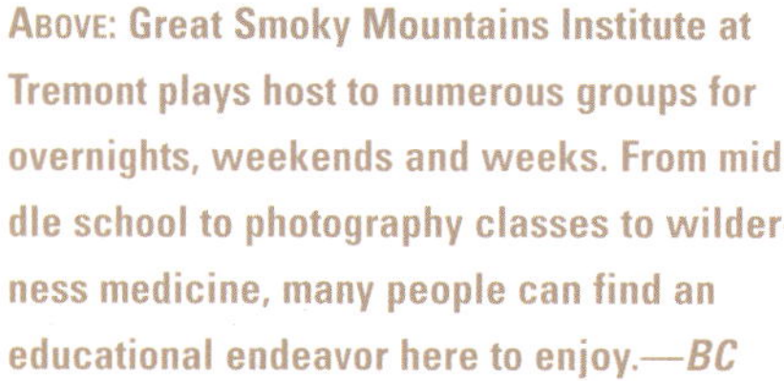

ABOVE: Great Smoky Mountains Institute at Tremont plays host to numerous groups for overnights, weekends and weeks. From middle school to photography classes to wilderness medicine, many people can find an educational endeavor here to enjoy.—*BC*

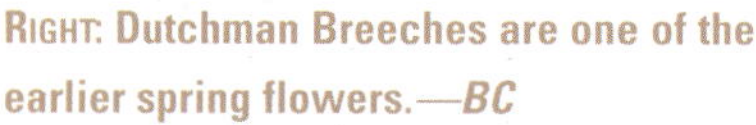

RIGHT: Dutchman Breeches are one of the earlier spring flowers.—*BC*

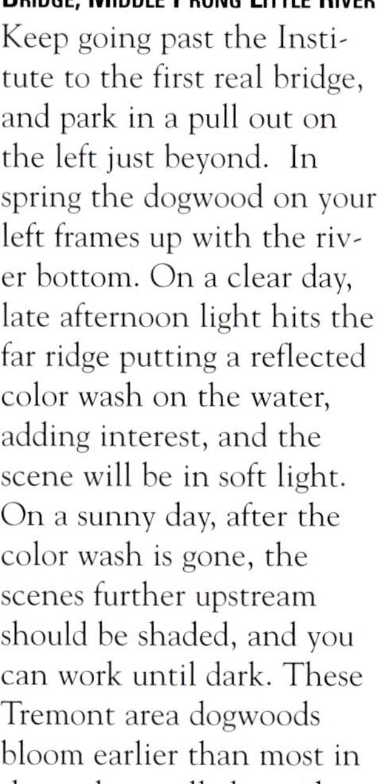

BRIDGE, MIDDLE PRONG LITTLE RIVER

Keep going past the Institute to the first real bridge, and park in a pull out on the left just beyond. In spring the dogwood on your left frames up with the river bottom. On a clear day, late afternoon light hits the far ridge putting a reflected color wash on the water, adding interest, and the scene will be in soft light. On a sunny day, after the color wash is gone, the scenes further upstream should be shaded, and you can work until dark. These Tremont area dogwoods bloom earlier than most in the park, usually by mid-April and are often past peak by the time the annual Spring Wildflower Pilgrimage begins.

MIDDLE PRONG LITTLE RIVER

The road will bend to the right, giving a fairly open view of the river beneath. Park where the shoulder allows and either work from the road for an aerial perspective, or carefully scramble down to the waters edge for a more intimate composition. The river needs to have enough water in it for this to be at it's best; if the creek is too low you lose the graceful pour over in mid-scene.

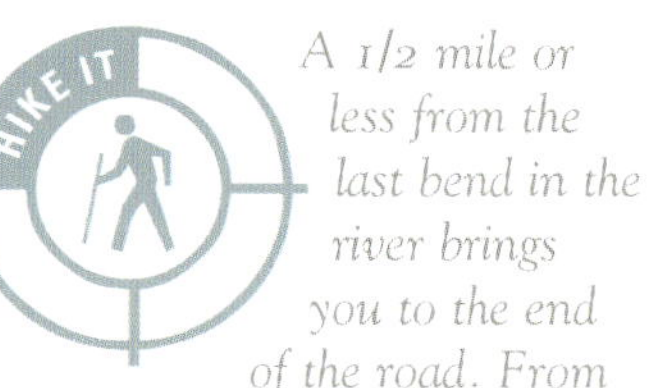

A 1/2 mile or less from the last bend in the river brings you to the end of the road. From here you can easily walk downstream to the scenes on pages 82 and 83, or hike on to ***Lynn Camp Prong falls****. A gentle grade on Middle Prong Trail brings you to the falls in less than a mile. Multiple compositions are possible, and a second set of cascades can be seen a little further along.*

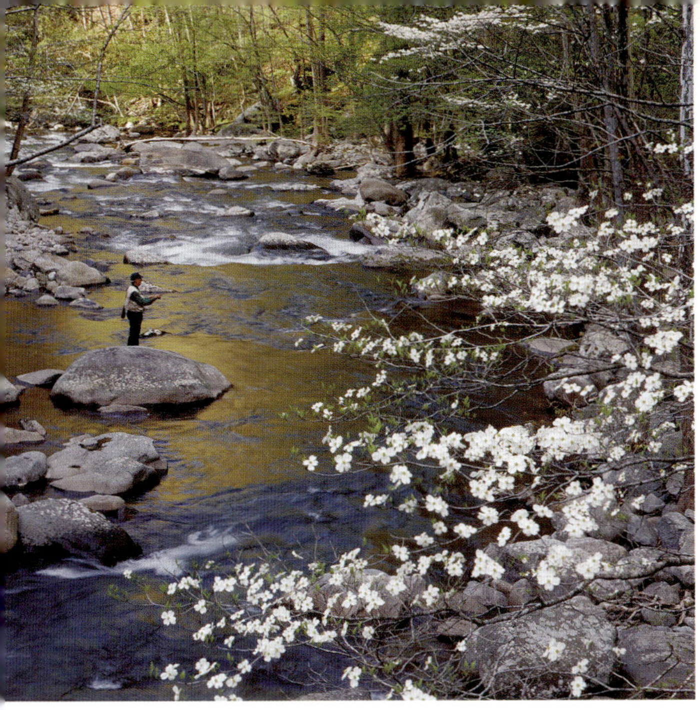

Left: Bridges offer a wonderful uncluttered aerial perspective otherwise difficult to find, but beware of vibrations. Other people walking around, much less vehicles crossing the bridge, can cause unnoticed camera shake even on a tripod. This bridge gives views both downstream and upstream. A fisherman adds human interest to the scene; often people or animals add a missing element that adds strength to the composition. The downstream composition picks up reflected light around 4-5 PM on the distant bank, while the foreground is in shade.—*NS*

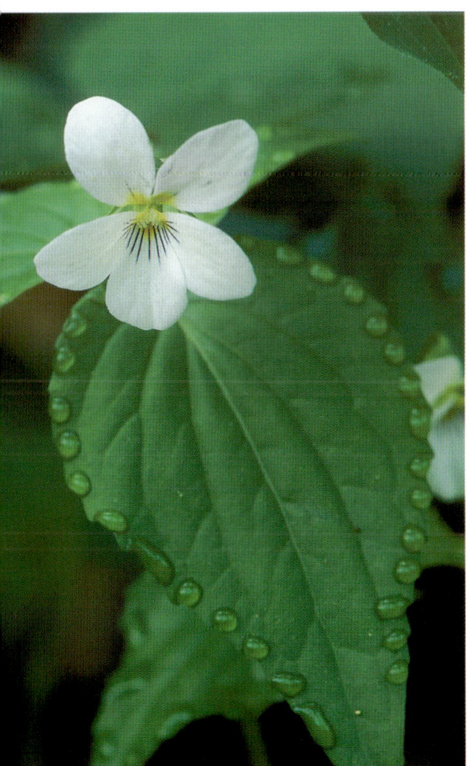

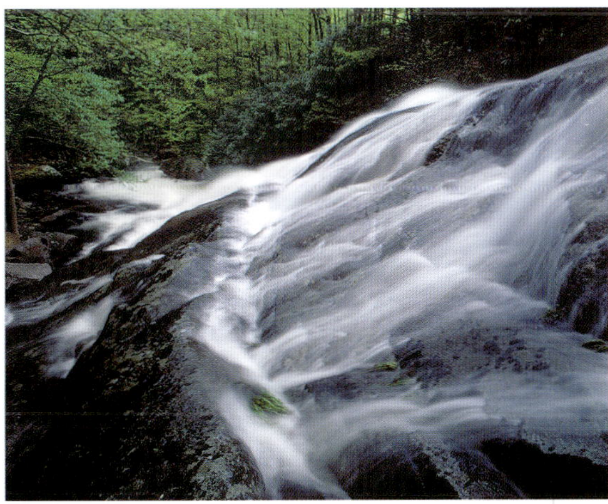

Above: Lynn Camp Prong Falls has many moods. Here very high water caused multiple braids to form as water spilled over the near shelf.—*NS*

Left: The necklace of water drops along leaf's edge is a phenomenon called transpiration.—*BC*

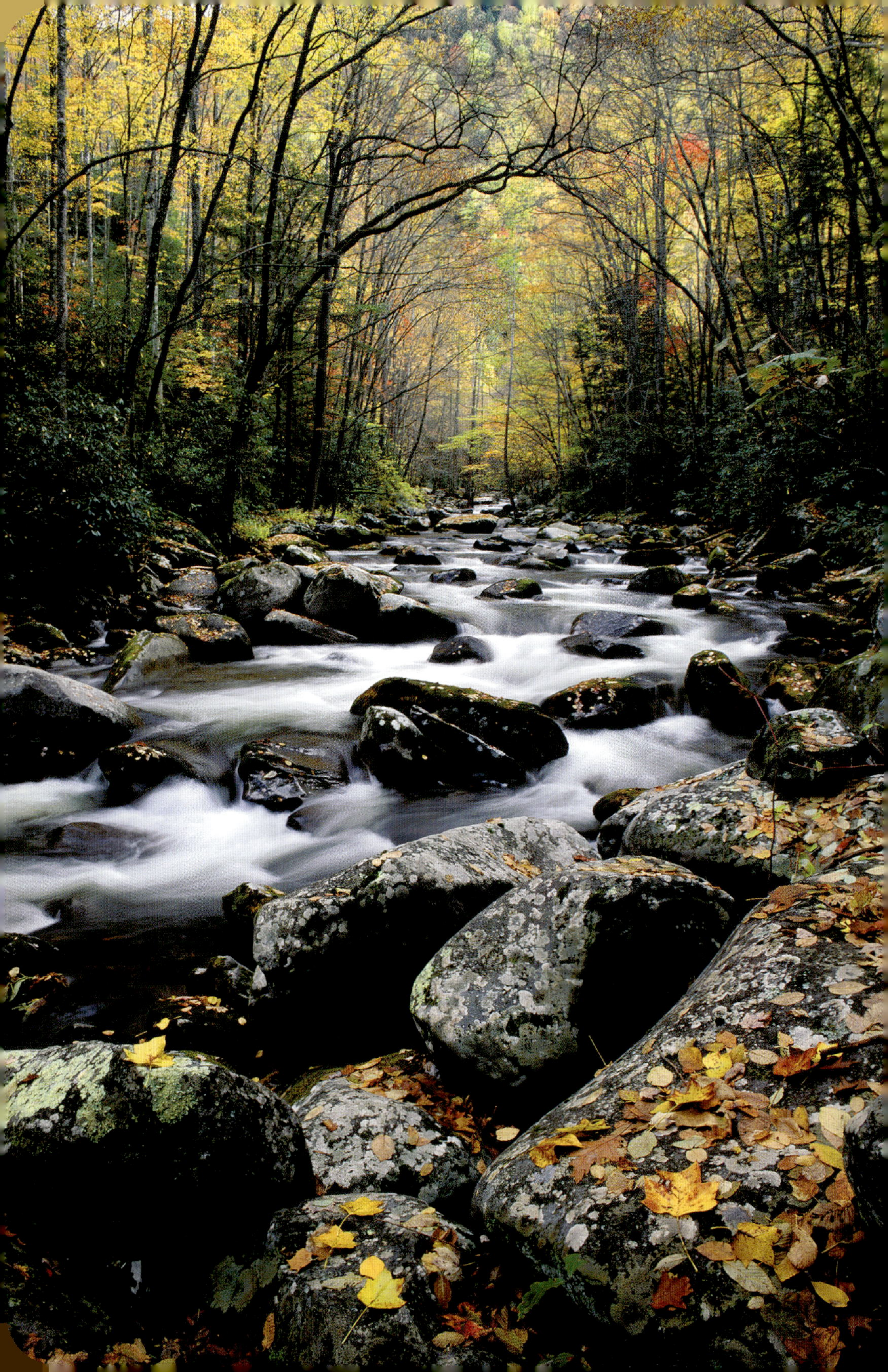

A grand scenic

Historic cabins, houses, and churches

Photo hike

Wildlife

Chapter Seven

Cataloochee & Big Creek

Big Creek offers classic Smokies scenes in all seasons. A photographer could become so bemused that he or she never reached Mouse Creek Falls. —*NS*

YOU CAN'T GET THERE FROM HERE. With that bit of encouragement you can visit Cataloochee and find out for yourself why it is lightly visited. This is a remote place, favored by those who want to get away from the crowds. Photographers who haven't experienced the Park could see more in a shorter period of time in other areas, but Cataloochee has charms of its own, and some unique features. The road is often closed in winter. Getting to Cataloochee requires some driving and a map. The directions make more sense with a map in front of you. Travel times are difficult to estimate due to numerous photographic distractions and the vagaries of traffic.

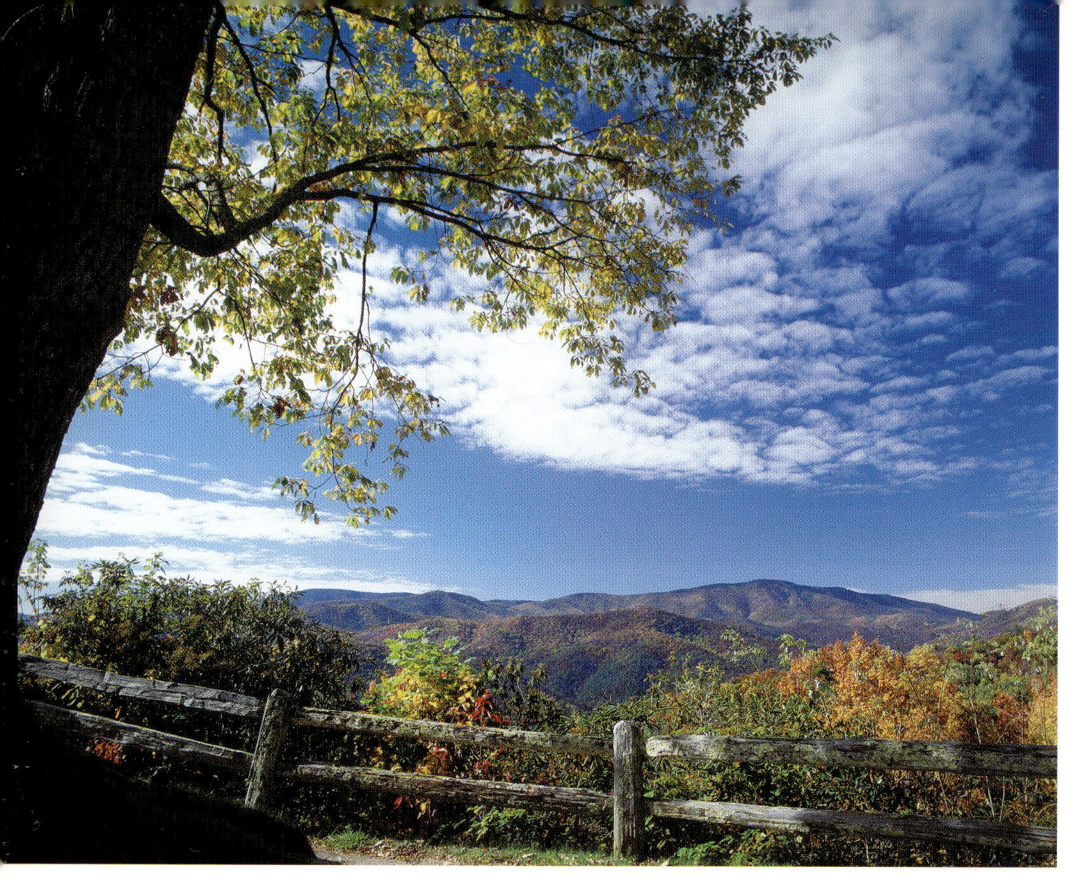

Obtain a map, and by whichever route is easiest for you, drive to I-40 exit # 20. This is signed for Great Smoky Mountains National Park, Maggie Valley and Cherokee, NC. Exit to the south on US 276, looking for Cove Creek Road, an almost immediate right turn (to the Northwest.) You will see a sign for the Cove Creek Missionary Baptist Church.

After leaving US 276, the road continues for about 3.5 miles before turning to gravel. Long before, it becomes narrow, steep, and winding with many blind curves. At a little over seven miles you hit pavement again; by now those prone to carsickness will have begged for mercy. This intersection is where you start counting miles again. Turn left to Cataloochee proper, or go straight to get to the trail to Little Cataloochee.

Overlook for Mt. Sterling Ridge, Big Cataloochee Mountain
0.2 miles

This is the best scenic vista in the area, and can be composed any number of ways. Fall brings intense colors, and the foreground trees and split rail fence offer options for framing or foreground interest. There are rhododendrons in the foreground to add color when in bloom. The overlook faces north, so you have good side lighting early and late in the day, and a polarizer usually works. Winter scenes are possible when the road is open.

After descending from the overlook with several stopping places for hillside scenics, and variations on what you saw at the overlook, you will reach the valley and cross a bridge at ***mile 2.7***. There is a campground with restrooms up the road on your left.

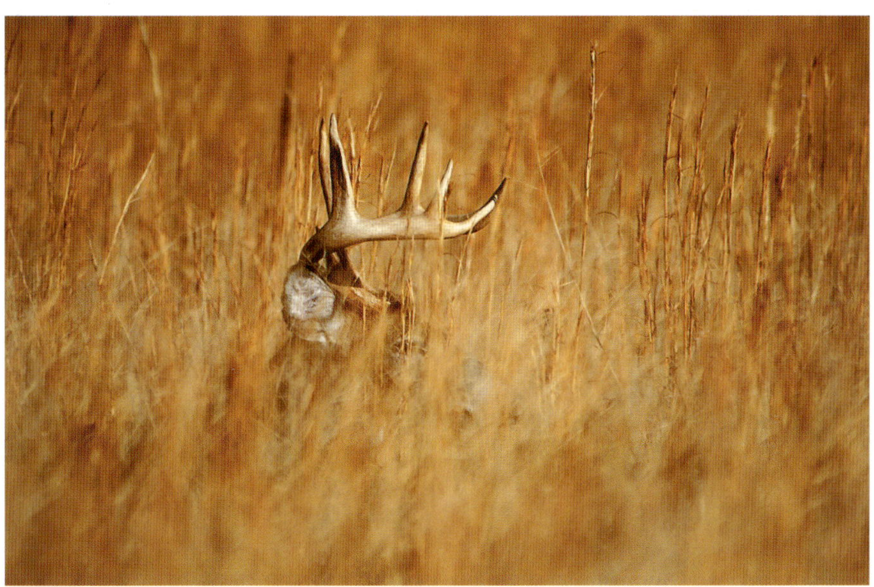

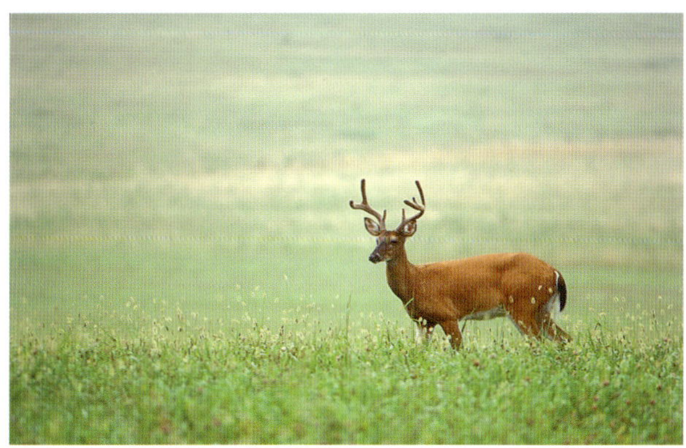

OPPOSITE PAGE: The lower sun trajectory makes for more hours of attractive light in the fall at Big Cataloochee Mountain Overlook.—*NS*

ABOVE: Cataloochee Valley is the second best place in the Smokies to see deer with much less companionship.—*BC*

LEFT: Bucks have their new racks covered in "velvet" from mid-summer until the beginning of the rut in October.—*BC*

RANGER STATION AND WILL MESSER BARN

3.3 miles

If horses are stabled here for the season, they add a nice touch to the scene. Next on the left is Palmer Chapel followed by the Caldwell house. From here the road continues to the end of the cove, with more open areas.

The creek is never very far away, and deer or elk may be close by. This is probably the second most productive place in the park for wildlife photography after Cades Cove. Its inaccessibility limits its popularity. The recent elk release may change all that.

Leaving Cataloochee proper, you can return the way you came to your right (south), or turn left (north) towards Big Creek and (eventually) I-40; this is NC 284. It is also the easiest way to get to Little Cataloochee Baptist Church. This road is rougher than the road from US 276; although neither requires 4-wheel drive, street sedans with low clearance will need to proceed slowly. The posted speed limit is 15 mph, and is a law of nature, not just a highway statute. It's about an hour to Big Creek, and the main attraction comes early, after about five miles.

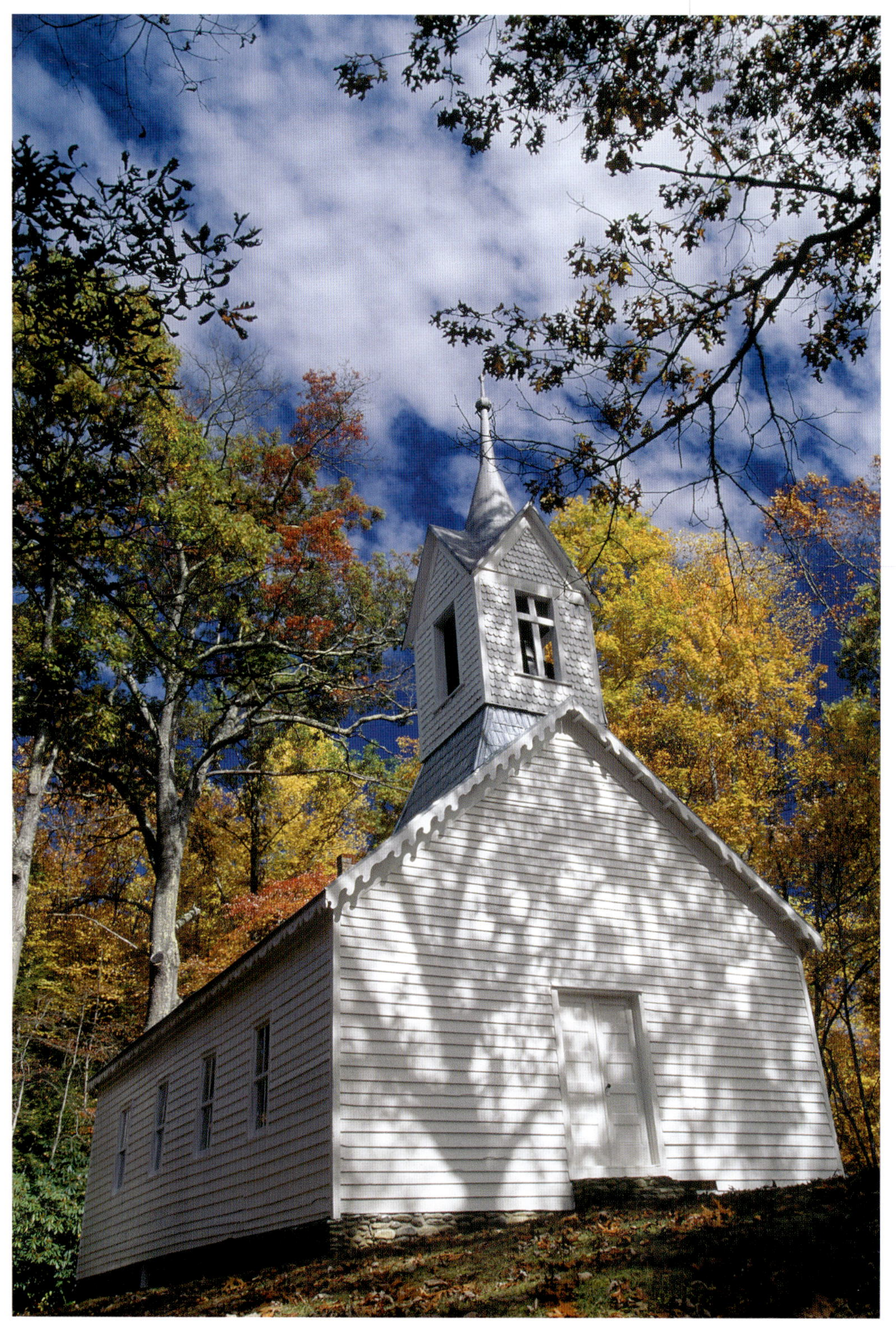

Trail to Little Cataloochee Baptist Church

mile 5.4 on NC 284

HIKE IT

This is a great scene in the fall when Little Cataloochee church is framed with color. Spring colors here are not as special and it's a big commitment in time and energy. Park at the trailhead sign (don't block the gate) and take the two mile gently rolling hike to the church. It photographs well in mid-afternoon light in fall. The adjacent cemetery is also interesting. On the way back take the short side trail to the Hannah cabin. Allow about 45 minutes each way if you are in average physical condition. From here, getting back to the Gatlinburg side of the Park, it is probably quicker to continue to Big Creek. Double back the way you came in to go back to Cherokee, the Blue Ridge Parkway, and the rest of the North Carolina side of the Park. With more hiking and less driving you can hike to the church from Cataloochee Valley proper.

Beyond the Little Cataloochee trailhead there are no compelling vistas, though the heavily wooded hillsides are close upon you. Mt. Sterling Gap is heavily wooded and unfortunately offers no usable views. At about 14 miles you will have signage for Big Creek and I-40 at the Waterville exit # 451.

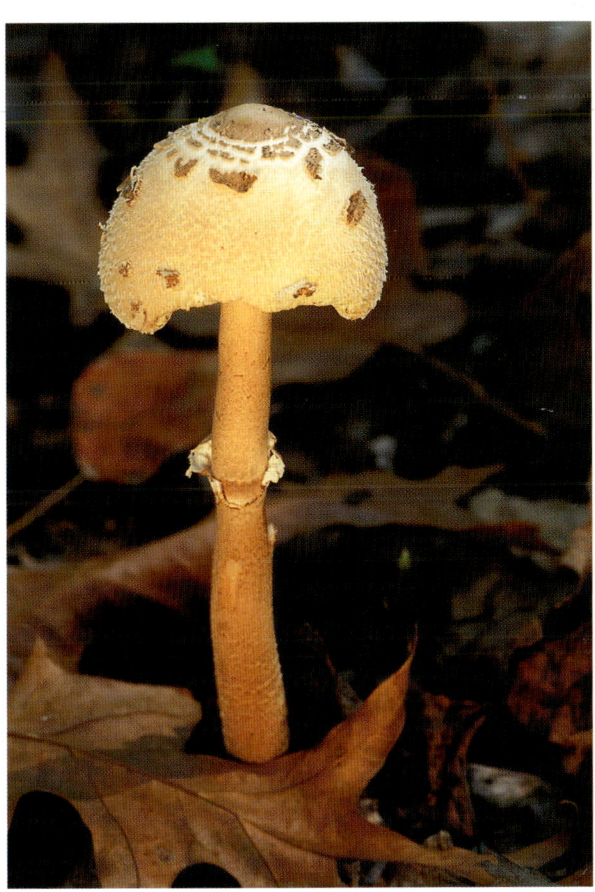

Opposite page: Little Cataloochee Baptist Church isn't easy to get to, but is well worth the effort; mid-afternoon light is superb here.—*NS*

Right: Mushrooms are easier subjects to photograph than wildflowers when a strong breeze in blowing. A soft gold reflector was used to add light to this fungus in the shade. —*BC*

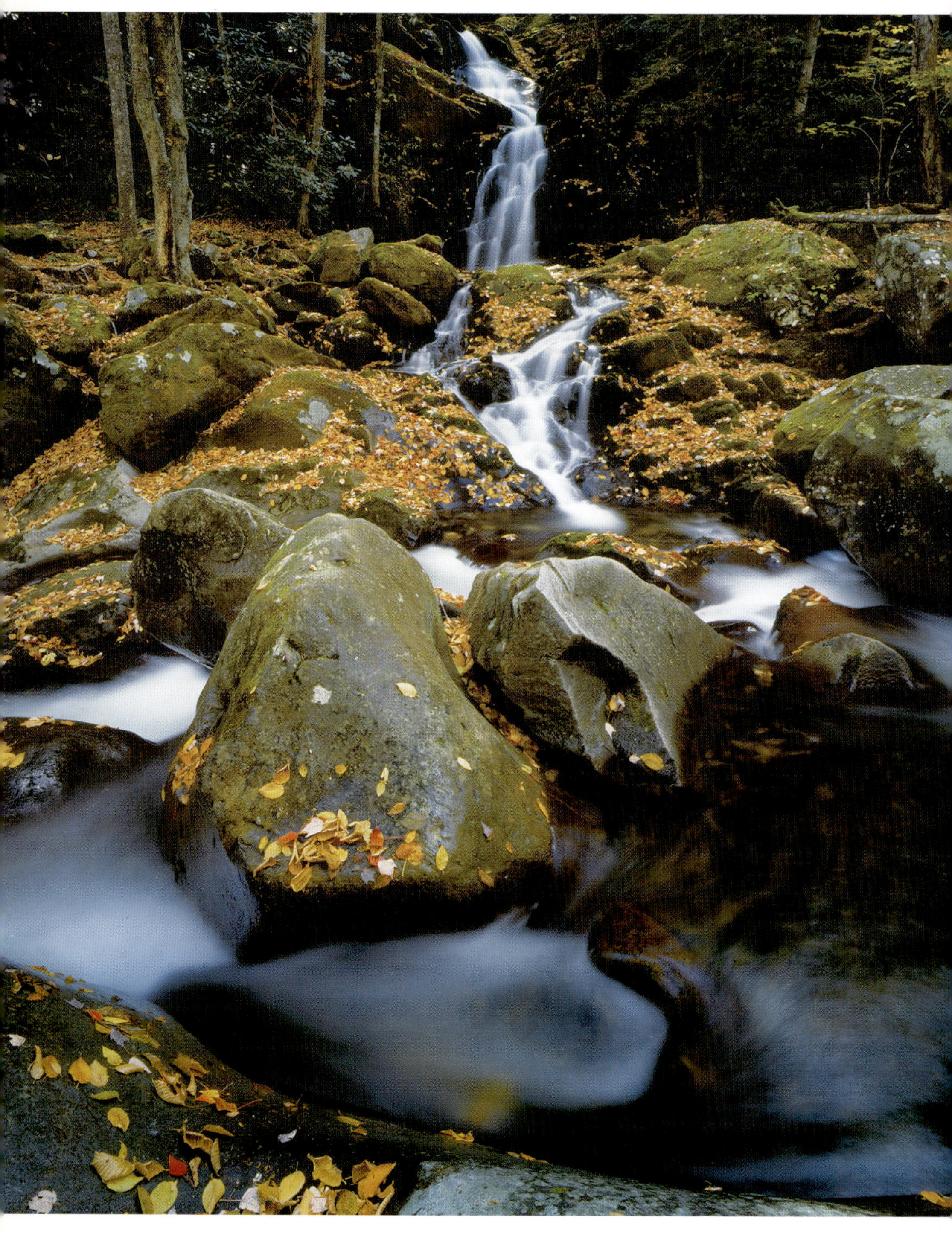

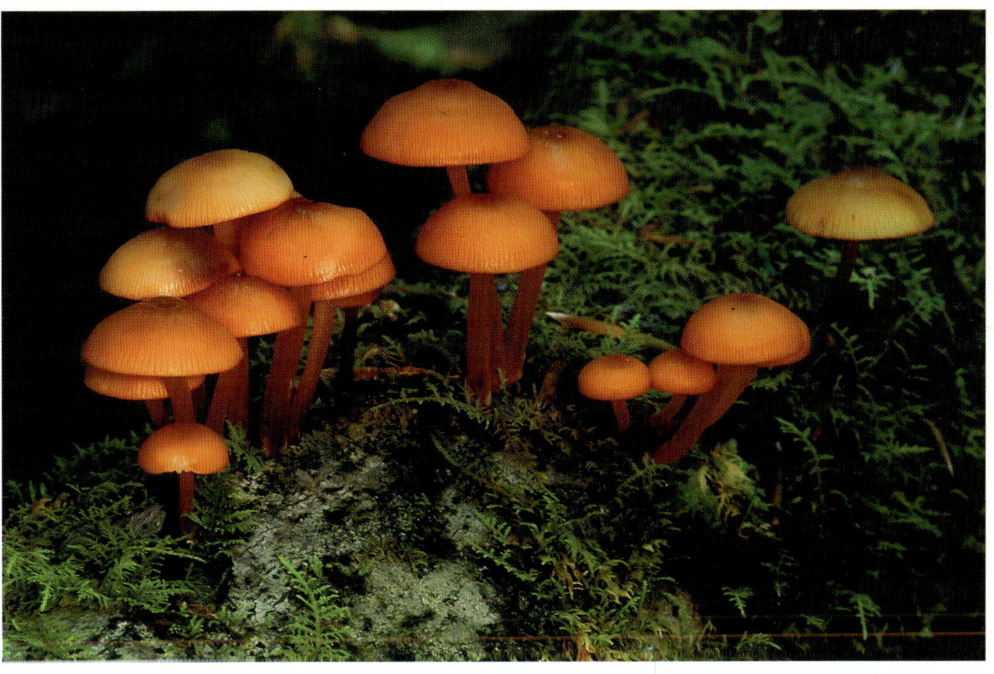

ABOVE: Orange Mycena mushrooms occur June to September. Cataloochee area plays host to a large concentration of different fungi.—*BC*

OPPOSITE PAGE: Mouse Creek Falls is an easy 1 hour hike (with no stops) along Big Creek, with countless opportunities along the way.—*NS*

Big Creek

HIKE IT

Big Creek is most easily reached by I-40; take the Waterville exit #451 and follow the road past the power plant, past Mountain Momma's store, past a small campground to it's end at a picnic area with restrooms. The real trail up Big Creek is to the right of the parking area; a small social trail on the far bank peters out after a couple of hundred yards. The real trail takes you along Big Creek, a gorgeous Smokies stream with larger than average rocks. The best scenes require hiking, but it's a great place to avoid crowds. Find Mouse Creek Falls after about 2 miles of gently graded trail, having passed numerous photo ops on the way. This area is often accessible in winter, though you may not be able to drive all the way in to the picnic area. The closest area services are at Mountain Momma's Store where you can find a pay phone, groceries, and a small deli.

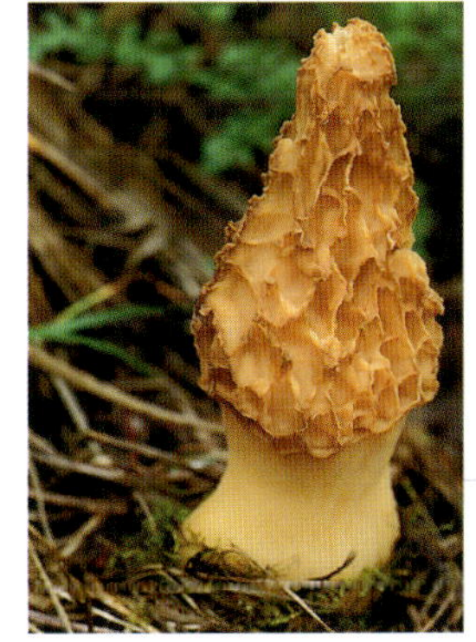

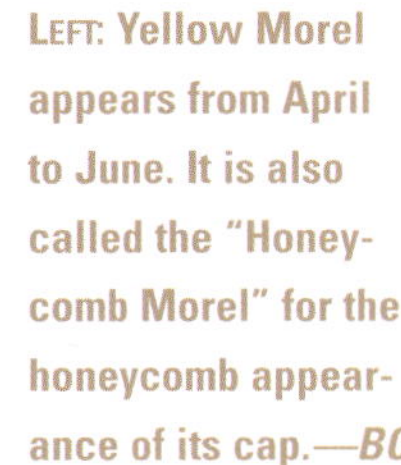

LEFT: Yellow Morel appears from April to June. It is also called the "Honeycomb Morel" for the honeycomb appearance of its cap.—*BC*

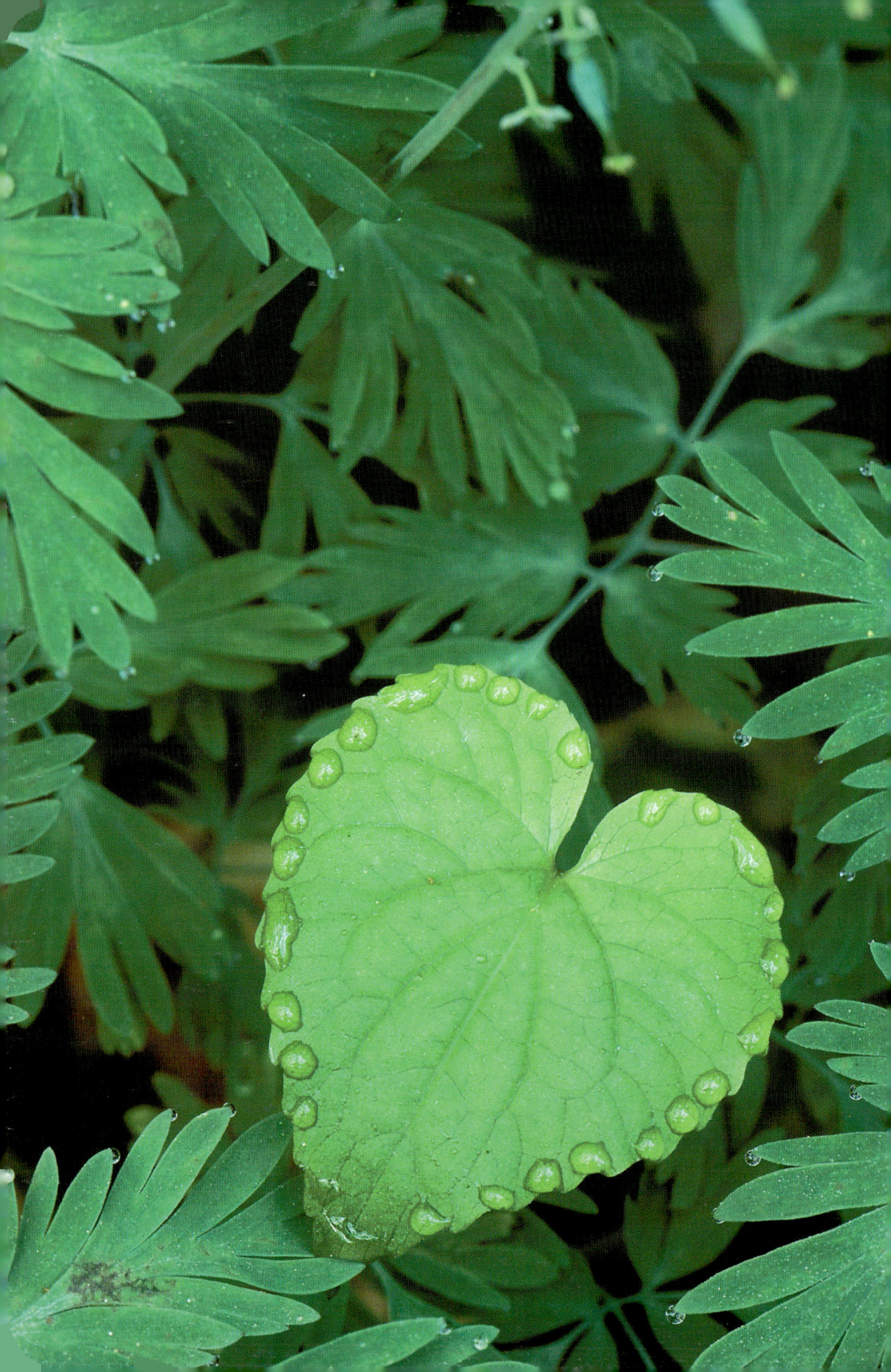

Stream scenes

Photo hikes

Wildflowers

Winter access

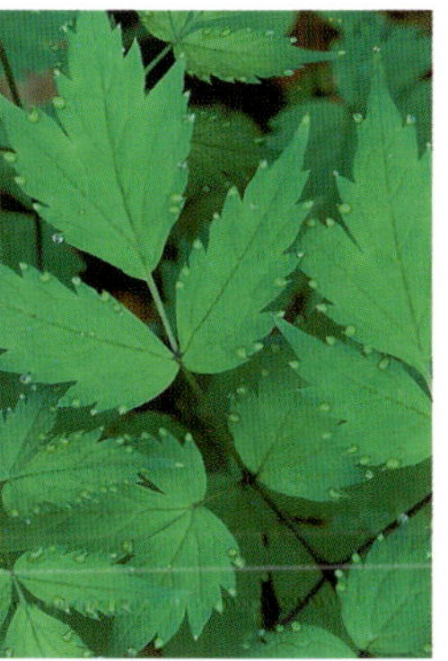

Chapter Eight

Greenbrier

Transpiration occurs along the edges of leaves when the conditions of humidity and temperature are just right.—*BC*

Drive five miles east of Gatlinburg on US Hwy 321 to the Greenbrier section of Great Smoky Mountains National Park, one of the least-crowded gems in the entire preserve. The Middle Prong of the Little Pigeon River flows along the road all the way to the end, offering endless opportunities for river scenes, as well as more intimate studies of the forest floor. Set your odometer to 0.0 as you turn off the road.

Maidenhair ferns are delicate ferns that branch out in a semi-circle. Try to keep the film plane parallel with the subject for sharpest focus throughout. —*BC*

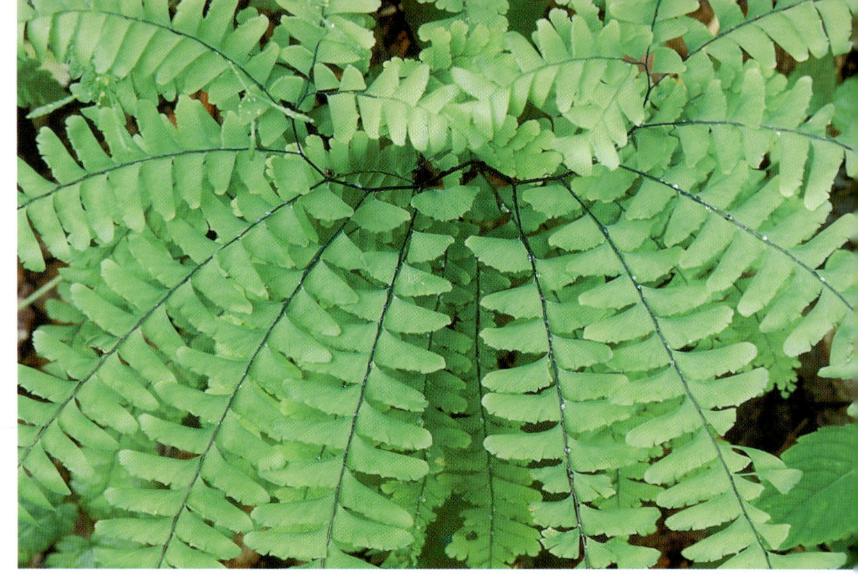

The road follows the river upstream past a picnic area with a pit toilet at 2.7 miles; it splits a little farther in leading to two trailheads at road's end. Early on in the first 1/4 mile you will see small rapids or rock shelves depending on season and water level. You can make various compositions here. Afternoon reflections from light hitting the east bank are good around 4 P.M. if there is direct light. In fall look for potholes catching reflections, in spring and summer a greenish bronze color wash gets reflected in the water.

In the spring, wildflowers and dogwood trees will keep you busy for as long as you have to spend. Occasionally in spring and after heavy rains, kayakers and canoeists descend these rapids, and the occasional fisherman may provide interest. Fall color is excellent due to the hardwood forest. In winter the road is usually open, at least as far as the Ranger station.

You will reach the confluence of the Middle Prong of the Little Pigeon and Porters Creek at mile 3.0, where the main road intersects a branch leading left to the Ramsey Cascade trailhead. You will see more stream scenes along the road until it ends in a turnaround parking area where the trailhead is. Going straight at the confluence soon leads to the parking area for the trail to Porters Flats, a locally renowned ***wildflower hotspot***.

The north south orientation of the main river lends itself to soft light early and late in the day and reflections as well. The east-west orientation of the fork leading to the Ramsey Cascades trailhead allows direct light in the creek soon after sunrise, and later into the afternoon.

Greenbrier Confluence

mile 3.0

Greenbrier Confluence offers a variety of scenes in spring, summer, and fall. Like most river scenes, this location works best when there is enough water to fill the creek bed; very dry years leave a distracting emptiness in the composition, although you may find a creative work around. Sadly, the beautiful dogwood situated so gracefully at the confluence has died, another victim of the dogwood anthracnose fungus. Still, it's a very pretty spot, ripe with potential. Park out of the way on the side of the road. It's an easy place to work on a rainy day.

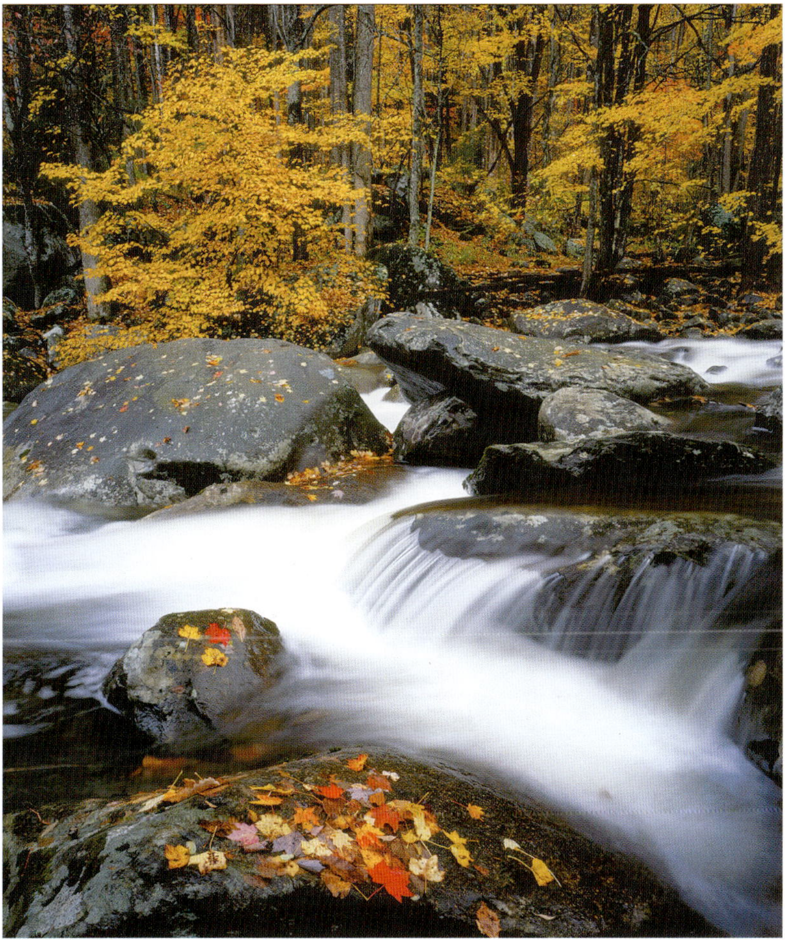

TOP: Once you find a good location, come back as often as you can. After a rain, fallen leaves are bright for a short while, then turn brown; polarization cuts glare and saturates colors—partial effect is often better.—*NS*

BOTTOM: Jack-in-the-Pulpit is a spectacular spring flower, but finding the fruit of the flower in June and July is equally impressive.—*BC*

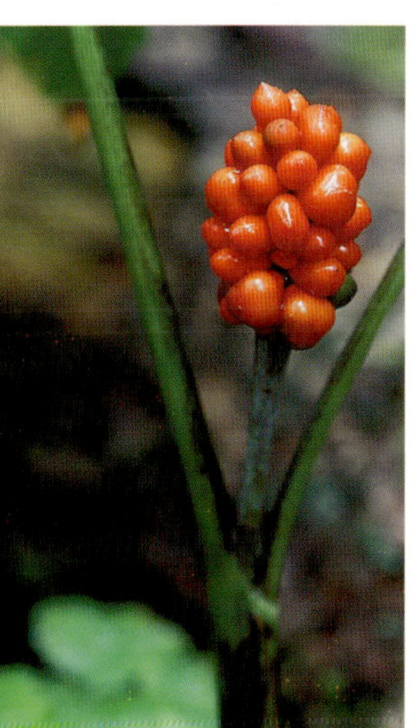

RAMSEY CASCADE PARKING AREA
mile 3.9

Turn to the left at the junction and drive another 0.9 miles to the end of the road. Plan to explore the riverbank in spring, summer, and fall (or make the hike in winter.) Depending on water level, the best vantage points will be on the bank (spring) or midstream (fall.) Walk slowly at water's edge, with an eye to possible compositions. The river has picked up gradient here so the rocks are larger and more dramatic. A large footbridge is 50 yards from the trailhead giving you more aerial perspectives. There are several large colonies of crested dwarf iris that bloom on the fringes of the parking area, and several more a short distance up the trail in mid to late April. You can find many of the other usual species here as well. Partridge berries turn red in fall, gracing the forest floor, nestled in a blanket of fallen leaves.

Ramsey Cascades Trail

This is a lovely four mile trail that gains about 2,000 feet in elevation. The first mile is relatively gentle which means you have to make it up in the remaining three. This is a tough trail if you are heavily laden, but you will need a tripod for highest quality images; your exposures may run several seconds. The trail takes you through some old-growth forest which escaped the saw when the Park was created; much of the section however is second growth. Recent storms have toppled some of the old trees; seeing those forest giants that have blown down is a sad thing, even though it is part of the cycle of life. At the end of the trail are the cascades themselves. They are at their best in wet times, but the spray then makes photography trickier, and you may not have access to all vantages points. In early to mid-June, the Catawba rhododendrons bloom close to the falls on the left, offering pleasing compositions. The rocks close to the falls get quite slick when wet; climbing is dangerous, and it's a long way back. People have fallen and died here; observe Park regulations.

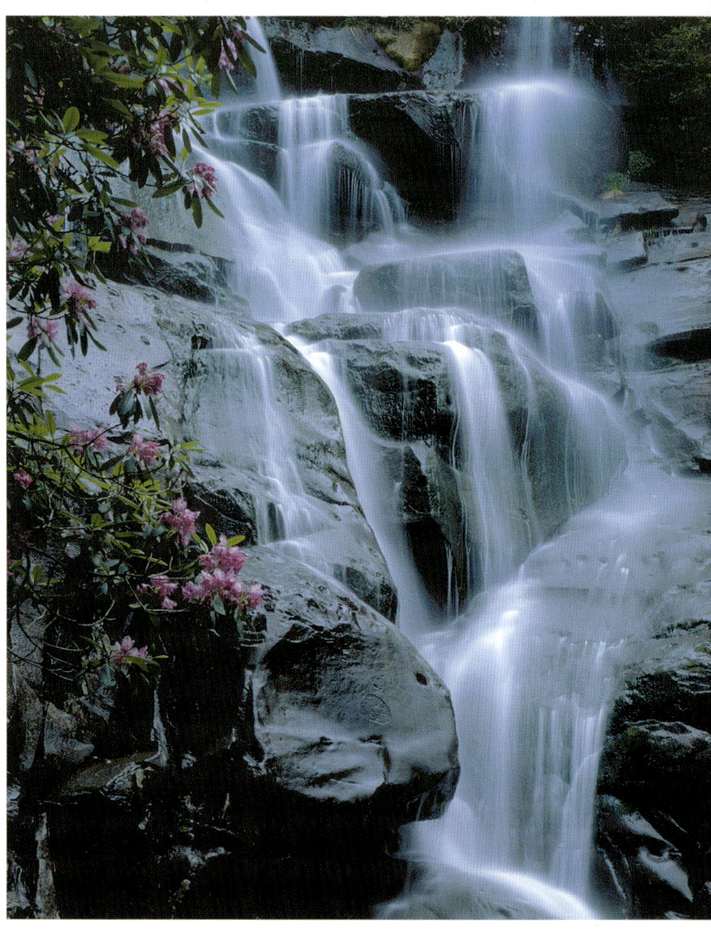

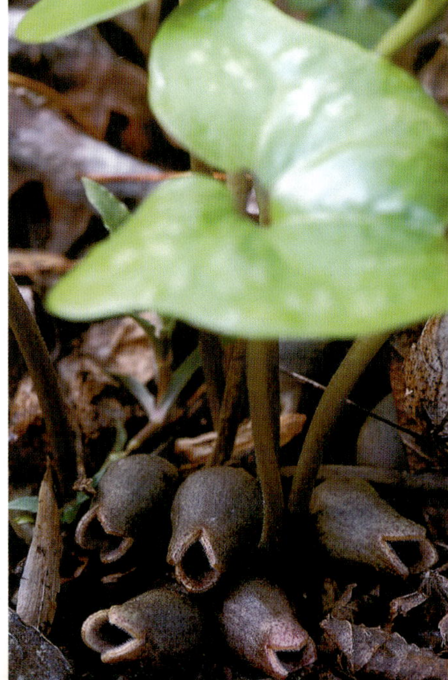

Top: Ramsey Cascades is a 1/2 day project, 4 miles each way, with special rewards in early June when the catawba rhododendron are in flower.— *NS*

Bottom: Little Brown Jug flowers are not as apparent because of their brown color and location on the ground under the heart shaped leaves. Ants pollinate this flower by crawling from one to another.—*BC*

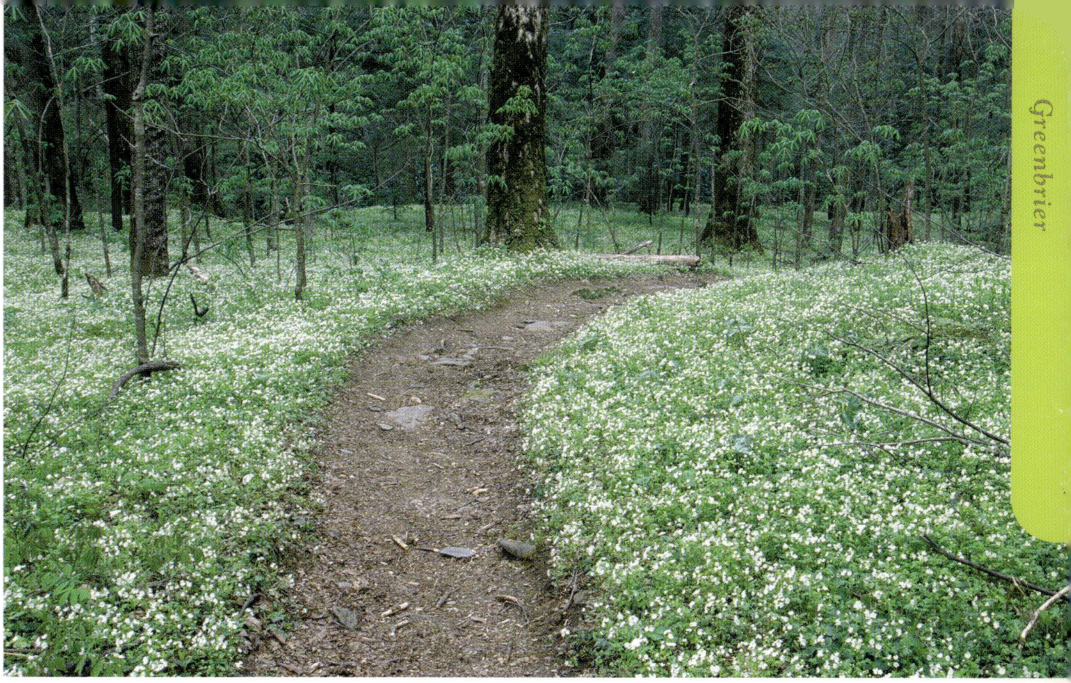

Porters Creek Trail

Porters Creek Trail is buzzing with activity in early to mid-April when the wildflower season hits high gear. The phacelia tend to peak here a bit earlier than the Chimneys area. Check with the Park Service for updated information. To get here, at the confluence, keep going straight (south) another 1.1 miles to a loop turnaround and parking area. From the very first steps you will find enough flowers to keep you busy for the entire day. Violets, iris, Dutchman's breeches, bloodroot, showy orchis, and various trilliums are but a few species in abundance here. Unless you find something compelling, hike to the destination and work your way back. Otherwise you may never get there! About a mile and a half hike in mid-April leads to an amazing display; carpets of fringed phacelia mixed with trillium stretch for hundreds of yards. You will find many other species mixed with them. Follow the trail, climbing easily, keeping to the left at trail intersections. Initially you will wonder what all the fuss is about and think badly of us for leading you astray with bogus information. However after crossing the 3rd footbridge you will seemingly cross through the looking glass, and like Alice, see sights wondrous to behold if your timing is good – check with the rangers or naturalists before making the hike.

This area is commonly referred to as Porters Flats, although correctly that is the area at the end of the old roadbed where the hiking trail proper started. The floral display continues on for another 1/2 mile or so, becoming less intense as you approach Fern Branch Falls. The falls itself are usually not striking, but it's a nice hike.

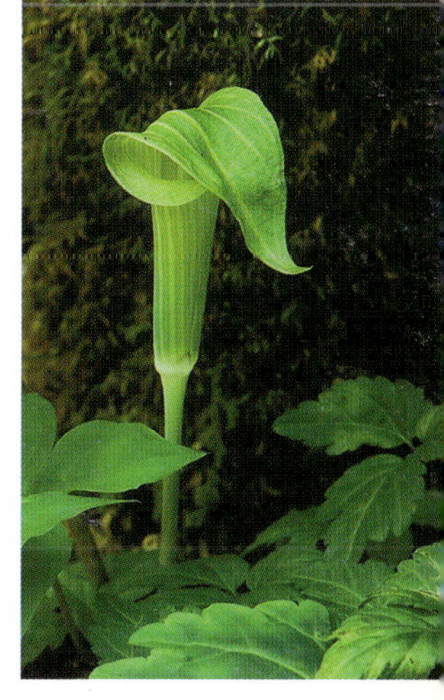

Top: Porter's Creek Trail, an easy hike, leads to a wildflower fantasy land in mid-April.—*NS*

Bottom: Jack-in-the-Pulpit are often located along Porters Creek Trail. The green color makes them harder to see at a casual glance.—*BC*

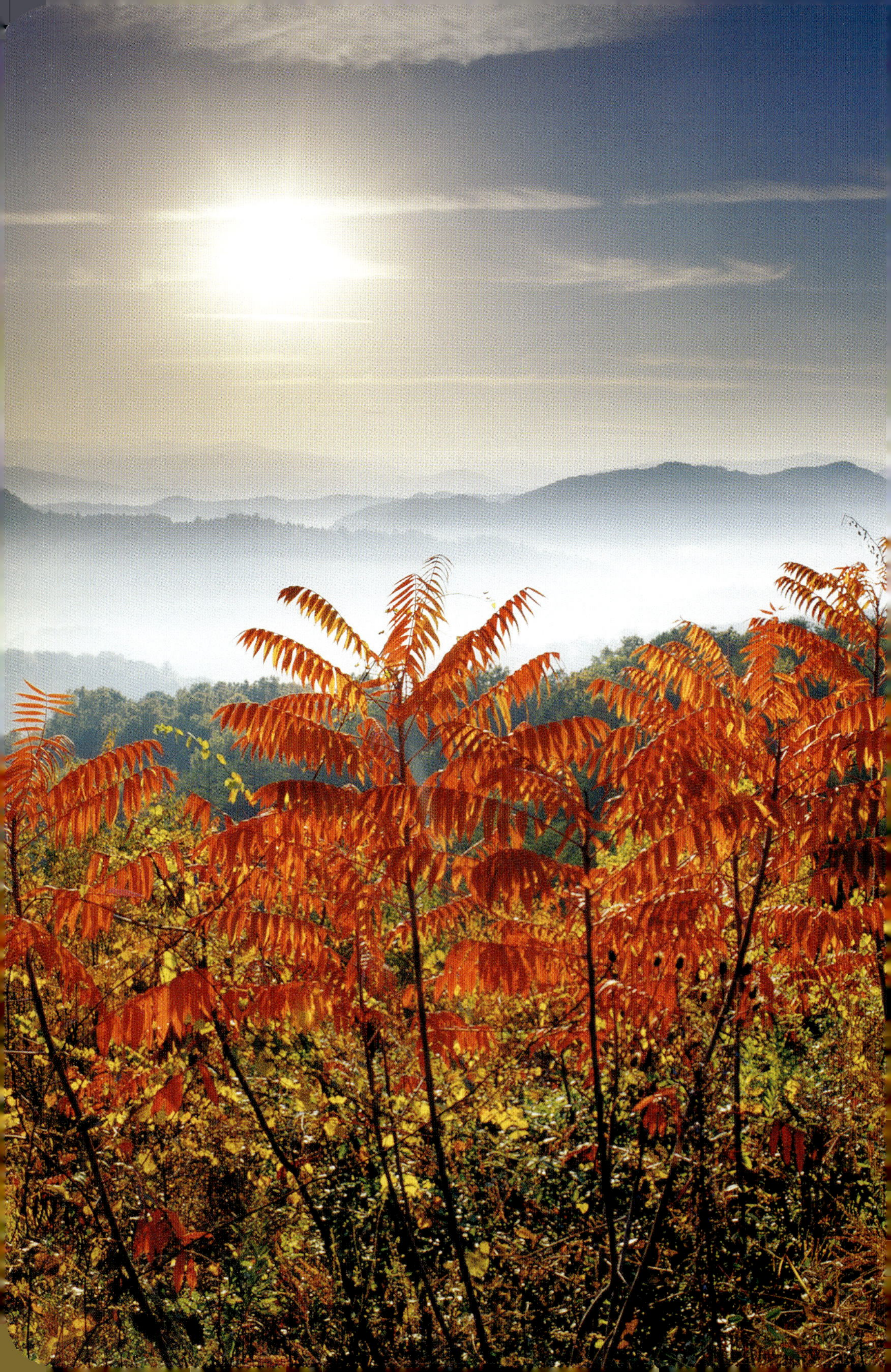

Grand scenics

Photo hikes to waterfalls

Wildflowers

At Foothills Parkway West ,the sun went behind a thin wisp of cloud, momentarily reducing lens flare; translucent sumac leaves glow at plus 1 1/2 . A 3 stop Singh Ray grad held it all in a range that Velvia could handle. —*NS*

Chapter Nine

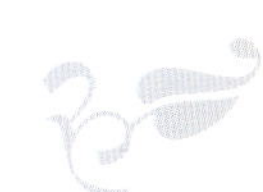

Other Points of Interest

What about the rest of the park? There are several other interesting areas not yet mentioned. All of them see light visitation and are off the beaten path. Local residents and knowledgeable visitors come to avoid the better-known and often crowded areas.

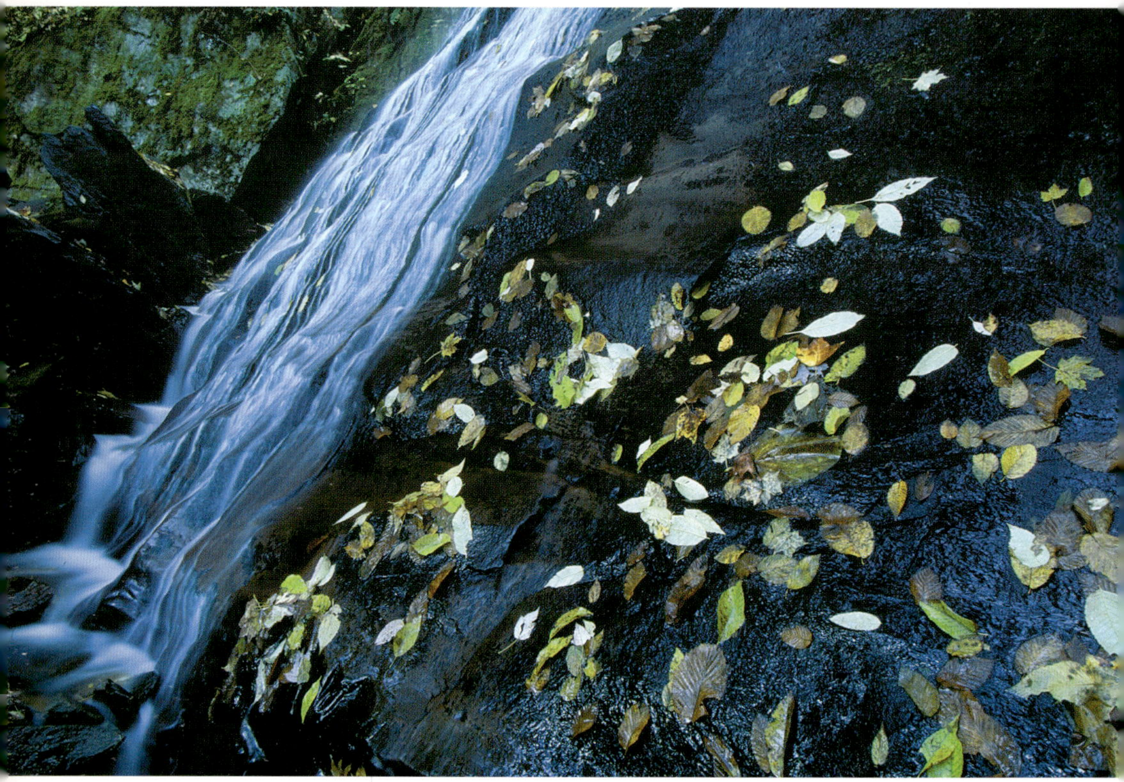

Many colored leaves plaster the wet rock wall next to the Hen Wallow falls. Watch out for water droplets on your lens; You won't notice them when composing wide open, but when stopped down to a small taking aperture, the blobs can ruin your image.—*NS*

Cosby

Hen Wallow Falls

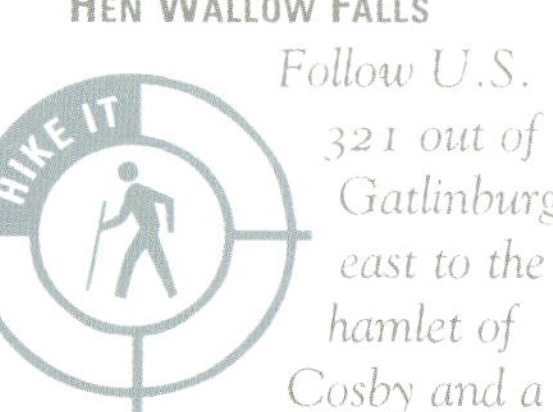

Follow U.S. 321 out of Gatlinburg east to the hamlet of Cosby and a "T" intersection, and turn right to Cosby Campground. This is a relatively secluded area where you can escape the crowds. The main photographic attractions are stream scenes, seasonal wildflowers, and an easy 4.2-mile roundtrip hike to the very photogenic Hen Wallow Falls. The trailhead is marked with a sign for the Gabes Mountain Trail; there is a large parking area just beyond the trailhead with restrooms. This is one of the better areas to find pink lady's slippers in late April and early May. Hen Wallow Falls slopes steeply down a slab of stone and at optimal water levels, divides into many rivulets. Freshly shed (and therefore still colorful) leaves plaster the wet rock in the fall after a rain. Use a long exposure for maximum depth of field and a cotton candy effect on the water.

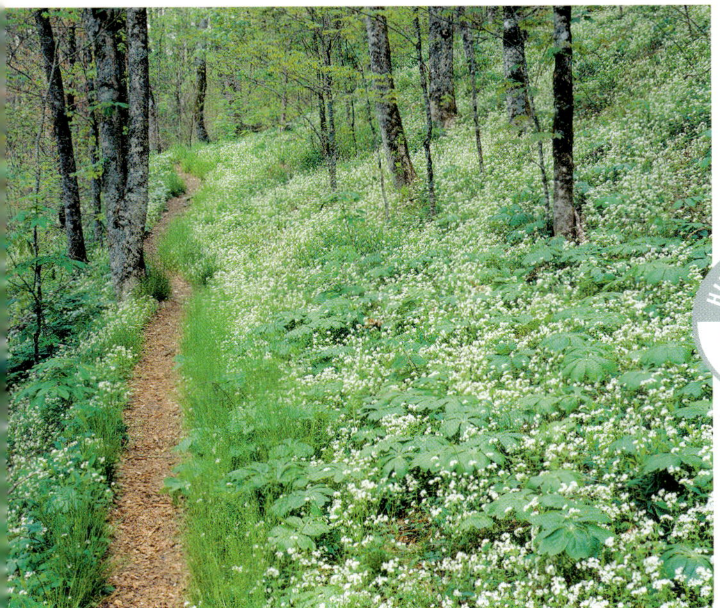

Flat Creek Falls trail gives a little-known high country option for wildflowers in early May.— *NS*

Heintooga Ridge—Balsam Mountain Road

HEINTOOGA OVERLOOK
FLAT CREEK FALLS

HIKE IT

Heintooga Ridge Road itself offers some nice views, becoming Balsam Mountain at the Heintooga Picnic Area where it turns from paved to gravel. There it offers an intimate forest experience, and in spring and summer, a profusion of wildflowers, but there is only one limited view. Access is from the Maggie or Oconaluftee end of the Blue Ridge Parkway. From the picnic area, it's a short walk to ***Heintooga Overlook*** *for a view of the distant Smokies crest, and sunset opportunities. In early May, the* ***Flat Creek Falls Trail*** *sports a profusion of wildflowers, including carpets of fringed phacelia. If the Heintooga Ridge Road is not yet open for the season, it's a short walk of less than a mile from the locked gate to the trailhead, and from there the flowers are at your feet. It's less than a mile to the best parts of the trail. Soft light, or shadows early and late in the day work well. The falls themselves are obscured by foliage. Balsam Mountain is the highest campground in the Park and is a great way to beat the summer heat.*

Deep Creek

TOM BRANCH FALLS
INDIAN CREEK FALLS

Access this entrance through Bryson City. Follow US 19 from Cherokee to Bryson City, and posted signs to the Deep Creek entrance, turning right at the train station. In summer there is a lot of tubing activity here, with several liveries offering their services. At the end of the road is a campground; park here and hike along the stream bed for scenics. Two small waterfalls are a short hike upstream, cascading in from tributaries to the side. The first, Tom Branch Falls, all but dries up in fall. The second, Indian Creek Falls, is larger and is about 20 minutes further on the trail. Fall colors peak here toward the end of October making this a good spot to hit if you missed the peak elsewhere. Dogwoods and rosebay rhododendron flower in season. The Deep Creek Trail connects this site with the Newfound Gap Road.

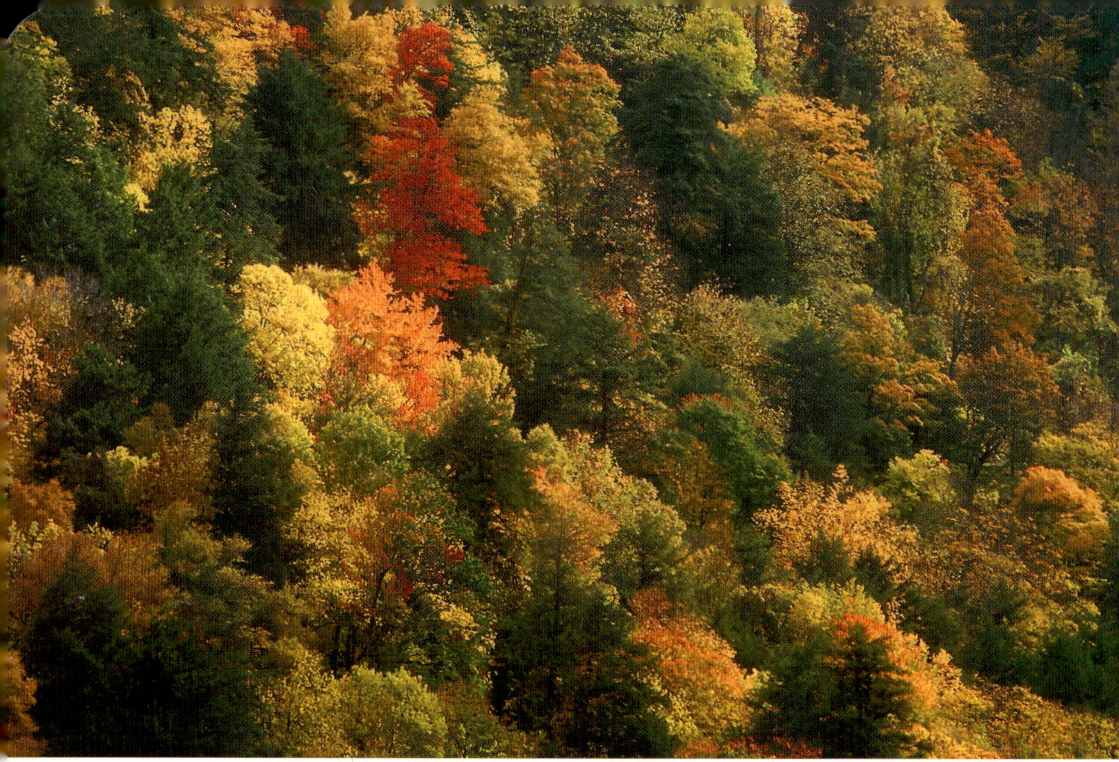

The Blue Ridge Parkway shines during fall color. There are many vistas with a combination of evergreens and hardwoods for a splash of color among the green. A polarizer helps cut down of some of the haze that is common in the Smokies.—*BC*

Lakeview Drive

This is the locally famous "Road to Nowhere" which began construction in the late 1940s but never saw completion due to mounting costs, engineering problems, and growing environmental concerns. It's a pleasant drive into a remote area of the park, but offers no compelling views or opportunities without hiking. At the Bryson City train station, continue straight up the hill (stay on Everett St.) and continue past a sign indicating Deep Creek Campground to your right and past Swain County High School. Approximately 2.5 miles from the train station you will re-enter Great Smoky Mountains National Park. 1.5 miles further, find two views (no pullouts) to the south and southeast of the headwaters of Fontana Lake, and a similar view at signpost #1 1.5 miles further. Almost two miles further is signpost #2 at the bridge over Noland Creek—there is a large parking lot just before. You are quite high above the creek here; the treetops have spread into a canopy mostly obscuring the creek below from view, making the photographic options more limited, and the creek below is all but lost in shadow. The road ends less than a mile further. Hiking options are plentiful, which will give you more stream scenes.

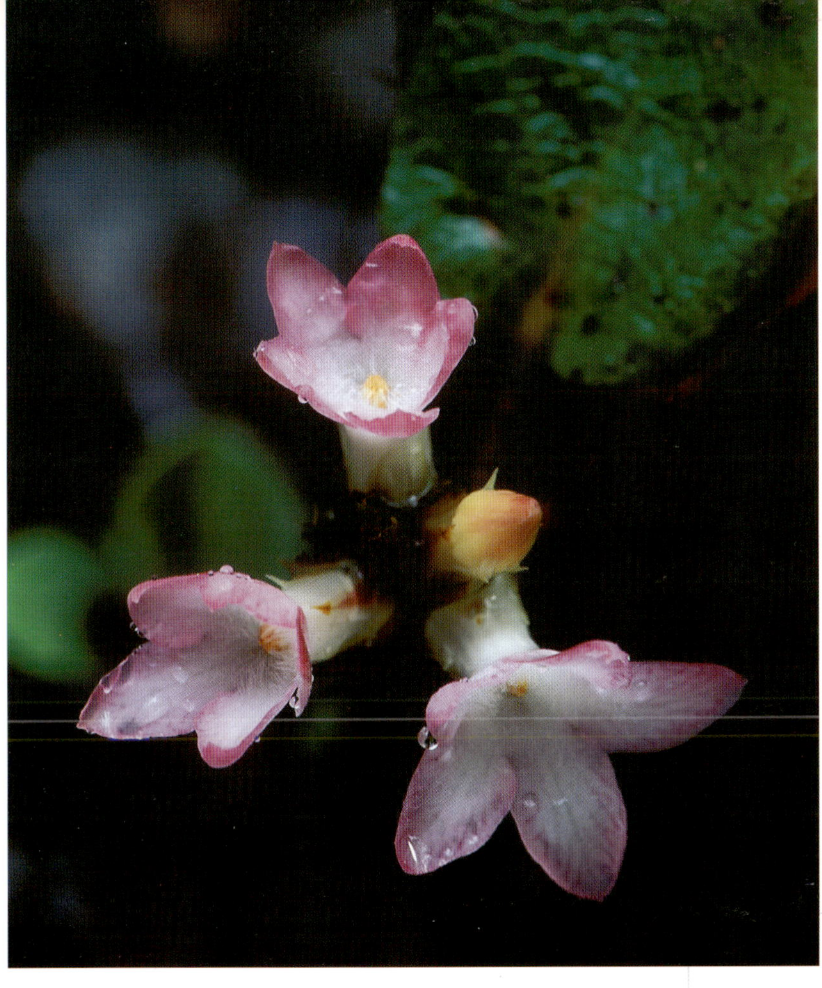

Trailing arbutus is one of the earliest flowers found blooming in the Smokies. The delicate pink edges give a nice hint of color to this white flower. A B+W KR3 filter with just a touch of magenta helps decrease some of the green cast in the white flower from the surrounding green canopy.—*BC*

Abrams Creek

This entrance is about 8 miles downstream from Cades Cove on a foot trail. By car it's easily a 90-minute plus drive from the Cove. From Cades Cove return towards Maryville, looking for the Foothills Parkway sign about 10 miles from the park boundary. Follow the parkway to its end and intersection with US 129. Turn left and follow the signs to Abrams Creek, almost an immediate left turn. Park outside the campground and follow the foot trail along Abrams Creek as far as you have time or energy. Afternoon in fall gives nice colored reflections in the river and pools along the shore. The stream has little gradient here and consequently few rocks. There are more hemlocks and rhodies in the area, so the fall palette isn't as intense as elsewhere. It is secluded, however, and a nice place to get away from the crowds. The occasional river otter is seen here, but don't count on it.

Foothills Parkway, West Section

This roadway offers excellent views into the park and a classic sunrise scene. From Cades Cove, turn north at the "Y" and drive towards Maryville, looking for the Foothills Parkway sign about 10 miles from the park boundary. From Maryville, look for the well-marked signs about a mile south of Walland where you will find a grocery store and gas station.

The first large parking lot on your left at 1.3 miles from the turn off on U.S. 321 is the best sunrise spot on this end of the park. The early morning fog fills in the foreground (Miller's Cove) with mist and on a cool morning the lower peaks seem to rise like islands in a sea of fog. The morning after a rain, after a cool evening, seems to be the best combination of weather. Sometimes the fog is too heavy and obscures the valley below and even the distant ridges; occasionally the parking area will be in fog too, and you can't see a thing. Late October has the sun coming up behind the peaks slightly to your left, at about 110 degrees by compass, while spring and summer see it coming up far to the left, down the road, almost out of the "picture." In late spring and early summer go on to the next pullout, and use the longest lens you have to compose up the valley to the east. This pullout offers a slightly different angle of view that gives just enough clearance to make it work; even here later in July is better, if you want the sun in the composition. The foreground brush here is more grown up than at the one you just passed, but that changes from year to year depending on maintenance schedules. The side lighting on the mist-shrouded hills below is dramatic; investigate compositions with a variety of focal lengths. This is a great place to try out a graduated neutral density filter to balance sky and foreground. If you don't have a graduated neutral density filter, compose with a long lens and don't leave a lot of blank sky at the top; the light pastel won't be objectionable if it's a small strip above the ridgeline. As the sun comes up more behind the ridges in front of you in late fall, a graduated neutral density filter becomes essential because the contrast range increases with the added light behind the ridge. Dynamic images have been made here for years. It's a great place for panoramic compositions. This section is sometimes closed in winter due to snow and ice. A new communications tower with its warning light blinks at short intervals. Time your exposure carefully. It is sometimes obscured by fog.

Follow the parkway for as long as you have time—it's 16.5 miles from start to finish. Periodic views to the east overlooking the Smokies and west overlooking the Tennessee Valley occur, but none offer any advantages until you reach Look Rock. Sunset views to the west can be found at mile 5.9, but beware of lights in the distance that come on at dusk—you may not pay them any attention when taking the photo, but they will be there when you get your film back from the processor. At mile 9 you will find the turn off to Top o' the World Community and Look Rock Campground and Picnic Area. Rest rooms are at the picnic area.

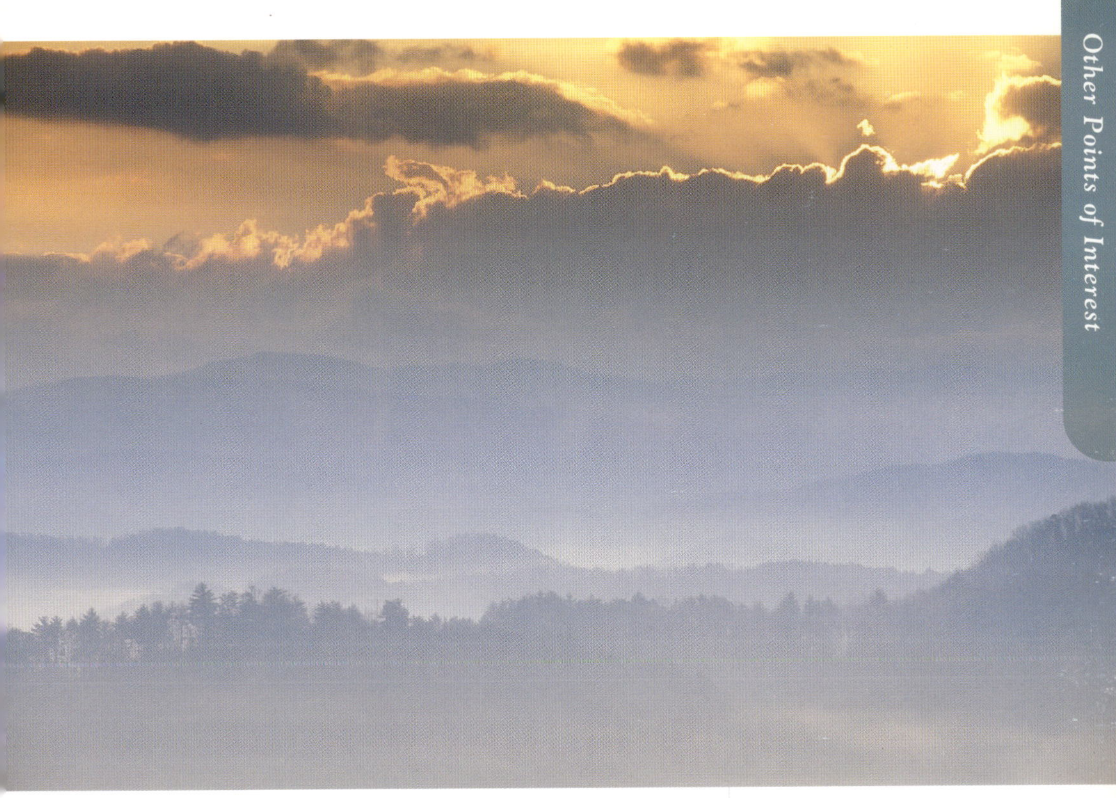

Look Rock

Look Rock at mile 9.4 offers great views and a campground. The formal overlook is a great place to snap a few frames at the west end of the parking area, but the best action is through the woods ahead of you. Spend some time exploring the climber's trails that lead to the rock ledges about 40 yards into the woods. In late May and early June the ***mountain laurel*** are beautiful here. There were many pines here, now sadly fallen victim to the southern pine beetle outbreak.

If you follow the parkway, there will be viewpoints about every mile or so, although none offers a distinct advantage over what you have already seen. Late light cross lights the ridge to your left and alpenglow will illuminate any clouds above the peaks. At the intersection with Highway 129, either turn right to catch US 411 back to Maryville, or turn around and retrace your path. Abrams Creek entrance is to your left across the small inlet, visible as you descend to the intersection.

Sunrise along the Foothills Parkway West is best at the first or second pulloff to the left going west from the Townsend end. This is one of the best places in the western section of the Smokies to see a sunrise with the typical ridges of the Smokies.—*BC*

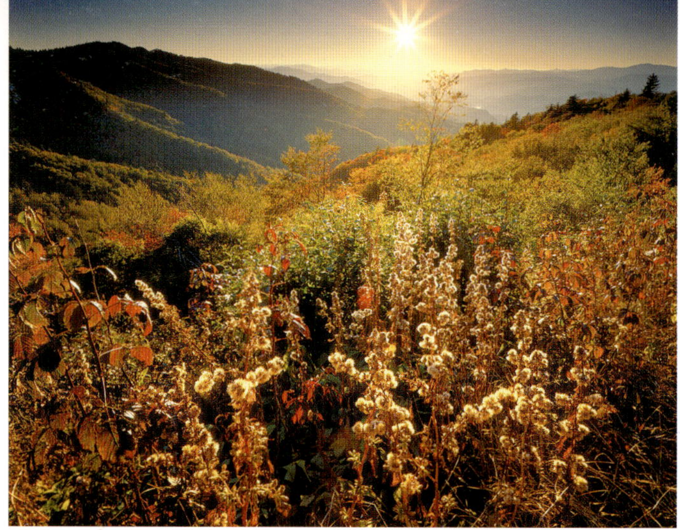

At Blue Ridge Parkway near Water Rock Knob, many of these overlooks face the setting sun; dried late summer grasses glow in back light. 3 stop Singh Ray grad.—*NS*

Foothills Parkway, East Section

Follow U.S. 321 towards Newport and I-40, 1.7 miles from the Cosby intersection, then turn right onto the Foothills Parkway. ***English Mountain Overlook*** is the second pullout on your right at mile 2.1. It gives you a picturesque cove in the foreground, albeit with more modern structures. Early morning light here is from your left which gives a nice cross lighting effect, and soft light works also with longer lenses. In winter the road is frequently closed because of snow and ice. Three and a half miles further is the intersection with I-40. There is one grand scene along this stretch (mile 2.1), and there are lots of maples in this area, so fall color can be intense, and intimate scenes abound.

Blue Ridge Parkway

Managed by the National Park Service, this scenic drive traverses the spine of the Southern Appalachians from Great Smoky Mountains National Park in the south to Shenandoah National Park to the north. Since the southern end provides the only practical access to the Balsam Mountain area, we included it in this guide. It also provides a link between Maggie Valley and the Park, bypassing Cherokee. Overlooks provide grand scenics as well as more intimate scenes, seasonal wildflowers and flowering trees, and glorious fall color. Blue Ridge Parkway milepost 469, at the Oconaluftee River Bridge (adjacent to the Mountain Farm Museum and visitor center) is the southern terminus of the Parkway. The first few miles have more limited views; ***Thomas Divide*** views at mile 464 are more open and receive attractive evening light. Past Big Witch tunnel at mile 461, overlooks develop more westerly views with various sunset and evening light potentials depending on season. Excellent intimate scenes can bemuse you for hours at ***Soco Gap*** (mile 455.) Here the Blue Ridge Parkway crosses U.S. 19 leading to Cherokee, Waynesville and Maggie Valley. From Soco Gap it's a short but steep 4 mile climb to ***Water Rock Knob*** with its small visitor center, rest rooms, and expansive views. Several overlooks between Soco and Water Rock offer sweeping views toward the setting sun with various foreground combinations. Spring is late and fall is early at these high (4,000-6,000 foot) elevations. The Parkway is closed much of the winter due to snow and ice, even when Newfound Gap Road (U.S. 441) is open.

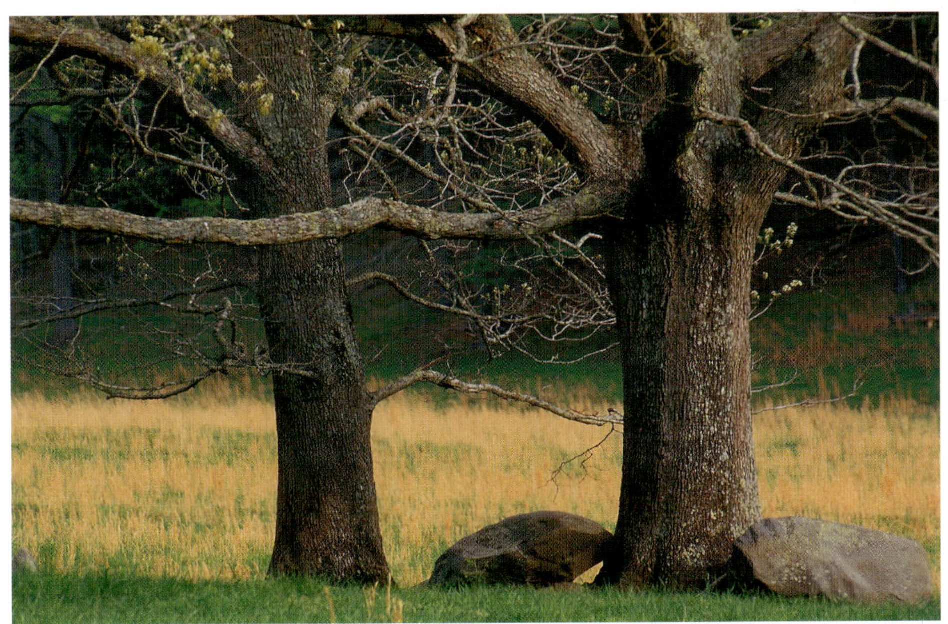

Chapter Ten

Getting the Most Out of Your Photography

Framing just the trunks and lower limb sections of these two trees makes the composition appear more dynamic than just trying to include all of both trees. On this day, the sky was very bright without interesting detail, so it was consciously eliminated from the image.—*BC*

There are numerous books (see our references for some that we think most useful) that offer excellent instructional material about the art and craft of nature photography. We do not have the space to duplicate that effort; this book is about the what, where and when of photographing the Smokies. But we would like to pass on some helpful hints and places to start if you want to improve your nature photography. Who knows, maybe the bug will bite hard and you too will ditch your day job for the long hours and little pay of a nature photographer We do have to admit that no one has a better office setting.

Nature photography is a synthesis of the art of using light and composition with the technical knowledge of cameras and film. Some of us have strengths in one direction or the other, but you cannot completely rely on just your art or technical knowledge to carry an image. Following is a discussion of the elements of nature photography, starting with the technical and culminating in four steps to better images.

Equipment

More questions are asked about the type of equipment used than the conditions surrounding an image. Equipment is important, but a good photographer can take any camera out and make a great image if he or she knows the limitations of the camera being used.

Any system that allows you to have a full range of lenses and flashes is considered adequate. One of us [BC] uses a Nikon 35mm system and the other [NS] uses a combination of Canon 35mm, Pentax 6x7cm and mostly large format view cameras. Neither system is perfect, but both do a wonderful job giving us good tools to use for our photography.

Tripods are considered a necessity by all professional nature photographers—they give stability for slower shutter speeds and encourage methodical work when composing images. Certain images are impossible to make without a tripod. Those silky images of streams are shot at 1/2 second to several seconds. Any hand holding and water won't be the only thing blurred. Even at faster shutter speeds, a tripod is better for very sharp images. Does that mean that you can't make a great image without a tripod? No, just keep the shutter speed faster than the focal length of the lens (i.e., if the lens is 300mm long, keep the shutter speed faster than 1/300 second) and you should be safe most of the time. A macro shot (where the image is magnified) needs a shutter speed of 2-3 times the focal length to keep the image sharp. Or use a tripod. See how the tripod can make life easier?

Filters are those little pieces of glass that go in front of the lens (or somewhere in the lens on big lenses) and can make or break some images. There are very few filters that are a must for the nature photographer—the polarizer, the warming filter and maybe a set of graduated split neutral density filters.

The most frequently used in the Smokies is a ***polarizing filter***. This filter allows you to cut down on reflections and, in doing so, increase the saturation of color in your image. All water has some degree of reflectance, and stream photography would be much less fun without a polarizing filter. Many plants have waxy leaves that reflect sunlight like a piece of glass. These reflections can appear as very bright spots (hot spots) in your image and are easy to control with the polarizing filter. Any filter cuts down on the amount of light reaching the camera, so shutter speeds will be longer for the same aperture when using a filter. This can be advantageous if longer shutter speeds are what you are looking for. To determine if you need a polarizer, just hold it up to your eye and see if it helps. Remember to rotate the filter, because this changes the amount of reflection that is eliminated.

A ***warming filter*** (designation 81a, Nikon A2, Sing Ray A13) will add a bit of warmth to the image color. Early morning light will look a little warmer with this filter. Any time you are in open shade (sunny day, blue sky but in the shade), the film or CCD will see the blue light reflected from the sky. Your image will appear to have a bluish or cooler tint, even though your eyes won't perceive it. This is because we use our brains to see with, not just our eyes. Our brains act like the warming filter and tell us to "filter" out the blue light, so the image we see looks correct. Sometimes you don't want to use a warming filter even if the light is "cool." Ice or snow on a blue day or overcast day may look better with a cooler blue cast. Again, place the filter to your eye and judge whether you like the effect.

A ***graduated split neutral density filter*** is a specialized filter used for controlling the balance of light between the dark areas and the light areas. Film and even digital cameras can't portray details in both the shadows and highlights in a single image if the difference is too great. A split neutral density filter can help compress the range of light so film or CCD can capture the entire image adequately. They come in rectangular sheets of plastic with a clear end (to go over the dark part of your scene) and then a dark end(to go over the very light part of your scene) with a split in the middle. There are hard and soft edged filters (meaning the edge in the middle) and their use is dictated by the separation between light and dark in your image. These filters are most useful when taking sunrise/sunset images where the foreground is dark and the sky is very light. Most cameras will meter the scene correctly if set to matrix or evaluative metering. Some photographers no longer use these filters when they are using a digital camera because they can expose two images, one for the highlights and one for the shadows, and then combine them within Photoshop for the perfect image. For a complete discussion on graduated neutral density filters, go to John Shaw's book, *Nature Photography Field Guide* or Bob Singh's website, www.singh-ray.com.

Film vs Digital

Film continues to be the standard we measure against. But most professionals are now shooting digital cameras, at least part of the time, and finding that they enjoy it. Many professionals shoot transparency film (slides) because that is what editors want from us. Print film actually works great and has greater latitude of exposure (able to capture a wider range of light from dark to highlights.) Shoot whatever you are comfortable with and whatever your needs dictate, but limit yourself to only several types of film so you will know how that particular film will work in any situation.

The digital revolution has presented a new set of problems for all photographers. How do I store my images? (Burn them to CD.) How do I share my images? (Email, prints from home, prints from service, slide show from camera to TV.) What about battery usage? (Carry extra batteries and a charger in your car.) None of the new problems are insurmountable, but it takes a new way of thinking.

Digital cameras are wonderful in that they can give you instantaneous feedback about your image. Is it sharp? Did I include and exclude everything I wanted? Is the light balance correct? For most images in nature, the cloudy setting or sun setting will work. If you don't want to think about the type of light, set your camera to automatic. This works most of the time, but the skies at sunset and sunrise may wash out. If this is the case, set the light to cloudy even if there isn't a cloud in the sky. This will give you warmer tones for those early morning/late evening shoots. Never shoot your camera until the battery is exhausted as this may corrupt the storage card and make your images unreadable. Change batteries once the low battery indicator comes on.

Image Design

Great images are not created by simply pointing a camera and capturing an image. Composition of the necessary elements into an image that projects your personal statement is an ordered, conscious decision. To achieve the statement you desire, first decide what you like about a scene and then eliminate everything else that doesn't support your statement.

Graphic design starts with a great subject. Then think about the graphic elements in the subject. How we use color, line, texture, form and patterns to emphasize our statement is the key to great images. The splash of bright color in an otherwise monochromatic scene, the leading line to the main subject, the delicate texture of the background, the sensuous curves of the snow-covered rocks, the repeating patterns of the flower blossoms—all of these add a depth to your image that goes beyond a simple picture.

Many images start out with a great subject, but the desire to include other elements overwhelms the statement. Instead of a simple phrase, you end up with a long paragraph for your statement and lose the viewer along the way. Remember to simplify, simplify, simplify.

Placement of the subject within the frame most often makes or breaks a great image. Many times the image ends up centered in the frame. We call this the bulls eye effect. This happens especially with wildlife. Consider where you want your subject to be in the frame and why. The direction of flow through your frame will help with subject placement. Photographers use a "rule of thirds" in which we divide the frame up into 1/3 divisions, both vertically and horizontally. Placing a subject on one of these lines or at the intersection of these lines, usually leads to a more pleasing image. This is not a hard and fast rule as all rules are meant to be broken at times, but it is a safe way to begin looking at your compositional placement. Get away from everything in the middle and your photography will take an immediate leap forward.

Lighting

The word photography means "painting with light." As a photographer, think about how to use the light you have to make the most pleasing image you can. ***Direct sunlight*** is what most film is balanced for and looks great if your image is well lit and has few shadows. If the direct sun gets too far overhead (noonday sun), then shadows will be cast from overhead on your subject. ***Soft early morning sunlight*** has a warmer tone than midday light. This light can last 5 minutes or 45 minutes after sunrise or before sunset, depending on time of year and atmospheric conditions. Meadow wildflowers, grand landscapes and wildlife usually look great in this light. ***Diffused light*** (light overcast day with minimal to no shadows on the ground) is the optimal light for forest interiors or streams or wildflower portraits. Without shadows to contend with, you get detail in almost all areas of your image without the shadows becoming jet black.

Side lighting uses directional light from the side of a subject and is a great way to bring out texture and form. The shadows cast by side lighting can also be a great compositional element. ***Back lighting*** can create a wonderful glow around a subject, but the subject may just be a silhouette if light is not added to the subject. Adding light to a subject comes in the form of a flash, a reflector or any kind of light source you can come up with. Candles, flashlights, campfires are all useable forms of light when adding to a scene.

Putting it all together

Once you have distilled your image from a confusing paragraph to a simple phrase, there are four questions to ask yourself. These questions are what set a great image off from a mediocre image. A great image will have all four elements.

1) Is this a great subject? A flower that is past it's prime or a buck with a small rack is just a mediocre subject. Look for the flower that says "WOW" when you see it or keep looking for that buck that looks like Bambi's father; big, majestic and proud. Once you find a great subject, keep working until you get all the other elements together. Always remember to give your subject some "breathing room" within the image. Composing too close to the edges might limit the use of the image when a crop is need or when a slide is mounted. Sometimes part of an element can be hidden underneath a slide mount if the element is placed too close to the edge.

2) Is this great light? You may have heard that great light makes a great photograph. Partially true, because a great subject in bad light falls flat. Conversely, great light won't make a mediocre subject come to life. That soft, warm light in the first 15-60 minutes of the day is why dedicated nature photographers roll out of bed so early. The color of light and the evenness of light is something that photographers learn to see the more they photograph. Light can set the mood, be it cold and blue on a snowy, cloudy day or warm and soft on an early morning sunrise with a light fog. Dark and foreboding light that comes with an approaching storm. The gentle glow of twilight just after the sun sets below the horizon. Look at great photographs and learn to judge the light. This will help you judge the actual light you see when you are out creating your own personal statements. Overhead sun is the most difficult light source to work in, but occasionally the subject matter will be enhanced by this light, so don't ever let anyone tell you that noonday photography is bad. It's not, it is just LOTS harder to use.

3) Is this a great foreground? Any element that is close to the camera is a foreground element. We've all seen pictures with a photographer's hand in the frame or a tree limb that got in the way. Make sure that everything you want in the foreground is in the viewfinder and everything you want out of the image is excluded. You might want to emphasizo a particular foreground element. Use a wide angle lens or setting and get really close to the element you want to emphasize. Some elements don't show up until you get the image back because they are very close to the lens. Get in the habit of focusing from near to far to check for stray elements and always scan the edges of your frame for uninvited guests. We call these guests "sneakers" as they seem to sneak into your frame.

4) Is this a great background? Many backgrounds tend to be too cluttered and detract from the statement of the image. Fog is a great tool for cleaning up a cluttered background. It obscures the other elements that many times are distracting. Looking around for a vantage point that offers less in the background should be part of setting up your image. Shifting a couple of feet so the bright sky behind your son's portrait is now dark red foliage can make or break the quality of your shot. If something is in your image and you cannot verbalize what it would do to add to your creation, get rid of it. Now we don't advocate physically removing trees or plants or even buildings, just remember that changing your position or even your focal length of lens can eliminate an unwanted background element.

The synthesis of your artistic expression and your technical prowess will continue to grow with each new image you design. Think through the steps leading to a great image and how the light and composition works best for the moment, and you will be creating better images in no time. Practice makes for perfection.

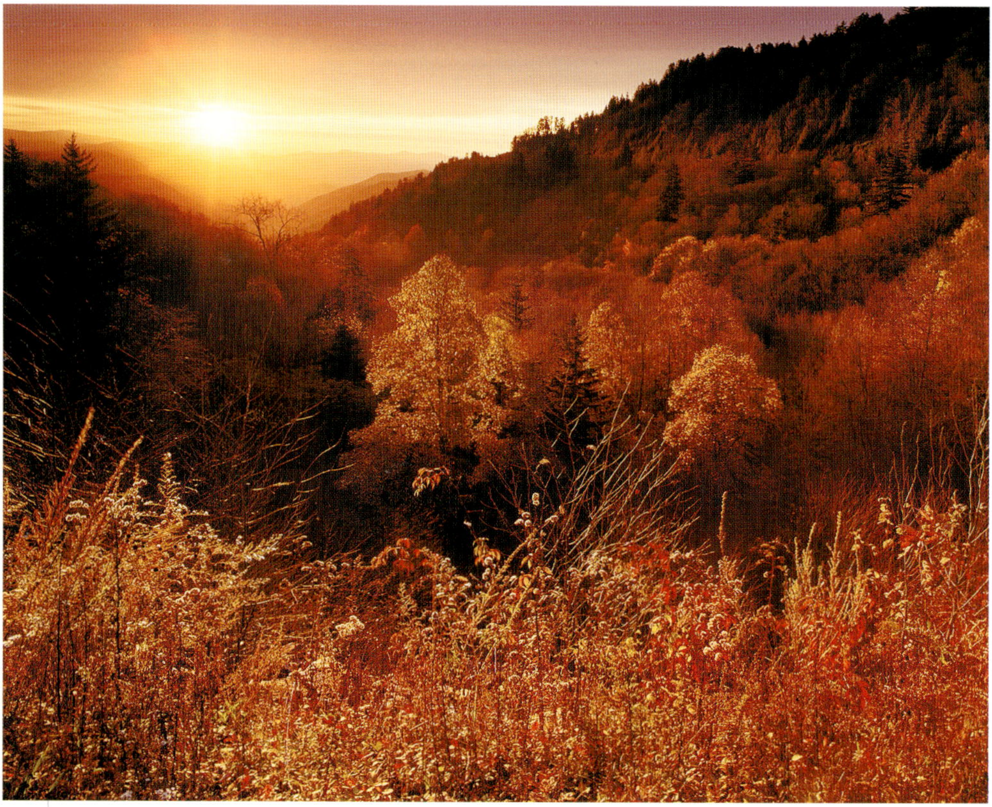

Chapter Eleven

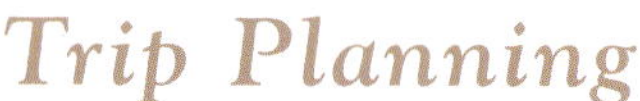

Trip Planning

Backlighted grasses glow as the sun briefly lights them before disappearing into clouds which help hide early morning contrails from flights leaving the Asheville airport. 3 stop Singh-Ray Grad.—*NS*

THE MOST DISAPPOINTED photographers we ever saw in the park showed up two weeks too early for fall color, closely followed by the folks that arrived here a week too late. Peak color and peak wildflower bloom change from year to year.

To plan a visit in advance, start with a basic knowledge of seasonal timetables, then find out if things are on time or not as time grows near. You can find this information online at several Internet bulletin boards devoted to nature photography, and by calling the Park. To get you started, here is an approximate chronicle of seasonal events in the park. Variations in weather can make long term planning difficult if you have to reserve vacation time far in advance; spring can be 2 weeks early, fall color has been 7-10 days late. Here is a seasonal almanac with highlights in italics.

January

Secondary roads such as Clingmans Dome closed for the season, and primary roads subject to closure depending on ice and snow conditions. Call (865) 436-1200 for road info; key in 631 when the recording starts to go straight to the road report. Some white-tailed bucks will still have their antlers; they look great in the snow in Cades Cove. **Ice formations at the weeping wall on Newfound Gap Road (U.S. 441) and streambeds.**

February

Most of the bucks have dropped their racks. Ice formations, and if it snows, winter landscapes. **Ice formations at the weeping wall on Newfound Gap Road (U.S. 441) and streambeds.**

March

The first spring wildflowers are coming up at the lower elevations in late March, red maples bloom, bears emerge from their dens. Higher elevations such as Chimneys and above will still be in winter mode for another 4-6 weeks depending on elevation. **Bloodroot blooms at lower elevations, forsythia at Davis House (Mountain Farm Museum) at the end of March.**

April

Spring is really here. Flowering trees and all manner of wildflowers peak mid to late April. The annual Spring Wildflower Pilgrimage is held in late April. Streams are full, waterfalls (usually) at their best. Clingmans Dome Road usually opens April 1. **Phacelia at Chimneys Picnic Area and Porters Flats, dogwoods everywhere.**

May

Follow spring as it advances to the higher elevations; it will still be early spring on the Clingmans Dome Road and upper reaches of the Newfound Gap Road. Bears with cubs more active in Cades Cove. Late May brings Mountain Laurel to lower elevations, Cades Cove, Little River Road. **Serviceberry trees bloom in the high country, pink ladies slippers at lower elevations.**

June

Bears active in Cades Cove. Newborn fawns early to mid-month. Rhododendron and mountain laurel start early at lower elevations and work their way up. **Flame Azalea at Andrews Bald peak mid-month, Gregory Bald often around the 21st.** Cades Cove Road closed on Wednesday and Saturday mornings until 10:00 a.m. for cyclists to enjoy the road unhindered (unthreatened) by auto traffic.

July

Sunset at Morton Overlook on Newfound Gap Road is a classic view, try to catch it with a clearing storm. Rosebay (white) rhododendron may bloom till month's end in a good year at higher elevations. Bee balm at higher elevations and Turk's Cap lily, wildflowers fringe parking areas at Clingmans Dome. Wildlife in the Cove, bucks start growing antlers.

August

Bucks in Cades Cove growing antlers in velvet, still herded up into bachelor groups. Early morning fog in the Cove is frequent, bears active. Look for them in the cherry trees at the west end of Cades Cove. **Wildflowers fringe parking areas at Clingmans Dome.**

September

Deer in the cove starting to shed velvet. Bears remain active. Hint of season change at highest elevations. Late wildflowers. Migrating hawks and butterflies pass through. **Blueberries on higher balds are ripening and their leaves are turning crimson.** Summer crowds have gone back home for school, fall season not yet upon us. Sunsets at Clingmans Dome, sun to the far right of the classic composition, sun no longer in scene at Morton Overlook.

October

The big month. If you have only one shot at a visit to the park, take this one. Some folks get here too early and miss out on the peak color, which is usually around the 4th week at mid-elevations. It starts out high of course and works its way down. Conventional wisdom recommends the middle of the month, but it is usually later than that except at the highest elevations. Straddle the third and fourth weeks and you will probably be just right. Critters and scenics are all dressed up in their finest.

November

The last remnants of color fade by the end of the first week at all but the very lowest elevations. **Deer are in their prime;** all the guys and gals want to look their best for the big dance. Bears finish fattening up and head for the den. The tourist season is over, and a semblance of sanity returns. Great time to visit the Cove. Snow and or hoar frost possible.

December

The deer rut is winding down for the white tails by mid-month. Landscape enthusiasts hope for snow storms and hoar frost conditions. Christmas slows things down a lot. Have a Merry one wherever you are. **Deer in the cove are a sure bet.**

Planning Your Day

Okay, you arrived at the season's peak. Now what? You have to make choices about what subject matter you want to photograph, then factor in where you are staying, season and weather. Our best images are the result of many trips into the Park; rarely were two images shown in this book taken on the same day. You can't get all the cookies out of the jar on one visit, much less one day. There are lots of choices to make. If you only have one day this will help you make the most of it.

The best compromise of wildlife, scenics, wildflowers, and accessibility is ***Cades Cove*** hands down. If your time is limited that's probably the place to be. The Cove can easily accommodate a group having diverse interests if you are with friends. That said, there are many permutations to choose from, and many moods to explore.

On ***a clear day*** if you want grand scenics, head for one of the sunrise overlooks; Foothills Parkway West, Clingmans Dome, or the high viewpoints near Newfound Gap on the North Carolina side. Vistas prefer clean light; dynamic light is even better. Early light is glorious in the Cove, and really special if it's burning through the morning fog. Deer in the mist are a favorite for breakfast while munching a granola bar, and scenic options often don't even require a lens change. When the sun is too high for your taste, look for shaded locations for close ups of intimate details or reflections in streams. The passing clouds of a partly cloudy day create peek-a-boo conditions, teasing us with moments of soft light. Wait for the sun to go behind a cloud and make the exposure. It can be very frustrating. Shoot when the sun peeks around the cloud's edge and gives the scene a fleeting glow. Very rewarding. If you want to make wildflower images in bright conditions, use a diffuser, wait for, or create your own shade. When shadows start to lengthen in the afternoon, be in the Cove for wildlife, or up high for scenics and sunset on 441 or Clingmans Dome Road. You will lose light in the Cove a bit before actual sunset. A mid-day nap is not to be scoffed at; you may need it on a nature photographer's schedule.

On *a cloudy day* the light is ideal for photographing the many rivers and creeks in the Park, as well as wildflowers and waterfalls. With the right kinds of clouds, you can be productive all day without periods of harsh contrast. It's not bad for wildlife either. If you know the day will be cloudy you can squeeze out some extra sleep in the morning and get an early dinner in the evening. Be flexible; it's easy to get locked in to a specific goal and miss a different opportunity unfolding before you. Sometimes there is a small opening on the horizon, and a cloudy morning or evening gives unexpected gifts, but you may also spend a lot of energy chasing phantom light, and miss other opportunities.

Rainy days are not the photographer's best friend, but it doesn't have to be a total bust. Usually there are some breaks in the rain when you can make images, and you get that precious wet look as a bonus. *Look down!* Raindrops beading up on fallen leaves and flowers make gorgeous images. Work near the car, use an umbrella or rain hood, plastic bag, whatever, and watch for raindrops on the front of your lens that may spoil your images. Too much rain beats down the blossoms and you have to wait for things to recover. At high elevations you will probably be in the clouds, with an opportunity for moody foggy scenes. Low lying clouds give you the fog without the hassle of rain, so head to higher elevations when you have had your fill of valley stream scenes.

OPPOSITE PAGE: A setting crescent moon adds an accent to bands of twilight color.—*NS*

Spring

Critters are still a bit gaunt and tattered from the winter and aren't as photogenic as they will be later, and newborns aren't really out yet, making this mostly a time for **scenics and wildflowers**. Peak wildflower time is elevation dependent but the displays most folks come to see are usually mid to late April. How you plan your day depends on whether you have specific images you wish to make, or just want a nice day in the Park.

For sunrise, if you're starting from Gatlinburg or Townsend, try **Foothills Parkway West**, the first pull out on your left, timing your exposure with the new flashing beacon so as not to be in your image. If you don't dally, there may still be time to get to **Tremont** or **Little River** before hot spots enter into the best compositions. The sweet light will be gone in the Cove by the time you get there, so you have to choose. If you get there 30 minutes before sunrise, and the skies aren't to your liking you can still make the gate when it opens. By mid-morning, look for shaded scenes in the canyons, or use a diffuser of some sort for wildflowers, get breakfast, take a nap, or scout for the afternoon shoot, or all of the above.

On the **North Carolina side, sunrise at Newfound Gap** is an option, but you will have bare trees, so you won't have great foreground options until later in May; longer lens compositions work fine. The Blue Ridge Parkway seems better suited to afternoon scenics. Follow to (or start at) the **Mountain Farm Museum** in early to mid-morning light, particularly in early spring when the yellow forsythia are in bloom at the Davis House. If the skies are nice you can make nice late morning images here too. Mid-morning light is good at **Mingus Mill** for a follow up, and it's close by. When you photograph the interior of the mill, buy some authentic stone ground meal—it doesn't get any better than this.

If **river scenes**, possibly with dogwoods, are tops on your list, try **Tremont Road, Roaring Fork Motor Nature Trail,** or **Greenbrier** at first light. You will have a couple of hours depending on which bend in the river you chose, on a clear day, and of course all day on an overcast day. Bop 'til you drop.

Morning light in Cades Cove is always nice, and there is often fog, which can be the accent you need for truly killer images. The **Rich Mountain Overlook** can be special if there is fog in the Cove but it's a one-way road out of the Cove, with at least 45 minutes driving remaining to get back to Townsend alone. It takes more commitment than a lot of photographers are willing to make for a single scene, and in the spring it's not as commanding as in the fall.

In **afternoon** look for soft light in the river bottoms for **scenics and intimate detail work**, wildflowers etc., basically reversing the morning routine. **Sunsets** are great from **Morton Overlook on Newfound Gap Road** (U.S. 441), and if you are staying on the North Carolina side, from the **Blue Ridge Parkway**. Late light is good in the Cove, although no fawns yet and no racks on the bucks.

Summer

Summer mornings often find the **Cove** foggy and moody, and it's the best place to be for the combination of **landscapes and wildlife**. When the light plays out, head for **Tremont, Little River**, or head up **Newfound Gap Road** (U.S. 441) looking for attractive river scenes; the white rosebay rhododendron blooms in June and July. **Sunrise** is attractive from **Clingmans Dome** with wildflowers later in the season. The sun is far to the left at Newfound Gap in early summer and moves across the scene as fall approaches. Early light can be pleasant at the **Mountain Farm Museum** with dewy grass and no crowds. **Evenings in the Cove** are often sublime, when **deer** come out to browse in the flowers. Consider **Morton Overlook for classic sunset scenes** and the **Blue Ridge Parkway** if staying on the North Carolina side.

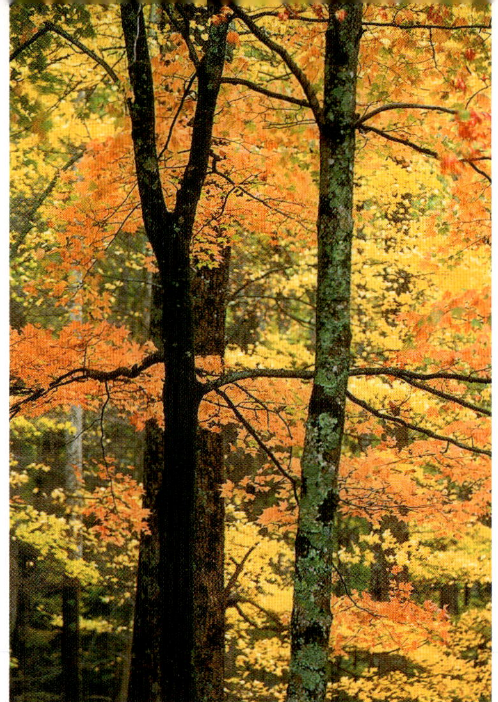

On a bright overcast day, the light shines through these translucent fall leaves and saturates the color. The composition of the two tree trunks set to each side of the middle help give a dynamic flow that a centered tree would not have had.—*BC*

Fall

Well, now is when it's happening! Fall seems to be the grand finale for the photo season, as well as for Mother Nature. At no other time of the year do photographers get more frenetic. It seems we don't want to waste even a drop of light. The sun is lower on the horizon in its course across the sky, so we can work longer without the harsher shadows and light quality of summer, and we have color to work with. It helps to be able to string first light together with scenes that come in to their best as the sun gets higher. First light choices dictate the follow ups, so you must chose what you wish to photograph, and make educated guesses as to how the day will play out.

Follow the light. A great sequence for landscape photographers starts up high on **Newfound Gap Road (U.S. 441), at the Oconaluftee Valley Overlook,** just on the North Carolina side of Newfound Gap (alternate could be Clingmans Dome or the Newfound Gap proper.) Play with first light here, **predawn** through the first 30 minutes or so, then move down the ridge to the various overlooks peering down the Deep Creek drainage overlooking Shot Beech Ridge. On a good day you will have **color, fog on the lake with peaks rising through it, and clean skies.** From here it's back over to the Tennessee side to the various Chimneys overlooks for various compositions of the **Chimneys** framed by fall color. A quick lunch in Gatlinburg, or sandwich on the road, and **early afternoon light on Mount Le Conte** around 2:00 p.m. It polarizes, so the colors get well saturated, and you might have nice clouds. Move back up to the Chimneys overlooks for various side light compositions that begin to polarize around mid-afternoon, or alternatively the same North Carolina overlooks where you did your second sets in the morning, before heading up to **Clingmans Dome for sunset.**

If you have been to Clingmans for fall sunset before, and you know your spot, you can linger near your next to last spot. If you need to scout, get there early. There is some jockeying for position, and your preferred tripod holes might be full. There will probably be some workshops there in addition to the usual throngs. Stay 'til you can't stand it for afterglow. Remember to look over your shoulder towards the east to see what's happening; there might be a rising moon and a magenta glow layered over a blue twilight wedge. Now that it's almost dark, start your drive back to town. If you have packed snacks or a picnic dinner, you won't have to sweat the restaurant lines, or the long lines of folks streaming

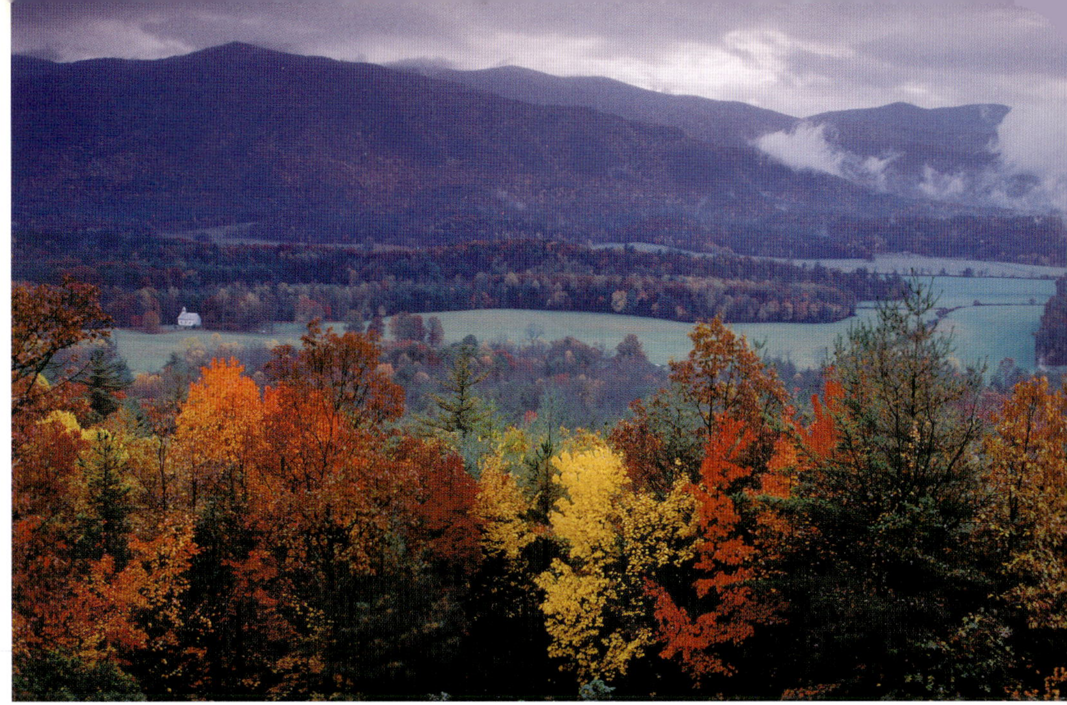

Rich Mountain Road Overlook shows a different mood on a stormy day. A 2 stop Singh Ray grad restored a heaviness to the clouds that otherwise would have washed out.—*NS*

out of the Park; traffic can back up quite a bit coming in to Gatlinburg, so plan accordingly. Traffic getting in to Cherokee is getting backed up too, with folks coming in to the casino. The **Blue Ridge Parkway** offers several overlooks facing the setting sun for a less crowded alternative.

Wildlife enthusiasts have an easy choice: **Cades Cove**. Be at the gate for **sunrise**, at least half an hour early if you want to be towards the front of the pack, and have snacks and lunch with you. Make tactical decisions as the light and subject matter unfold. **Rich Mountain Overlook** is wonderful in early morning and late afternoon light, and it's an American landscape icon, but you have to play the light (wait too late and shadows hurt the scene) and wait for cars to disperse (here comes our old friend Photoshop.) It's difficult to get back to the Cove in time for deer; if you want to make this image it requires commitment to that scene. If you do make that choice, try a stream bottom once it goes into shade like **Tremont or Little River** for a follow up, or find glowing back lit fall foliage to work with.

You can spend a lot of time sitting in traffic in the Cove, so don't cut your times too close. Traffic jams are unpredictable; a cooperative bear can tie things up for an hour or two. Traffic leaving the Cove is often bumper to bumper because the whole world wants to see the deer come out at dusk. It is less crowded during the week. **Escape the traffic via Rich Mountain Road,** crossing on Hyatt Lane before the gate gets locked after dusk. You can easily make dinner in Townsend.

On the Tennessee side, for **sunrise**, try the **Foothills Parkway West** at least once. From there move down to streambeds in **Tremont, Little River,** or if you didn't hang out too long at Foothills Parkway, try to get in to the **Cove**. Then head up to the **Chimneys**, watching for reflections on the way, and tie in to one of the other sequences.

If you opt for **Cataloochee Valley**, give the elk and other critters your best shot early, then work churches and cabins, and intimate scenes. You can come here in the early afternoon and have a productive visit for scenics, but probably miss most of the critters. **The Little Cataloochee Baptist Church** is great on a fall afternoon; see that chapter for details. You can come back out and catch late light over the ridges from the overlook or high tail it towards the main park. You could photograph **sunset from the Blue Ridge Parkway**, a few miles from Cherokee or Maggie Valley with a lot less driving, or leave earlier and get to **Clingmans Dome**. Allow at least two hours to get from the Little Cataloochee trailhead to Clingmans Dome via Maggie Valley and the Blue Ridge Parkway.

Winter

Because of access problems, winter is the toughest season to photograph in the Park. These are mountain roads, some at high elevations, with restrictions on what road treatments can be used for environmental reasons. **Newfound Gap Road (U.S. 441) over Newfound Gap is usually closed for the first few hours after a storm,** and sometimes before dark when things start to refreeze. You may be asked to drive down before dark if Park Rangers are worried about the roads icing up, and you might get stuck on the opposite side of the mountain from where you are staying. **To make plans, call the Park for road information at (865) 436-1200** to hear the latest report; when the tape starts key in 631 to take you directly to the road report. It's updated immediately whenever there is a new closure or opening. If you have Internet access, you can get additional weather information to try to predict what's going to happen. When planning your day, you must consider where you are staying because various roads may be closed, preventing an easy return.

After a snow, it doesn't stay on the branches for long, sometimes only an hour or two, so you have to work quickly and be on location when the last flakes are falling. **Rime ice** usually goes hand in hand with snow at high elevations, and will often stay on the branches longer, giving you a couple of more hours of grace. Sometimes you get rime (hoar frost) by itself. Rime is deposited when temperatures are below freezing within a cloud; these clouds move through the high ridges and whip over them at high speed. Usually the road doesn't get iced, just trees and everything else. If you can predict when this will happen, you will have access to the higher elevations at first light.

You can usually drive to the **Townsend "Y," the Greenbrier entrance or Sugarlands,** and on the North Carolina side to the **Mountain Farm Museum or Deep Creek** near Bryson City, regardless of how much snow fell. From there you can walk along the stream, working scenics as well as close-ups.

A storm that shuts down Newfound Gap Road (U.S. 441) might leave **Cades Cove** accessible, and a couple of inches is all it takes to pretty things up. If Cades Cove Loop Road is open you can follow it around looking for scenics and wildlife as opportunity presents. The Cove offers your main **winter wildlife** opportunity, and the **cabins and churches** make much-sought-after subjects in the snow. Get a very early start, because footprints will soon mar the scene, and children like to knock down the snow that settled on rail fences. It is an easy 20-minute walk to **John Oliver Cabin** if the gate at the start of the loop road is closed. If the campground is open you could try to get "snowed in," but this will require walking to the various locations; have everything with you, there aren't any services in the winter. **Laurel Falls** is an easy hike, even after a snow, and often holds snow on its foliage longer because it receives less direct light in winter. **Noah "Bud" Ogle place and the Mountain Farm Museum** are also relatively accessible after a snow.

If Newfound Gap Road (U.S. 441) is open, try to get up high for first light, working your way down after the best light is gone. Stop at the weeping wall for icicle formations mixed with lichen (this location is always in shade in the winter so it works in all conditions and times of day.) If the road is closed in the morning, work in whatever streambed is accessible, and if the road opens try afternoon light from wherever conditions look best. Check out the **Chimneys overlooks, Newfound Gap, and the high ridges on the North Carolina side**, possibly walking a way on the closed Clingmans Dome Road. The North Carolina ridges melt off quickly because they get much more direct sun, while the high ridges in Tennessee are more shaded. **The Oconaluftee Mountain Farm Museum and Deep Creek** are good options on the North Carolina side. If you end your day on the North Carolina side, you may not be able to get back over U.S. 441 if the road closes; Interstate 40 is the alternate route.

From **Townsend** you can easily go to the "Y," park and hike in to Tremont or Little River in both directions, and work from the car if the road opens. **Meigs Falls** can be gorgeous with the right amount of snow. If the road to Cades Cove is open, go straight there and walk in if the Loop Road is closed. Afternoon light is good in the Cove and if conditions are right, you could spend all day there.

From **Gatlinburg**, work **Greenbrier or Elkmont**, hike to **Laurel Falls** or the **Noah "Bud" Ogle Cabin** in the Roaring Fork area, and wait for the road to open. If Little River and Laurel Creek roads are open, the Cove is an option.

The Sun and Moon

The moon, whether full, crescent, or something in between, adds a great accent to an image, and sometimes "makes" the image. Knowing where and when the moon rises and sets is key. You can get the information you need from many different web sites and publications; you need to know time of day and compass bearing (azimuth.) On the day of the full moon, the moon crests the horizon a couple of minutes before sunset. The day before the moon is full, it will be up an additional 40 minutes or so before sunset, and an additional 40 minutes, give or take for each day before that. You have to catch the moon with enough light in the sky and on the land to even out the exposure, so the day before full moon seems to work best. The moon is always receiving direct sun when you are able to see it, so expose for the overall scene, if the land below is still lighted. Otherwise the contrast range may be too extreme so bracket liberally, or use a graduated neutral density filter. The moon moves constantly; after a few seconds it will be distorted on film, and it's worse with longer lenses. Pursuing the nuances of lunar movements is beyond the scope of this guide. The same sites can give you azimuths for sunrise and sunset. The US Naval Observatory web site has detailed information. Typing "sunrise" in most search engines will give you several hits, or use this URL; **http://aa.usno.navy.mil** and follow the site map. If you don't have that information with you, the following table will give you a rough guide.

The sun and moon swing around quite a bit during the year, causing compositions to change. For instance, when the red setting sun is in your frame at Morton Overlook it's not at Clingmans Dome and vice versa. The following table of compass bearings for sunrise and sunset is for mid-month. During July, August, and September, the sun picks up about a half degree of westward drift per day. This can be crucial if you are trying to line up the sun behind the Chimneys. Come back a couple of weeks later, and the scene has changed. Notice that positions will be about the same 6 months later, as the sun journeys back across the sky, turning from one solstice to the next.

Month	Sunrise compass bearings	Sunset compass bearings
January	120	248
February	109	259
March	96	272
April	81	287
May	70	298
June	64	304
July	66	301
August	76	292
September	90	278
October	104	264
November	116	251
December	122	245

Waterfall and Stream Guide

Waterfalls	
Abrams Falls	*Cades Cove*
Meigs Falls	*Little River Road*
The Sinks	*Little River Road*
Laurel Falls	*Little River Road*
Grotto Falls	*Roaring Fork*
Place of 1,000 Drips	*Roaring Fork*
Rainbow Falls	*Roaring Fork*
Ramsey Cascades	*Greenbrier*
Hen Wallow Falls	*Cosby*
Indian Creek Falls	*Deep Creek*
Juney Whank Falls	*Deep Creek*
Tom Branch Falls	*Deep Creek*
Mingo Falls	*Big Cove Road*

Streams	
Abrams Creek	*Cades Cove*
Laurel Creek	*Laurel Creek Road*
Little River	*Little River Road*
Middle Prong Little River	*Tremont*
West Prong Little Pigeon River	*Newfound Gap Road*
Middle Prong Little Pigeon River	*Greenbrier*
Little Pigeon River	*Greenbrier*
Cosby Creek	*Cosby*
Big Creek	*Big Creek*
Deep Creek	*Deep Creek*
Oconaluftee River	*Newfound Gap Road*
Cataloochee Creek	*Cataloochee Valley*

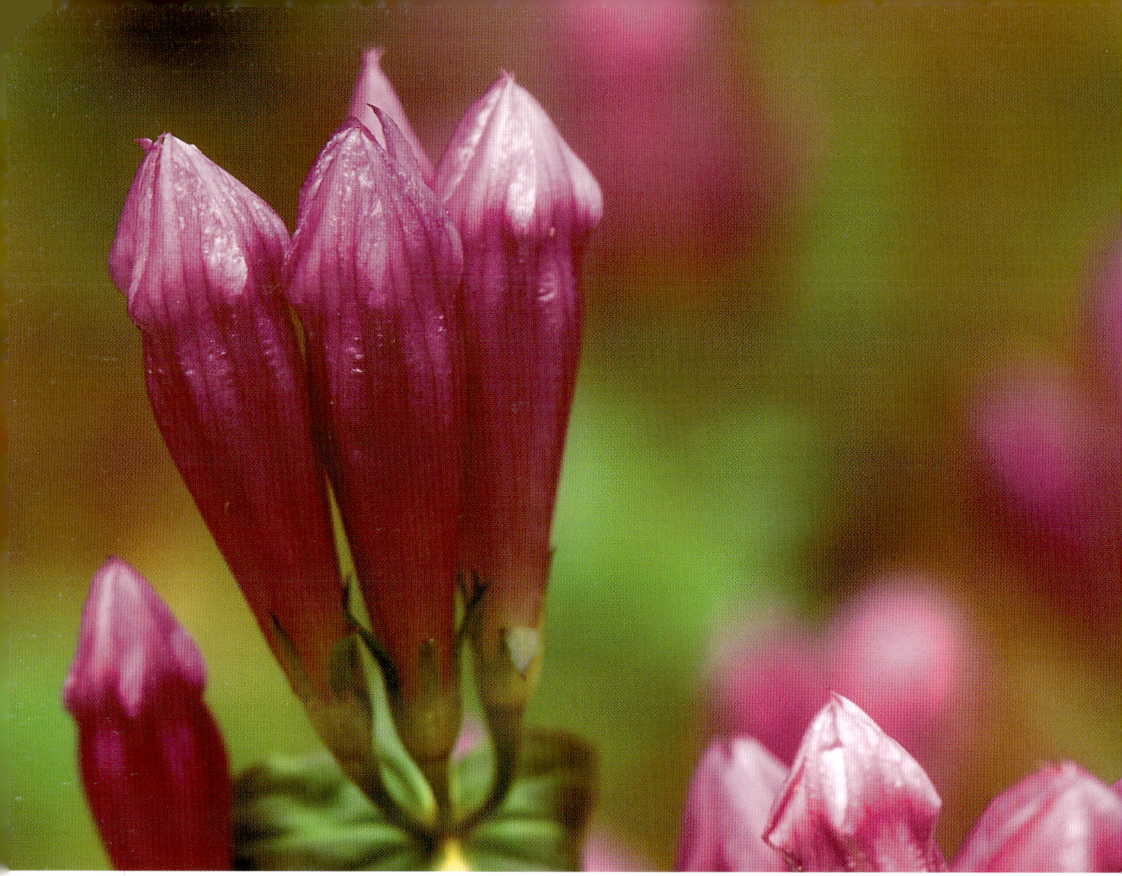

Chapter Twelve

Advanced Photography: The Next Level

ABOVE: Gentian in the fall.—*BC*

FILTERS

Filters are an essential part of any photographer's equipment. Here are a few hints on uses that will help you learn the intricacies of their function without the trial and error that most of us have had to go through.

Polarizers: Use any time you wish to reduce reflections on streams or shiny leaves. Rotate until you see the result you wish. If you use a polarizer with a blue sky, rotate to maximum polarization (darkest sky) and then rotate further by about a 1/4 turn. This prevents your blue sky from becoming so dark it looks black. Polarizers can also be used to cut down on the amount of apparent haze, especially for scenics of far away mountain ridges. These filters can also be used to slow down the shutter speed for stream shots and for increasing the saturation of color in wildflowers. This filter is often the most used filter in a photographer's bag.

Warming filters: See chapter eleven, *Getting the Most out of Your Photography*.

Color Enhancers: These come in both a general filter and a color specific (red, green, blue) variety. Used with fall colors, these filters can give an added punch to the colors, especially on a day where the light appears to be somewhat flat.

Graduated Neutral Density filters: Described in chapter eleven, these filters are essential for the grand landscape that includes a bright sky and a darker foreground. To use this filter, spot meter the foreground area where you wish to keep detail and the brightest area of the sky (don't meter the sun, but meter the bright sky to the side of the sun.) Calculate how many stops of light difference there are between the bright areas and the dark areas. This difference allows you to choose which filter strength you will use. If the difference is three stops, choose a two stop filter, as you want the sky to be at least one stop brighter than the foreground (otherwise it looks unnatural.) Choose between the hard and soft edge transitions based on the elements within your image. If a tree sticks up into the sky, choose a soft edge so the transition won't turn the tree dark. Once you have chosen a filter, place it in the holder (always use a holder as the filters scratch easily) and stop the lens down to the aperture of your final exposure. Move the filter up and down.

With the lens stopped down, the transition line will become more apparent and be easier to place in a proper position. Remember that even hard edge transitions become softer with longer lenses. Exposure is fairly straight forward once the filter is positioned, just use a matrix or evaluative meter setting and shoot away.

Protective Filters: A common recommendation during a camera purchase is to buy a "protective" filter for the front of your lenses. Skylight or UV filters are the ones usually recommended. However, we believe filters should only be used if you can express the reason you are using that particular filter. If you have read about the infamous Jack the Scratcher who goes around and scratches the front element of lenses, then by all means use a UV or Skylight filter all the time. At least until Jack is caught. If you are not worried about Jack, then using a UV or Skylight filter when there is sand, dust, or spray may be a more appropriate use. Think about it this way: why would you want to routinely place a $20 piece of glass in front of your very expensive front element?

Stacking Filters: There are times that placing one filter on top of another (stacking) is the only way to achieve the filtration you desire. But this may cause unwanted flare with your lenses or cause vignetting with a wide angle lens. Stack filters only when absolutely necessary.

Light, Film and your Meter

Before discussing exposure, we must consider how light reacts with film. Understanding how film "sees" light and how that is different from our own natural camera (our eyes and brain) is essential to making better exposures. The understanding of how your meter measures light is also critical for advanced photography.

Transparency film records about five "stops" of useful light which is much less than the 12 stops of light the human eye can perceive. A "stop" is a doubling or halving of the amount of light recorded, so a move of one stop will either double the amount of light or halve the amount

Transparency Tonal Range Chart

+2 $1/2$ Light without detail Generally overexposed whites (highlights) whether snow or whitewater; a small area won't necessarily hurt you, and is sometimes a necessary compromise.

+ 2 Light A good target setting for the white foamy water in waterfalls, cascades, and rapids and bright white clouds. Clean white snow with some detail in soft light; however, snow is tricky, and the optimal exposure varies depending on lighting conditions.

+1 $1/2$ Light with detail Delicate white blossoms, average pastel colors, a good starting point for back lighted spring or fall foliage. Snow and white-water in sun.

+1 Medium Light The palm of your hand, a good starting point to render sky or some lighter colored rocks. Skies seem more natural a little brighter than medium. Yellows that appear medium will actually meter closer to +1.

Meter your palm and learn where it reads relative to what you consider a medium tone. Most of us will be 1-1 $1/2$ stops brighter. Unless your hand gets dirty, you will have a constant reference with you.

0 Medium Many grasses, gray rocks, tan tree trunks (unpolarized blue sky looking north at mid-day) and any other color you can think of. Moderately weathered barn wood will be close to mid-tones. If you would describe the color as "medium," it will probably be pretty close. Exception: yellow, see above.

-1 Medium Dark Good shadow detail. Darker foliage, but not evergreens or rhododendron—these are difficult values to assign. Black bear fur, receding ridgelines that are approaching the horizon in a sunset scene from Morton Overlook or Clingmans Dome.

-1 $1/2$ Dark with detail Receding ridgelines in a sunset or sunrise toward the middle of the scene, darker streambed rocks with detail, mountain laurel and rhododendron leaves, a different rendering of the black bear.

-2 Dark The practical limit for shadow or dark detail in slide film.

-2 $1/2$ Dark without detail Silhouettes or as a background to make a primary subject stand out.

Exposure

Most cameras will give adequate exposures on matrix or evaluative meter settings, but learning when to trust these settings and when to meter the scene yourself is part of becoming an advanced photographer. Sunrise, sunset, strong backlighting and extremely bright situations (snow, bright fog) are situations where manual metering will give better control of the exposure.

Sunrise, Sunset Spot meter the bright area of the sky not too close to the sun. Make this exposure +1 stop above medium (0 on your scale) and the colors in the sky will be closer to what your eye perceives than if you use automatic metering.

Strong backlighting Spot meter the area most important to you, and expose for the desired effect. If left on automatic, areas in shade may be darker than you intend.

Snow or bright fog Bright fog is easy to meter, just spot meter an area without detail and set this area at +1 to +1½ stop exposure (one stop lighter or brighter than 0 or medium tone.) Snow is similar, but varies depending on light direction and quality. The brighter you set the exposure for snow, the less detail the snow will have. A very dark and overcast day may need even more exposure compensation than brighter days.

Bracketing is a technique of over and under exposing an image around the suggested proper exposure. Some cameras can even be set up to bracket automatically. While bracketing every exposure makes your film company and developer very happy, it is not a routine that everyone should aspire to use. Bracketing is important in those situations where lighting is difficult and the situation will not be easily reproduced. We find that bracketing toward a lighter exposure is more advantageous than getting darker exposure. In the long run, it pays to know your film, your meter, light and how they interact. One day you may have one frame left when Elvis walks out in front of you. Not enough film to bracket, no time to reload, got to get it right, no second chances.

of light available. In shutter speeds, to go from 1/125 second to 1/250 second is halving the amount of light allowed to strike the film. This is one stop. A move from f4.0 to f5.6 aperture is one stop of light, also. Learning to think in stops of light is a key to advanced photography.

A camera spot meter is designed to force whatever it meters to look medium toned. Matrix or evaluative meters use complex software to evaluate the entire tonal range of light and decide what the best exposure will be. However, this won't always be right and part of becoming a better photographer is learning when not to use matrix metering. If you spot meter a black object (say a bear), the meter will give you an exposure that will turn Mr. Black Bear into Mr. Medium Gray Bear on film. If you meter a white subject (snow), the meter will give you an exposure that turns nice white snow into dirty gray snow. If you spot meter a medium tone, then mediums will be medium, whites will be white, and blacks will be black. A useful reference to meter is the palm of your hand, which is about a +1 exposure and usually difficult to misplace.

Sometimes there is a greater range of light in the scene than the film can capture. If you measure the brightest spot and the darkest spot and they are more than five stops of light apart, then you cannot record everything in the scene. The darks will be too dark with no detail or the brights will be too bright with no detail. This is when you have to learn to modify the light, come back another time, or just enjoy the scene. Having your shadows go black is usually better tolerated than blown highlights if you have to choose. A 1/2 stop variance in exposure can push highlights over the top or shadows into featureless black. The chart (opposite page) will help you understand the range that transparency film can handle. Many camera systems now have 1/3 stop increments to give more subtle control of your exposure than the 1/2 stop increments listed in the chart.

Double exposure

We will limit this discussion to film cameras as most digital cameras do not allow in-camera double exposure, but you can duplicate the technique in your image editing software. The effect of the double exposure can be varied. You must be able to set your camera to take a double exposure. If you are looking to buy a new film camera, make sure it has this feature. Two different effects are:

1) to combine a sharp image and a soft image to create an ethereal feel by throwing a halo around the sharp image

2) portraying both a near subject and a distant subject as sharp.

The first method to create an ethereal feeling is rather simple. This works well on flowers, even when they are occasionally moving. First, set your camera to double exposure (remember to turn this off after you are finished.) Next, you want to under expose each image of the double exposure by one stop. This can be set on your exposure compensation dial to -1 (don't forget to turn this off when finished.) Frame up your subject and set exposure (under expose by one stop if setting manually and you haven't used the exposure compensation.) You want to use a moderate depth of field (f8 is a good starting point) for the first exposure, which will be the sharp image. Once you have exposed the sharp image, set your aperture to maximum opening (f2.8-f4), reset your exposure, and focus in (set focus closer than first image.) Capture the second image on film. This exposes both images onto one piece of film.

The art of this technique comes in experimenting with different amounts of soft focus to create different feelings. You can also adjust the exposure by making the sharp image more dominate by exposing it at -2/3 stop and then the soft image at -1 1/3 stop. The resulting exposure is the same as the first technique, but the visual results will be different.

The second method is used to portray both a foreground image and a background image in sharp detail. Try this method when a small aperture (great depth of field) is not an option. Use the exposure compensation as above and remember to set your camera to double exposure mode. Focus on the foreground element and use a moderate depth of field (start with f8), take your first exposure. Don't change the exposure or aperture (except as described above to achieve the overall proper exposure) and then focus on the background element you want in focus. Take your second exposure. This method works well with telephoto lenses where your depth of field seems more compressed or where you need more shutter speed (and larger aperture with shallower depth of field) because of movement of the subject.

Reflectors and diffusers

How to modify light is an essential technique for every advanced photographer. Light conditions are often not ideal and learning how to control lighting will save many a day of shooting. Full sun streaming down on a flower *usually* will not make a pleasing image of the flower. In the wildflower section you learned that soft light works best, but sometimes you can't wait until the next time it rains or is overcast to take the image of the flower you found.

The most natural way to control lighting on your subject is through the use of reflectors and diffusers. These can be any size, material, or color, but commercial reflectors come in white, silver, gold and soft gold (or sunlight.) They are light and fold down to 1/3 their open size, so a 42 inch size folds down to 14 inches. Rule of thumb for size for field use is 12-30 inch size for reflectors, and 30-42 inch size for diffusers. There are several combination packages that have both reflector and diffuser material, but make sure you have at least a reflector and a diffuser to use.

There are two advantages to modifying light this way. The first is a more natural appearing image because the use of flash can cause a color shift in the subject, and second, you can see the results in the viewfinder before you take the image. To use a diffuser, unfold and place the material as close as possible to your subject without being in the image. The closer you place a diffuser, the softer the light on your subject. Think of it this way, the further away a diffuser is the more like a shadow and less like a soft cloud it becomes. Sometimes diffusers are referred to as pocket clouds. Take string or Velcro ties to help keep the diffuser in place. Leaning it against your tripod leg works, but any movement of the diffuser could vibrate the tripod and hence your camera.

Reflectors work best if there is direct sunlight to bounce into your image. Without direct sunlight, the reflector must be much closer and the effects will be much softer. You can bounce light using multiple reflectors for multiple sources of light and use it to backlight a subject, lighten up the background, or take the shadow out of a side lit subject. The soft gold reflectors seem to emulate sunlight more closely and tend to be used more in nature, but experiment with the colors. You might find that the silver works well in certain circumstances.

Macro Photography

Micro photography, macro photography, and close-up photography all mean essentially the same thing, making an image look much larger than it appears in real life. Specialized lenses work extremely well, and if you do much macro work, you might want to consider investing in one of these lenses. For nature field work, a 200mm macro seems to work best, as your working distance (how far away you are from your subject) is far enough not to affect those subjects such as butterflies, spider webs, flowers, insects, reptiles, etc. But you don't need to invest in these lenses. The close-up diopters made by Nikon and Canon are superb and screw right in front of the lenses you already own, just like any other filter. There is no light loss and most of the time you can still auto focus. With a 70-200mm range lens and close-up diopters, you can do most of what you could do with a specific 200mm macro lens.

The greatest difficulty of macro photography is depth of field. As you magnify your subject, the depth of field shrinks. You may go from a depth of field (the area of apparent sharpness from foreground to background) of several feet to less than an inch. Thus, using as small an aperture (greatest depth of field) as possible becomes a necessity. This leads to slower shutter speeds and more difficulty with movement of the subject or camera or lighting changes. Camera instability you can take care of by mounting on a tripod. Subject movement takes patience (waiting for the wind to stop blowing.) Try to use an aperture of f11 and greater (f16 and f22 commonly used) to get the greatest depth of field. Critically focus to make sure the nearest portion of your subject will stay in focus. Follow the other elements of image design and have fun with a whole new world.

These techniques and thoughts should spur you along to attempting different images and a creative expression of your inner vision.

What's in the Bag?

Bill Campbell's equipment

Cameras:
- Nikon F5, F100, D1x and CoolPix 5000, depending on space

Lenses:
- *All the time:* Nikon 17-35 f2.8 AFS, 28-70 f2.8 AFS, 70-200 f2.8 VR
- *When needed:* 200 f4 Micro, 85 Tilt/Shift Micro, 300 f2.8 AFSII, 500 f4 AFSII, TC20EII teleconvertor, TC14EII teleconvertor

Flash:
- SB80DX

Tripod:
- Gitzo 1348 MKII or 340

Ballhead:
- Kirk original ballhead and plates

Bag:
- Lowepro ProTrekker or PhotoTrekker AW
- 500mm goes in Kinesls Long Lens Case

Accessories:
- Nikon A2 warming filter and circular polarizer
- B+W KR3 filter
- SinghRay graduated neutral density filters (1 and 2 stop, hard and soft edge)
- Cable release
- flash remote cord
- 30" Diffuser
- soft gold reflectors

Nye Simmons' equipment

For landscape adventures close to the car, or involving easy hikes:
- KB Canham 4x5 / 5x7 camera
- KB Canham 6x17 roll film back
- Assorted lenses to approximate 17mm to 135mm equivalents in the 35mm world

For hiking:
- Gowland 4x5 pocket view camera with assorted lenses to fit the day
- 6x9 Calumet roll film back, or Pentax 67 medium format system with 45mm, 75mm, 105mm, 135mm macro, 200mm lenses

When 35mm gear is called for:
- Canon EOS 3 with 20-35mm, 28-135mm, and 400 f5.6 lenses

Filters by Singh-Ray:
Grads, polarizers, Singh-Ray Color Intensifier, and A13 warming filter

Resources and Suggested Reading

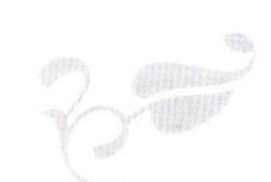

Books by the Great Smoky Mountains Association:

- *Hiking Trails of the Smokies* by various authors.
- *Trees of the Smokies* by Steve Kemp.
- *Exploring the Smokies* by Rose Houk.
- *Wildflowers of the Smokies* by Peter White.
- *Reptiles and Amphibians of the Smokies* by Tilley and Huheey.

Other resources and references:

- *Waterfalls and Cascades of the Great Smoky Mountains* by Hubbs, Maynard, and Morris.
- *Wildlife Watchers Guide to the Great Smoky Mountains National Park* by Mike Carlton.
- *Wildflowers of the Southern Appalachians* by Kevin Adams and Marty Casstevens
- *The Sibley Guide to Birds* by David Allen Sibley
- *The Sibley Guide to Bird Life and Behavior* by David Allen Sibley
- *Nature Photography Field Guide* by John Shaw.
- *Closeups in Nature* by John Shaw.
- *Focus on Nature* by John Shaw.
- *Landscape Photography* by John Shaw
- *Beyond the Basics* by George Lepp.
- *Beyond the Basics II* by George Lepp.
- *How to Photograph Animals in the Wild* by Len Rue, III and Len Rue, Jr.

Specialized Equipment:

- Wimberly—Specialized tripod heads and accessories. On the web at *www.tripodhead.com*
- LL Rue—Everything for the wildlife photographer, general use equipment and books, hard to find items. On the web at *www.rue.com*
- Singh Ray—Filters. On the web at *www.singh-ray.com*
- Kirk Enterprises—Ball heads and camera and lens plates. On the web at *www.kirkphoto.com*